"This is unlike any public-policy book I've ever read: part *Catcher in the Rye,* part *The Road to Wigan Pier,* part *The Federalist Papers,* it is mesmerizing, rueful, painfully honest, and never, ever dull. As a personal account, it makes vivid the experience of an idealistic generation that has watched helplessly as the country moved away from its dreams. As a work of social philosophy (which it is, without putting on any airs), it gets far beyond the political byplay of the moment and makes us understand, and want to change, the structural forces that have brought about the failure of the national ideal."
—Nicholas Lemann, author of *The Promised Land*

"A truly strange and wonderful book. Who knew that political autobiography and a restless, dead serious meditation on the meaning of American citizenship could be so funny? Tom Geoghegan attacks the New Federalism, ponders labor economics, compares Chicago and Washington, attends tedious meetings, and talks fiercely to himself—all in a voice like nothing you've ever heard before: playful, self-effacing, erudite, and breathtakingly earnest. He also dates au pairs from Poland."
—William Finnegan, *The New Yorker*

"Tom Geoghegan's *Secret Lives* is an extraordinary piece of work. It has the essential trait of a memorable book, in that after reading it you look at daily life in a lastingly different way. Geoghegan's style is unique in modern nonfiction writing—quirky, funny, accessible, but at the same time successful in dealing with complex and weighty matters. I don't know anyone who has such an inviting, winsome way of addressing really major questions of how we live and how the world works."
—James Fallows, author of *Breaking the News*

"*The Secret Lives of Citizens* is, above all else, a book about longing. Longing for the days of the New Deal, for a time of 'Central Government,' for a politics of one man, one vote. . . . Through his candor and his questioning (of himself and others), he has written a book that is not only compelling to read but provokes us to seriously reflect on the choices we make and how we spend our time."
—Jonathan Coleman, *Washington Post Book World*

"Thomas Geoghegan has written a book urging the rehabilitation of the civic idea in America that isn't the slightest bit boring, or pious, or given to bland generalization. That Geoghegan has achieved this won't surprise readers of his previous book, *Which Side are You On?*, about his experiences as a labor lawyer. . . . If the White House domestic policy council—and, more importantly, a lot of citizens—were to read this book, it might stimulate the national imagination to think big again, just as it did during, well, the New Deal. Less grandly, Geoghegan's book should be read simply because it's elegant and funny and sharply intelligent."
—Timothy Noah, *The Washington Monthly*

"Thomas Geoghegan approaches the mechanics of government with the sensibility of a Romantic poet; he's the Byron of the bureaucracy and *The Secret Lives of Citizens* is a brilliant account of a doomed but lovely passion for the American dream."
—Ron Rosenbaum, author of *Explaining Hitler*

"In 1991, Chicago lawyer Thomas Geoghegan flung open a window in the airless room of American political and social discourse and let in a blast of fresh air called *Which Side are You On?* His passionate, funny, angry memoir, which won the Chicago Sun-Times Chicago Book of the Year Award, chronicled the decline of unions in the 1970s and '80s and challenged America to live up to its promise of a good life for all, including the working class. *The Secret Lives of Citizens* reiterates that challenge in a new context: the frightening contraction of American public life."
—Wendy Smith, *Chicago Sun-Times*

"In an era in which public discourse is dominated by propagandists and professors, Thomas Geoghegan is a prophet. *The Secret Lives of Citizens* is an impassioned, witty, and wise report on the decrepit state of our Union."
—Michael Lind, author of *The Next American Nation*

The Secret Lives
of Citizens

To Ian
who does
not keep
his
civic life
a
secret !

N
Ym

The Secret Lives of Citizens

PURSUING THE PROMISE

OF AMERICAN LIFE

Thomas Geoghegan

THE UNIVERSITY OF CHICAGO PRESS

Reprinted by arrangement with Pantheon Books, a division of Random House, Inc.

The University of Chicago Press, Chicago 60637
Copyright © 1998 by Thomas Geoghegan
All rights reserved. Originally published 1998
University of Chicago Press edition 2000
Printed in the United States of America
05 04 03 02 01 00   6 5 4 3 2 1

Library of Congress Cataloging-in-Publication Data
Geoghegan, Thomas, 1949–
    The secret lives of citizens : pursuing the promise of American life / Thomas
Geoghegan.
        p. cm.
    Originally published: New York : Pantheon Books, c1998.
    ISBN 0-226-28764-5 (pbk.: alk. paper)
    1. Geoghegan, Thomas, 1949– 2. Civil service—United States—Biography.
3. Lawyers—United States—Biography. 4. Labor unions—United States—
History. 5. United States—Social conditions. I. Title.

JK693.G46 A3 2000
340'.92—dc21
[B]   99-054671
                                                                                  CIP

To Leon Despres

Contents

The Secret Lives
of Citizens

ONE

There Is No One City

WHEN I WAS THIRTY AND SICK OF D.C., I THOUGHT: "OH, GO! Just pick out a city and be a citizen of it!"

It was 1979, everyone was going. I decided, there must be a city, maybe to the North.

But for an American the problem is: There is no one city. Not like Paris is for the French, or London for the British.

Oh, there's Boston, Seattle, Cities of the Fabulous Coffees. And New York and L.A., Cities of the Fabulous Jobs.

But each one I picked up and turned over like a silver goblet, I always thought I saw a flaw.

Boston? Too many kids. Toy town. Seattle? City of Silly Bicycles. L.A.? Or for that matter, Atlanta?

How do I know I'm not there now? Maybe there is only one city in the U.S., and the airlines just circle one airport, and I get back on the same interstate, and check in the same Radisson.

Ever notice on the interstate how the "green" on the ramp sign is the same green in every city? That's odd, isn't it?

But then there's New York, where the Radisson is unaffordable.

"Oh New York!" my old teacher Sam B. once said. "New York, it's still the mecca, isn't it?" Oh Sam, if only it were! If it was 1940, and it was the New York of Auden and Frank Loesser, my life would have been simple. But by 1979, when I had to choose . . . uck, all the old wet New Yorkers, lying sodden on the sidewalks.

"It was the only city," I told Steve, "where even the orange juice looks pestilential."

"The only city," he said, "where you can take a shower and not get clean."

Anyway, who can be a citizen in New York? It's a place one would go to dial a "900" number, like "1-900-I-C-O-N-F-E-S-S," and at the other end there's the mayor, whispering some private repulsive fantasy.

No, I wanted to be a citizen, like Cincinnatus. Roman farmer, who left his plow, saved the city. I was born in Cincinnati, and I thought of my grandfather like that: he had left his business, insurance, to be a county commissioner in the Depression, 1932. I remember him as an old man, hands out, blessing his grandchildren. It would take us half an hour to walk a block, people coming up to shake his hand.

"Maybe," I thought, "I can live like he did, end my days, with my own grandson holding my hand."

But I needed a city, right?

It's what Aristotle says in *The Politics*. It's the lesson of the Buddha: "You need a base."

It's what they all said to Kafka, when he started out: "You need a base."

Sure: a base, then it's a block, soon it's just a single room.

But I had to take a risk, find a city to vote in, use up half an hour to walk a block.

Because I remember the famous story of the man who said: "In the 1920s I went to Paris, because everyone went to Paris then; and later to New York, because everyone went to New York then; and later to L.A., because everyone went to L.A. then.... And really the whole time I should have just picked out some place and stayed there!"

Well I did do that. I knew the city I wanted: I wanted a big, disheveled city, Catholic and alcoholic, to shut myself up in:

To breathe into me an immortal soul.

Be a citizen and a voter, for a thousand and one nights.

I picked out Chicago, our political city. Precinct workers knocking on doors. It would get me out of my room.

And the whole thing ended badly. Now in one or two city elections, I've lost even the heart to vote. Walk a block, know no one, OK: But stop voting?

I'm unsure of the exact year I first tried it, maybe 1991. I was getting off the El and thinking, "I can still make it," but I now know I was trying not to. Then I panicked and began to run, past the Red Tomato to Bert Weinman Ford.

Are you shocked? Want me to say what happened next?

A cop was standing at Weinman's. "Sorry. All over."

"All over? No," I said, "it's 6:59!"

"It's *closed*."

And at that moment I felt a thrill. I'd come to vote against Daley, and I couldn't remember his opponent.

But though there was a thrill, the shame was: I'd never live like my grandfather. Or even have a grandson.

So why had I even come to Chicago? It was a good city, I thought, to cast my ballet.

I thought I could have it all: Augustine, *The City of God*. And *The Adventures of Augie March*.

I wanted it ethical and elegant.

Urban and urbane.

And dark bars like the one, the other night, where Ann was in the black dress, and singing.

I once thought this would be such a serious city. And out here I could concentrate on being an American, not like being on the coasts with people peering in from abroad.

But slowly even this city became, well . . . silly. But that's the problem: every city in America seems the same now, doesn't it?

One half: Girls, in tennis whites, dawdling over cat calendars.

The other half: Babies, in crack houses, sitting in feces.

I feel at times split in half myself. But is it the city's fault I'm split like this, or is it really mine?

THIS MUST BE THE CITY!

When I came here, I had the sense that Chicago was the best place to be a citizen. I got this idea from books I'd read in college. I think of the great writers on republics.

Machiavelli on small republics
Harrington on compound republics
Madison on large republics

They wrote the great prophetic books. From these I got my reasons:

First, number. Chicago had three million, the same as the U.S. at the time of our founding. As late as 1960, that was still enough people to elect a John Kennedy! The Founders whispered, "This is the right number."

Second, wards. It was divided into wards. One alderman or "councilman" per ward. Fifty aldermen. Too many? It was the one alderman city, big city, that had so many wards.

It's easy to drive around it, since it's all blocks, and grids, and wards. "Now why," you think, "is that important?" It's the ward, Hannah Arendt wrote, in her book *On Revolution*, that is the "organ" which comes, spontaneously, from every revolution. Paris, 1789. Paris, 1871. Petrograd, 1918: suddenly, there's the ward. Even Thomas Jefferson, she wrote, tried, at the end, to cut the country up in wards.

In his Northwest Ordinance, everything is blocks and grids. So in the Midwest, we'd be wired like cable to think in terms of squares and wards.

That's why, I always believed, people in Chicago do "think politically," and why it is our political city: it's the "red" city. Haymarket, Grant Park, always on the political bubble.

Anyway, it's Jefferson, not Daniel Burnham, who did this. That's the second reason the Founders said, "Go."

Third, and this may sound odd, flatness.

My brother, when he first saw the city, hit on it: "Nothing, not a hill, between these neighborhoods, rich and poor, white and black. . . ."

A flat city crackles politically. When there's a big storm, electrical, we're all out in the open, in a public square.

My first days! September 1979, I was thrilled. First, I'd found the right ward. Up north in Rogers Park, on the lake, I could pad to the sand in my bare feet. And drink two cans of Old Style, and smoke cigars, and toast the seagulls, circling.

By municipal tennis courts: as bleak as the New Deal's.

Second, did I ever meet aldermen! Everyone I knew:

My roommate, David, was an alderman (ward 49).
My employer, Len, had been an alderman (ward 5).
On the El, I met a girl, red hair, the niece of an alderman
    (ward 48?).

The numbers 49, 5, 48 . . . and how many more would I know by the
first snow? I could see myself asking a date, "Dinner in 8?" Back then I
seemed to table-hop wards. And 49 was deli, 48 Vietnamese, and 44 was
Sather's . . . and I just didn't notice as the years went by (1983, 1987, 1991)
how with each election the city was shrinking. Maybe not in absolute
terms (though it was), but relative to the bigger suburban darkness and
beyond.

Then one day after grazing in every ward, I noticed: it's shrunk! Sure
I was still a citizen of the city, but what happened to the charge?

I'd go in, pick up my ballot, there wasn't even a little spark.

I should have seen it coming, when Ed Sadlowski said he was at a ball
game, "And I saw a guy actually TIP THE VENDOR!"

Yes, the city as a boxing gym, and now it all seems punchless. The old
Chicago gone . . . the Chicago where the median age was sixty-two, and
people were fat, and I was the youngest guy in the bar.

"Who lost Chicago?" I sometimes blame it on the kids.

The other day I sat in Tucci Milan with a friend.

"Don't quote me," he said.

"I don't want to be quoted either."

"But I think all the cities were more exciting in the 1970s."

"Of course it could just be our age."

"No, the city is dull now, don't you think?"

But what appalls me is these kids, corporate types, little earrings, who
sip martinis, they don't even know where their wards are.

The noodle shops have all smudged the lines. And with the kids,
being here, and not voting, they've taken the punch out of the city.

They roam from noodle shop to noodle shop, they don't know the
numbers of their wards.

Oh sure, blame it on the kids. It's just as much my fault, when I
stopped going to meetings. Now Tocqueville said: that's the first duty of

an American, to go to a meeting, to "associate." The older I got, the harder it was to go to a meeting that starts at 7 P.M.

First, I had to have my fix, *i.e.,* my jogging began to get worse.

But which came first, the running or the running from meetings? It's all a form of "fight or flight." At 6:00 P.M., I can go over to Lake Shore Drive, and see people like buffalo in Nikes thundering up the cinder paths.

What are they running from? They're running from meetings. Because now we meet for a living, and we meet all day.

And at night, we run faster, and now this in turn creates another crisis: "I have to eat!" Running is a kind of a drug, after all, so now people have the munchies, and they have to go out to eat. Who can go to a meeting?

It's true, I could come late. But then people would stare, "Oh, his hair is wet," and shake their heads, "Oh boy, he's on endorphins."

Second, wasn't I scared of the people in there? These are people who have been in meetings all day! Oh sure, in Tocqueville's day, the 1830s, I'd have gone to a meeting at night! Out in the woods, lonely all day. And if I went to one, everyone else would be an amateur like me.

Now if I walk in, it's a roomful of . . . pros, foundation people. Meeting vampires. All day at other places out at O'Hare, the meeting airport, where they've been sucking blood from conferees around the U.S.

Finally, our jobs, the hours. Even if I could come by at 7:00! They'd whisper, "He can't be much of a lawyer!" Oh sure, if I were in Europe I could meet, but I'd be out of work at 4:00 or 5:00. But we work 1,700 hours a year, on average, they work 1,400: apart from vacation differences, the hours spent at work each week are not much different. Maybe two extra hours off a day. But doesn't Civil Society live or die in these one or two elusive hours?

Of course we could just shorten our meetings.

That's my agony . . . how to get the things to stop? I've tried it all: summing up, not summing up.

Lately I've tried grinning at people, grinning until they stop . . . the way, they say, Davy Crockett tried to "grin a bear."

And as Chicago became punchless, I even came to blame the mayor, Rich Daley. Now my old activist friends like C. rage at him: "I hate him, I

HATE HIM!" C.'s an organizer, and she hates the way he goes around and tells people to stay in their homes. "Don't come out, the city'll take care of this!"

It's not his fault, is it, that the city can't punch in a president or even a governor?

No, it's not Daley. It's just why punch at all in a city that's shrinking?

Once, the Second City. Now? Not even second in Illinois. We're third. The first is suburbia, especially DuPage County, out to the west. DuPage is where you can get a job: that is if you're out there already, with a house and a car. It's mean, white, Republican: its boss, "Pate" Philip, is the head of the state senate. Now in Springfield, DuPage outclouts us all. Pitiful for me to blame Daley for that. In a way the mayor is even . . . well, disarming. Even now, over fifty-six, he's still "Rich," the boy mayor. It is disarming how he's not in DuPage. He is still in the city, even though he seems to belong, almost umbiblically, to the Weber grill.

Of course, where in the city is he? The old mayor, he was in a bungalow, people could drive by.

His son, in a private complex, who really knows where?

But he's still here, right? Since 1960, just think . . . over 1.5 million ethnic whites have left!

It's true he has voting stats like Dad. But here's the one stat that shows his real power:

Suburbs (six counties)	4.5 million
Downstate	4.2 million
City	2.8 million

"The Suburbs," which are the Lost City of Old Dick Daley, wandering like the Ten Tribes, are not just out of Rich Daley's control. They're in control of him! *Chicago,* the city magazine, asks each year:

"Who Runs Chicago?"

Of course, the magazine always lists Daley as No. 1.

He's number one, because he can still tow away my car? But guys like Pate and Jim Edgar, the governor, who don't even live here, can tow away the whole city.

Now in theory that's impossible because Chicago has home rule. But what is home rule? "We don't have to wear our motorcycle helmets if the State tells us."

But on anything really important, we in the city are like flies to wanton boys. Three examples:

1. In 1995, over the screaming of city Democrats, the State simply abolished . . . poof . . . the city's school board.

Well *now* Daley says, oh that's what I wanted Jim Edgar to do. Sure. And it's true that he did get the power to appoint a new board, so he would now get the blame for the city's collapsing public schools. But Daley had no choice. It was the State of Illinois, unilaterally, that had lined him up against the wall.

(And did other mean things, like crippling the city teachers' union.)

2. Then it almost took away O'Hare! Our *airport*! What is the city but O'Hare! But the suburbs wanted it, and Daley saved it, i.e., city property, only by signing a pact with the city of Gary, Indiana, to help Chicago run the airport. So now, technically, it's an "interstate" airport, and under a special federal law, the State of Illinois can't grab it away.

But what an escape! I thought we'd have to go out, like militia, and ring the airport, to keep the National Guard from seizing it at night.

Boss? Hard to be boss, when they can break and enter at will.

3. And what about the bread of the poor? Even that, it turns out, is now handed out from Springfield. Medicaid, welfare, we have to go there and beg. What if we run out of food? Springfield, where is it? How do you get there?

It's 197 miles away. Too close to fly, and too far to drive, as people say, and devised, almost maniacally, to always be beyond our reach.

When did the state take over the city? I began to notice, going to ball games, and one day I nudged a guy, who was tipping a vendor:

"Say, when did all the ball teams begin to come from states?"

Colorado Rockies
Texas Rangers
Florida Marlins

Was it when states started to seize airports? And impose martial law on the poor? And more troubling, when I'm at the park, when I think about this as a citizen, what is the team . . . city, state, or federal . . . that I'm playing on now? How confusing now to be a citizen activist. Once, there were three or four ways any young activist could "change the world."

Now I doubt that any of them really work. What would?

1. Go to D.C.? Too much gridlock.
2. Sue in the public interest? The courts are too scared.
3. Work for the unions? They're busted, mostly.
4. Cities? They've been busted too, in terms of power.

Indeed, I have brooded about this: I think the one great thing now would be to run for state rep.

Now when I came here, that would have seemed nuts. *Alderman*: that was the great thing. I actually dreamed, once, I guess, sort of, it was a fantasy, of being an alderman. Walk around. People would know my name.

Now the paradox is, if I really want to help my city like this, I'd have to leave it, I'd have to be a state rep. It's odd, I used to think the horror of politics was . . . well, knocking, going to their apartments. Now, why worry? As the voting rate drops and drops, I think, "I can invite them to *my* apartment."

Of course my place isn't big enough. Yet.

But if the voting drops at the 1950 to 1996 rate for presidential races (i.e., from nearly 80 percent to under 50 percent), I could, one day, have them all over.

In some suburban elections I could invite them all over for brunch.

Here's something chilling I saw in the paper. In Belarus, the president canceled the election because only 60 percent of the voters showed up. Now, I know this is a pretext, but at least, they could even think of it as a pretext!

Anyway, I no longer worry about going door to door. No, the sad, evil thing now would be: to give up my city, the reason I came here.

Drive . . . 197 miles, slowly, like Lincoln's funeral train. I see myself surrounded by kids, on rollerblades, the "voters." I'd say, "Kids, to save the city, I have to leave it. . . . Go down there and talk to your parents."

They'll weep and oh . . . pierce their ears. It sounds strange: that to be a state rep, that's how one really is an alderman now. How many even know their state reps? Or better, how many know, for sure, the last time they voted for a state rep? One year ago, or maybe two, or fifteen? If they canceled the office, how many years would pass before anyone would really notice?

ANYWAY, THE PROBLEM IS, where is the place I can connect with the whole city? I mean even the parts that lie outside the city walls. Oh, they're out, sometimes past O'Hare, out among the trees. Oak Forest, Forest Oak, Oak Lawn. Dark places, no sunlight, where people have to file Freedom of Information, just to get the names of their mayors. What if I lived there? One day a hearse honking: "We're taking you to Forest Lawn." The weird thing is, at moments, the people out there still think they're living in Chicago.

The kids, out there, as they grow up, have a strange way of talking: "You from Chicago?" "Yeah." "Which suburb?"

But it is a good question, isn't it? Which: There's Oak Park, where they sell the *Financial Times.* Or Riverdale, with a crime rate worse than ours. "There is no one suburb." Yet every night at 10:00 they all sit down for the Channel 2, or 5, or 7 News, to watch "us" back in the city, see what "Chicago" is doing, which aldermen are fighting their indictments, all to entertain "them."

The saddest thing of all: to watch another person's government on TV. I think about some of them after they flick it off, go to bed, begin to sob, shaking in their sleep. They know they used to live here, or should live here. And now . . . they don't even have a government to watch.

It's why I believe they're so enraged about city crime. "Why?" says an academic. "It doesn't affect them." Even when that's true, it's still taking place back in their homeland, the ancestral home. It's back in the old public square, where they used to gather. It seems wrong for it to be there. Who cares about crime in Riverdale? But the city . . . and each year, it's more and more gorgeous, like a wedding feast from which guests in RVs have been turned away. And what have they been given? Villages, untelevised.

Water districts, like handfuls of dust.

I too would be in a rage.

THIS BUILT-UP OUTER GOVERNMENT is baffling. No rational account of it is possible. A lawyer friend who deals with local and state government says, "Even I can't understand it."

Ms. Radtke of the Northeastern Illinois Planning Commission tells me: In our six-county area, there are nearly 1,300 "governments." OK, some are like mosquito abatement districts, etc. But there are, she says, 268 municipalities.

Now, just imagine, from the top of the Sears Building: out there, 269 municipalities! Maybe 240 with the mayors elected for life. No one even knows them on the street. Ms. Radtke claims we have more governments in our . . . uh, area, if that's the word . . . than there are even in Massachusetts.

What kind of vision, broken up like this, can we have of the city now?

James Madison and the Founders wanted a large republic, because a large republic, he said, would enlarge our views. We'd think in bigger terms than, say, O'Hare.

So I can moan about how we live in little burblets, how they're so small, too small even to haul away the trees.

Indeed, we seem to live among the trees, Oak Forest, etc. That's the problem with having 1,300 governments: they're too small to check and balance the state. And with no one looking, and the local governments like cities becoming smaller, the state usurps their role. For example, as few seem to know, the state here has put caps on taxes that local governments can levy. So in the case of Cicero, it's not Cicero but the state that puts a ceiling on what Cicero spends.

Then there's the secret government, or the government that's not just off TV, but virtually off the books, for example, the "state-city boards." As my friend Myer says, "*They* control the real prizes . . ."

Who builds the Bears stadium?
Who builds the third airport?
Who builds . . . if they do build . . . the casinos?

So I laugh, I scoff: This is what Daley and Springfield fight over. Does the mayor get two seats on the board, or one.

But come on . . . do I really want Pate Philip to get them *all*? Sometimes, I think, we *do* have to go down there.

YOU HAVE TO GO DOWN THERE

Yes. Bring back a skybox. No, I had other reasons to run for state rep. What? Well, defend the poor. It's now the state, not the city (and *not* Washington), where one does the battle.

And, well, I had other reasons.

One night in Laschet's, a bar, I complained to Tony how I'd gotten a fundraising letter from an old crush, and now she was running for office.

"So?"

"So? Well at least she put a personal note at the end. But she's . . . being a citizen, you know? What am I doing?"

"Want to run for office? Run for office!"

"No, no, I'm not worthy, etc."

"But your issue. Why would you run?"

"Yes, why would I run, really? I mean other than envy? She's doing it, so why can't I?"

I tried to think of an issue. . . . "Well, it might improve my social life."

He lit up. "That's it! That's the issue . . . Looking for the right girl."

"I can't run on that!"

But later Tony and M. took me to lunch, to talk over, well, the race. "Have you seen a map of the district?"

"No."

"You should."

"Yeah," Tony said. "Get a copy of the paper, the B__."

"I, I have to read that?"

The B__ is a neighborhood newpaper, pictures of grade school kids who got into high school.

"Well," said Tony, "how much money will he need?"

"Hm." M. gave a figure, which I can't remember.

"But look," I said, "nobody knows me."

They laughed.

"You can *buy* name recognition."

Not with my name, I thought.

"What you need," M. said, "the one thing you have to have, is a lot of friends."

"But," I almost wailed, "if I run for office, I won't have any friends."

Of course who cares once you're in, right? But that's the paradox: at first, to run, you really do need a lot of friends. Too many friends.

"But isn't this what you wanted?"

I argued it over and over. What if I'd lose?

I had a friend who lost. I remember how I came across him wandering around the Loop. It was his first day back, he said, after his loss. I took him to lunch. He sipped tea. He smiled, "This is a good day."

He'd lost and now was $40,000 in debt. I stared in horror. What if this were me?

Friends would take me to lunch. I'd sip tea. Say slowly, "This is a good day."

No, no no. But on the other hand, what if I won?

Well, I'd be in Springfield. "He so loved the city," he went down there and gave it up. What agony. The hotel every night! Yes, but I could do something for the poor. That's where the battle is.

But what about the "stings"? I read now about the mass indictments of aldermen, over ten of them in the last five years.

In a story the alderman with the "wire" is quoted as saying, "You know a guy is on the take if, when he's offered a bribe he says, 'Oh. That's not necessary.'"

I gasped when I read this. "Might not I, being polite, say, 'Oh. That's not necessary'? And then click. Handcuffs. Ten years in Statesville.

And what of other horrors? A friend of mine was telling me what she saw outside her window. Friday night, at 2:00 A.M. A car pulled up, with a spotlight, and shone it all over a local pol's house. The guy had a mega-phone, on the car roof, and was shouting, "X, YOU ASSHOLE, COME ON OUT! COME ON OUT!"

He shot the spotlight wildly all over the house, and kept screaming, "COME ON OUT!"

I told Tony, "See, that'd be me! What would I say to the neighbors?"

"Say: 'I'm just happy that people feel they can come to me at any hour.'"

No, no, I'm out.

One thing that haunted me, though, was a remark from my friend Gus, "Think of all the deals you could see."

I could see them from up here. No, he was right, I should go down.

And if I cared about the inequality, the poor, that's where I could do something. But do what? Government by discussion . . . with these guys?

I backed off from running. Later I had an experience that made me feel I'd done the right thing, I guess.

It was on Good Friday, at night, I was light-headed, I'd fasted . . . that means, for me, I had postponed dinner.

Anyway I went to a Whole Foods and saw J., a woman I knew, com-ing out of Transitions, a New Age bookstore.

Now it's true J. lobbies for the good causes in Illinois, but she's tough, hard-knuckled, so I was surprised to see her coming out of . . . well, that store.

"Oh," she said, "I was buying tapes."

Let it pass, I thought.

She went on, "Yes, from over there. I play them when I drive down to Springfield. When the Republicans won in '94, I thought, 'What am I going to do? How am I going to deal with this?' I mean, they'll cut everything. But still I . . . I couldn't do this job if I think of them as evil."

"Sure."

"So . . . I buy tapes, and I try to think positive thoughts, kind thoughts."

"About . . . about these Republicans?" (It was a question.)

She frowned, "Yes, what else am I supposed to do? Am I supposed to hate them? I can't be like S."

"No."

"And the other thing I do, I get these Rush Limbaugh tapes and pop them in, for the drive, the whole three hours. By the time I pull into Springfield, some of these . . . legislators, they seem almost reasonable."

I was dizzy.

"Now," she said, "you could say, 'Well, why do this?' But lately I've been able to get some deals. Now maybe I'm kidding myself, and none of these deals will hold, but . . ."

I was starving.

Later, eating alone, I thought, "Maybe, to deal for the poor, you do have to play the tapes."

I NOW THINK, "Forget Springfield, build a city up here." Try to heal the broken vision, and think of city and inner suburb together as one city. "Yes, the battle really is up here in Chicago," I think.

A while ago, I went to a speech by a state legislator from Minnesota. His topic was "building bridges" between the city and (inner) suburbs. Cicero, Maywood, Riverdale, they have many of the problems of Chicago: crime, poverty, even gangs. In some cases, their tax bases are in decline, while Chicago's has shot up. The outer suburbs are the common foe, sticking us with the poverty, crumbling schools. Pitiful to drive past the old malls of the inner burbs: some are just used car lots.

Forty people in the room. Where were they from? the moderator asked.

"Who's here from downtown civic organizations?"

A few hands.

"Who's from the governor's task force?"

Sounds like a chain gang, doesn't it?

"Who's from the better housing groups?"

The roll call went on. The associations seemed to outnumber even the people in the seats. Then came our speaker from Minnesota. He told us how in his state, the city and suburb even work together on tax issues. He said they sought to replace the local school property tax, which is inequitable, with the income tax.

"What?" someone yelled, "That would put us even more in the State's power!"

"Why is it," Mary next to me said softly, "why is it these guys are always from Minnesota?"

The legislator went on with the story of Minnesota, how the churches helped heal things, etc.

"So, yes," he said, "we have to think region wide."

"This is Chicago!" someone said. "We don't even think city wide." But how wonderfully high-minded it would be for us in the city to march out to DuPage, and say, "Bad enough to abandon the city . . . did you also have to abandon the poor little Inner Burbs?"

THE OTHER DAY AT THE ITALIAN VILLAGE, in a kind of darkness-at-noon, I had lunch with Tim, who used to work with Harold Washington the mayor. At the end of his life, Harold thought about a city-suburb coalition, Tim said. As a black mayor, he didn't want to become isolated.

Oddly enough, Daley seems to think less about it, we agreed.

At the time there was much press as to how Daley had unified the city, made it stronger. No more arguing, turmoil, as there was under Harold Washington.

But as a result, the voting has dropped. Especially for blacks, who, as an academic friend moaned, "are so isolated, cut off, even from Hispanics."

Yes there was turmoil under Harold, but didn't people come out to vote? "Tim," I asked, "don't you think Republicans in Springfield used to fear him, because he could turn out so many voters?"

"Sure," he said.

"In Springfield, didn't they worry that Harold . . . well, in a statewide race, he could take a guy out."

Tim said, "And did."

Now he's dead.

Now Daley's unified the city. And so no one votes, which is fine by him.

In Springfield now, well, what's to worry?

THE CITY BLOOMS

But the city blooms, even as it becomes weaker politically. When I say the city blooms, I have to explain what I mean by city.

As my demographer friend J. said, there are two cities. "There's the old Chicago, the old city . . . that's dead. But inside that old city, there's another city. It's white hot. It's . . . it's not Lincoln Park, it's what I'd call 'Greater Lincoln Park.'" He meant: the spiraling out of the primal ur-Yuppie neighborhood. He got me to think of it as a city.

"It has a population of 1.1 million, it's a city the size of greater New Orleans."

And Daley is like a master of revels of this little city, the white hot "New Orleans."

Meanwhile, in the outer-shell city, cold and dark, the ball is swinging, bam, bam, knocking the houses down.

There's much talk of public housing coming down, Cabrini, etc., but it's the private housing stock that's going too. In the first half of 1996, a reporter found, the city was knocking down private buildings at the rate of TWO CITY BLOCKS A WEEK.

OK, they're crack houses, etc., where children are dragged in and raped, but even if it's true . . .

Two city blocks a week?

I said this to J., and he said, "Look, we have to tear the city down if it's going to come back."

"All of it?"

"We aren't tearing down all of it."

He was annoyed, so he took me to a map: "Look at the little green lines. These are little rivers of green . . . That's all new development." Looking at this map, I had an image of snakes: Loop professionals wriggling into places where I didn't think they belonged.

I kept thinking of the two cities, the white-hot little one, throbbing, in the corpse of the old one.

It turns out even the taxes are set up this way. More and more the Mayor is using "TIFs," or "tax increment financing" districts. Only a policy wonk like me would care about TIFs, but they really are the new "shame of the cities." A TIF is supposed to help a "blighted area," but someone decided the Loop is blighted. So that means all the new tax revenue from the Loop, fabulously wealthy, can only go back to the Loop. That's why the rich areas, taxwise, are like gated compounds. Their taxes can't leave!

The rich get more fancy lampposts, while the poor get cut out of the city's boom.

So, starved of tax money that belongs to me, my friends, the outer city crumbles. "But still," I thought, "how can the city tear down so much?" I asked Len, my colleague, about this.

"Oh," he said, "they send out inspectors, who find building code violations. Then they go to building court, then they wait, till they collect a lot of judgments. Then they go and knock down a lot of buildings all at once."

He paused, "And the owners are very pleased, often. It saves them the expense."

Do I want the city to be full of these rotting crack houses? Of course not.

But I feel badly that by kicking out the poor, the city is pushing its problems, the poor, I mean, over the city line.

Now it's true, as J. cautions, we don't know if the poor are moving out to Riverdale or Harvey, or some other place, some suburban Devil's Island. We have to wait for the next census. But Riverdale and Harvey do have more poor. Does it matter if the poor are "out there"? Sure, because out in these midget burblets, there's no Big City for the poor to march on, no Daley to corner: "Give us food, give us jobs!"

As the city, the "new" Chicago, becomes smaller . . . and yes, weaker . . . it is so much easier in a way to push out the poor. Push them, ah, just over the city line. Now it's the burbs' turn to cry: Maywood, other places. So as the city becomes weaker, it becomes stronger. As it loses people, it runs budgets in the black.

Now that seems at first counterintuitive: the fewer people, the more the tax base of the city rises. That's true all over isn't it? I keep thinking of those numbers:

Chicago (1947): 3.7 million

Chicago (1998): 2.8 million

And it seems to me that the smaller the old city gets, the more our civic imagination shrinks.

It makes it easier to cut back food stamps and turn our glance away from mass poverty.

But if Chicago is no longer as big, it actually looks like a bigger city. I mean the new postmodern buildings, glass, and the tops with little turrets and needles and minarets.

I stare at those little turrets and minarets, many a night from my window.

Maybe I can't be a citizen now of a big old-fashioned city but at least I can imagine how it used to be.

It's ascended now into the sky like a skygod. There it is, every night.

It burns and burns, but it never seems to burn up. From here, I can feel like I'm standing on holy ground, and should take off my shoes.

It always reminds me how in cities once there were live men and women with large hearts, and they had the nerve, the imagination to see the country whole, and do such bold things—the New Deal, the Great Society, which had floors and minimums that no one in the city could go below. Still, I miss the time when the city wasn't just a view, but something that, as Madison might say, "enlarged our view."

But unlike those days, it's easier to stand at night and see the city, oh, as a unity, as one work of art . . . subspecie aeternitas.

Sometimes I think, Oh, go live in a burb. Stop looking at a line of boxes.

Yet I can't seem to stop looking at it, the way it hangs up there, and burns. What does it mean, this light that seems to travel from the distant past?

Oh, I like to drive to Halsted and Chicago Street to look at it . . . and, just stop, and look up at it. To see, every night, one city, all of us in a single city, the whole republic in a single glance.

TWO

City of Fabulous Jobs

WHEN I WAS IN HIGH SCHOOL, MY TEACHER SAID OF ME, "You were meant to be a civil servant."

Be a citizen, and run for office? No, I was meant to be a civil servant. Even now I feel, "How could it have happened that I'm not in the civil service?"

Even my boss at the Department of Energy said to me, when I left, "Don't you think, one day, you'll be coming back?"

Oh God, and don't I still wish it! And when Clinton was elected, and I thought I was over all this, I . . .

"Oh," I thought, "O, D.C.! City of Fabulous Jobs!"

I wish I had one!

Even now, I still miss it. Everything. I miss . . . , the DNC, the SEC, the PBS.

I miss the free concerts at the Library of Congress.

I miss the restaurants—Nora, the Tabard Inn, where the waiters look like interns at the *New Republic.*

I miss it all, now that Clinton's in.

I almost went down. I should have. Really. When he was elected, I did go to D.C. for a visit, I asked people about the inauguration.

"It was," my old college teacher said, "like the opening pages of *The Charterhouse of Parma.* The young French officers storm in, and there's dancing, and balls, and freedom of the press, and they throw out the corrupt old Austrian Catholics . . . oh, sorry, Tom, about the 'Catholics.'"

"No, no, it's all right."

But when the young French officers stormed in, what was it they came to do? Reduce the deficit?

"Well, that's good enough for me," my friend Mike said.

"Yes, yes, and we should raise the savings rate, too," I agreed.

Oh, that felt good to say. I was sick of being a "local" Democrat, and talking of Pate Philip, and Jim Edgar, and Rich Daley, and the—what? The disposition of the garbage.

A friend who came out to visit when I first moved to Chicago marveled one night at a restaurant under the El: "This is, so . . . unlike D.C.! I mean people out here talk about . . . things that matter!"

"Like what?"

"Like . . . the disposition of the garbage."

O, D.C.! I felt sick, because I knew *I* was always first of all a citizen of this city, Washington.

I miss the red light blinking on the Washington Monument.

The fire in the fireplace at the Tabard Inn.

The way the fountain in DuPont Circle would leak, all August, like a broken toilet.

When these pictures haunt me, when I think of the taxis at the 7-Eleven, and the drivers who throng around like Special Forces from the U.N., I'm a citizen not of Chicago, but only of D.C., and always will be.

I'm a citizen of D.C. because deep down, I'll always be a "national Democrat." And I care more about the interest rate, the savings rate, the growth of inequality in the U.S., and I just don't give a damn about the disposition of the garbage.

Besides, how can I be a citizen of Chicago where I didn't go to high school and know the local teams?

No, no, I'll always be a "national Democrat," and what does that really mean? It means, out here, nobody knows my name. I still feel like K., who because of her work moves from city to city. And she told me how she has a way of getting people in a new city to "know her name": she sends flowers. Flowers to the druggist. Flowers to the laundry lady. Flowers to the florists. I often thought I'd have been a better citizen if when I came to Chicago I'd sent more flowers to people.

But I already knew the names of people in D.C., so why did I ever leave? Oh, take me back! When Clinton was elected, I was desperate to go back.

Yet in a way, the city of D.C., my true city, has shrunk even more than the city of Chicago. There are now, outside the Beltway, not just 1,300 governments, but over 85,000 governments, and often, the way we talk, D.C. seems like just one government among many, no better than the rest, or maybe lesser than the rest.

It's shocking today how much the city has shrunk, just one among the 85,000, from the time I first saw it when I was a child. And it's been shrinking and shrinking, sick at heart, unable to issue commands.

But in May 1962, my grade school tour, John Kennedy was president, Robert was attorney general, and Washington, D.C., was the greatest city I had ever seen.

To me, when I first saw it, and had a Kodak, and took pictures of the green statues of Stephen Decatur, this was an island city, a holy city, outside and floating above the fifty states.

I still half-feel, the way I fully believed then, as a boy, this was the only city in which I could be a citizen, and be a lawyer, and spend my life, among the green statues of Stephen Decatur.

I read *Profiles in Courage,* like a book of boys' stories. And just as there are boys who dream of growing up and being pilots on the river . . .

Well, I dreamed of being a lawyer in D.C.

But then, I have to say, my uncle worked for Robert Kennedy, and on that eighth-grade school tour, May 1962, I stood at midnight in the Department of Justice. What a place to be in, at midnight, when the clock strikes twelve!

I'd been invited out, away from the other kids, to have dinner at my uncle's house. But as the night wore on, he still hadn't come home, and after eleven o'clock my aunt drove us to see him in the Department of Justice.

It was a dream to be here, a boy, in the dark, next to Athena in the lobby . . . *wow*! We took the elevator, up, and up, and . . .

A blaze of light! Young lawyers, white shirts, picking up the phones. That very night they were sending federal marshals into the South.

Both Kennedys, I learned later, had kind of had it with Alabama, where a bunch of goons one night had actually beaten up one of Robert's aides.

But that night all I knew was that white men with dogs were chasing little black children.

And here I was! The other kids back at the Hotel Harrington were bouncing on the beds—but I was here, at midnight, on the same floor with Robert Kennedy!

(In fact, I don't think he was there.)

It was May.

Cherry blossoms were opening.

Little children were being locked in jail.

I had a Kodak and could see it all.

I should have taken a picture: back when the North ruled the South, and in D.C., young lawyers, white shirts, picking up the phones, were standing over the states. Now isn't it just the reverse?

Anyway, I walked around in a daze, I went back to the hotel, and to the cafeteria, with all the patrol boys from Alabama. I looked at them with disgust—orange crush smeared all over their mouths. The master race. Did they know what was going on?

I kept thinking: I wanted to grow up and live here, in this island city, off the coast of the fifty states, and spend my life being a young lawyer, and moving among the green statues of Stephen Decatur, my country, right or wrong.

When I did come back, it was in college, and it was Stop the War, Stop the War. By then I was a lot more interested in Stephen Dedalus than Stephen Decatur.

You know: Washington (1970) as a nightmare from which we're all trying to awake.

Except even during Kent State, it was my dream to come back. I wanted to be in the Department of Justice next to Athena; I wanted to be one of her lawyers.

I still do, really.

Sure, when Clinton came in, I blush to say, I thought about it again. I was over at P.'s house, and we began to laugh. After the suits, his, mine over the years . . . the very idea, that he or I could represent, well, the government, the United States!

"Can you imagine after suing them, to be on the other side?"

I thought: "Can you imagine the look on the faces of these judges, like

Judge ___?" I'd walk in right before him, and say, "Your Honor, the United States is now reconsidering its position . . ."

Or: "Your Honor, the United States takes the view . . ."

And all the time what I'd really mean, right in his face:

"Your Honor, *I am the United States*!"

Just like my uncle, when he worked for Robert Kennedy.

And just to imagine this, that night, at P.'s house . . . I remembered what it was like to be fourteen years old, and to stand, alone, at midnight in the Department of Justice and, even now, in my forties, I still want to work for someone like Robert Kennedy and say, "I am the United States."

WHILE D.C. SLEPT

It seems over the years we lost the art, the old art, of running a Central Government.

I tell myself now that people who were in the time of FDR, *they* knew. They built the New Deal: they raised wages; they "founded." They should have been, for us the grandchildren, *our* "Founders," just the way that Lincoln and his generation thought of Washington, and Jefferson, and James Madison.

But the problem is, the Founders of *our* national government, the one we inherited, never wrote up what it was they were doing. They never passed any Constitutional amendments (except the noble Twenty-first, repealing Prohibition). They never left any *Federalist Papers*. They simply never wrote it up, the science, the art of running a Central Government. Maybe they were too busy. Maybe they themselves were not aware exactly of what they were doing.

Even by the time of the Kennedys, people older than I were beginning to forget. And the forgetting has gone on and on even though we all laugh and we say, "We're post–New Deal," when no one knows anymore what the New Deal was. And by the New Deal here I simply mean the art, the lost art, of running a Central Government. And I saw it best the first time, the moment my uncle and the other lawyers, at midnight, were picking up the phones.

Oh, I'd love to come back, just the same. I remember the week after

Clinton was elected I wrote in for a copy of the Plum Book, which is a list of federal jobs, appointments.

I flipped the Plum Book open to see if my old favorite job was still in there—"Battlefield Monuments Commission." As the old-timers told me, you make sure the grass is cut at some battlefield in France. Then it's off to lunch at a two-star Michelin. But they'd never give me that. And I felt, well, immoral, flipping through, and I noticed how the book is not "plum" really but yellow, unripe, like a book of drawings by Aubrey Beardsley.

I put it down, it's immoral. It's possible I wouldn't even be in D.C. Many of the agencies have been moved out to the burbs, as if the city, the idea of a capital, is now under siege. I could end up, not in France, but in Landover Mall, or out past New Carrollton or beyond I-270. Where the new congressmen are. And what's eerie is from out there, there is no direct road into the city, *i.e.,* the downtown. Impossible to find. Wisconsin Avenue? I seem to hit every red light.

ONCE, D.C. WAS A BIG DEAL. Back then it was a little white marble city, and emanating out, the sixteen silver cities of the American and National Leagues. Now there is something called New Carrollton, and what emanates out? A few high-tech "corridors," which lead, I guess, to the fifty states. But I saw D.C. before they had a New Carrollton.

Now I should say here that while I was never a waiter at Nora or the Tabard Inn, I was in fact an intern at the *New Republic.*

I was twenty-two. I was supposed to be a staff writer. My job that first year was to write little editorial notes.

I remember my first, it was a little one, "The Arms Talks in Berlin."

When I came home that night, my roommate said, "What do you know about arms talks in Berlin?"

"Nothing."

"Well then, how . . . how can you write this?"

"It's easy," I said. "You call up a staffer on Capitol Hill, and he tells you what to say."

"Oh, God," he said, "this is so depressing!"

How could I answer?

Later he got a job at the *New Republic,* too, so I didn't feel so bad. But wasn't he right?

I mean, did I know, personally, that there even were arms talks in Berlin? There might not be.

But I loved going up on the Hill. It was, they say it is now, an incredible place, the way everyone is twenty-two and twenty-five, and a guy can meet a girl in a cafeteria and just get her first name. I could call Bob: "I didn't get her last name, but I met her outside the Library of Congress." He'd phone Nora, who'd phone Jill, who'd phone Tim, and sometimes— within an *hour,* I once timed it—I'd get a call back, and know:

> Last name
> College major
> Is she seeing anyone now or not?

Even better than the Hill was the "Inner Circle," which was a movie house. Every time I went, I'd see a pal or friend. Not two, or three times, but thirty, forty times, *every* time, and I was keeping count, like DiMaggio's streak.

There is something wrong with that, right? That's what I said to Mike.

"No," he said, "I think it's kind of nice."

Yes, of course. But I was uneasy. "Oh," I scoffed, "it's like living in the burbs, with the same people all your life . . . I just wish I could go to a film and not see anyone at all!"

(Wait, even Alessandra, when I saw her at *Sinbad the Sailor,* the Hungarian Film Festival? No, except for her.)

Then one night I did go to the Inner Circle, which was showing Part IV of the seven-hour Louis Malle documentary *Phantom India.*

And I was watching the Ganges River flow very slowly, and then suddenly it hit me, "I don't know anyone in the theater . . ."

And when the lights came up, I knew why—I was all alone, no one was there at all.

Calvino, in *Invisible Cities,* says the city contains in it all desires, both conscious and unconscious.

I must say when I was young, D.C. contained all *my* desires. If D.C. did not desire it, me neither. I went no deeper than D.C. did.

Anyway, my job, at the *New Republic,* was, really: to read the papers. Each morning I read the *Washington Post* and the *New York Times.* But first I'd go out and get a big cup of coffee, a double cream. All morning I'd sit there with my cup of coffee and two almond crescent rolls. Oh, I can still taste the double cream, and the two rolls with the icing, and the icing dripping all over the almonds . . .

They say, "Write about what you know." Oh, if only I could have written an editorial about the two almond crescent rolls!

Alas, I needed a subject, or just to "know something," other than those two almond crescent rolls! And for some reason I picked the rise of New Federalism, and the states. And in time "the rise of State Government" became hypnotic to me, as the flow of the Ganges in the movie *Phantom India.* Just as at the Inner Circle that night, I also seemed to be watching it alone.

THE TWO BIG CHANGES INSTITUTIONALLY IN MY LIFE, the big ones, that might alarm a true conservative like Edmund Burke, are, I believe: (1) the collapse of American labor, and (2) the rise of big state governments, where once there had been nothing but paper governments before.

The first change, concerning the collapse of unions, took a while to see. But under Nixon, in Washington in 1972, anyone could see the new rise of the states.

Indeed, Nixon bragged about it constantly: it was supposed to be his big idea.

But it was not Nixon but John Kennedy who had started it long before. That's what my old college teacher said: "Back in 1962, the federal government had so much money coming in, Kennedy didn't know what to do. 'How am I going to spend this?' And one of his advisors, Walter Heller, said, 'Let's do revenue sharing with the states.'"

Remember, at this time, the economy was booming, and Washington, D.C., was just awash with money.

Tax receipts: Up, Up! Wages rose over 23 percent in real terms just from 1957 to 1962. And the New Deal had never spent much. The idea of a central government then was, well, picking up a phone, and giving orders, to Wall Street, business, as they did in the FTC, the FCC, the SEC. Much of what John Kennedy did as president was pick up a phone and talk to Walter Reuther of the Auto Workers or Roger Blough of U.S. Steel. This "big" government costs little money. So as tax revenue went up and up, Kennedy's problem was, "What do I do with all this cash?"

Then came Lyndon Johnson, the "Great Society," and spending real money. Kennedy's solution was revenue sharing, big blocks of money to states. Johnson gave them programs to run. It was not just D.C. but the states, especially the states, that would run the Great Society. But why? Why did Johnson want to build up the states? His hero, FDR, hated the states. The New Deal had no use for states. It was the states that had made such a botch of relief programs during the Depression. Until the 1960s it never occurred to any Democrat to give the states much to do.

But Johnson? He wanted to build up the states to lobby for his Great Society. He saw the governors as being a vested interest for spending more.

Then came Nixon. And back then Republicans were spending money, too. That's what S. has always emphasized. "Remember," he says, "in the 1960s even Nixon and Rockefeller were raising taxes." Why not? Wages were going up. As pointed out by Daniel Moynihan: as people's income goes up, they usually have a taste for more government. People were tired of Ike. By 1962, America could afford a Jack and a Jackie Kennedy and even sent them to Paris.

As people became more generous, the government—the government!—was even willing to do something about race.

But Nixon wanted to go back more to Kennedy's sharing of revenue. And waking up, as after a long dream, some Democrats, old New Deal liberals like Joe Rauh, began to grumble: "Why give all this money to the states?"

Answer? Nixon's Southern strategy.

It was the South that gave Nixon a narrow electoral college win. It was chilling even to hear the words: "Southern strategy." I could hear in the background Neil Young, singing "Southern Man."

Why were we giving all this money to the South, with no strings?

And really deep down that's how I stumbled on this as my subject. New Federalism. It seemed to me we should keep Alabama and the rest away from our treasures, the bounty of the New Deal, our seigniorial right in D.C. to levy the Big Tax. Lock it up. Don't give it away to Dixie.

Did I overreact? I now wonder.

Maybe I did because I found I had begun even living a bit like a Southerner in D.C. I'd eat at Scholl's Cafeteria ("Religion and patriotism make this a great place to work"). I'd stay away from Duke Zeibert's with its Northern-style martinis. I was abstemious like Southerners.

Every day I ate rhubarb pie.

It reminded me, after my years in Boston, how close in my life I had come to being Southern.

AFTER ALL, CINCINNATI, where I grew up, was a kind of border city, one that sits on the border of Ohio and the South. When I was a child, I could stare and stare at Kentucky, like *Phantom India,* on the other side of the Ohio River, which I longed to swim across. I had a dread of Kentucky: it was creepy how kids born a few miles away could have a "Southern accent." What if it had been me? Thank God for the Ohio which separated me from . . . well, our own "Phantom India." I was told that by my grandfather's house, high on a hill, was a tunnel that ran down to the banks of the Ohio, and was part of the Underground Railroad used by the fugitive slaves. I begged and begged for some adult to show me the tunnel and used to imagine I'd go down one day with a candle step by step, lower and lower, until I landed at the water's edge and could look across the river to slavery and the South.

It was a relief to know my mother, father, all of us, were in the North on the other side.

And in high school I read Faulkner, the white Random House editions. White like the color of terror. The first one I read, *Sartoris,* shivering in the library, I closed it on the last page.

"But it's only a region." This isn't the United States.

No, the United States was the North, and the North was:

> Crisp fall air
> The idea of progress
> Libraries built by Andrew Carnegie

Like this one, the one across from the Shell gas station. While the South was a region, and it was:

> No air conditioning or the idea of progress
> *Absalom, Absalom*
> Rape
> Miscegenation
> No martinis or even beer

The North, the real U.S., was where I'd wake up. Like being in Kansas after *The Sound and the Fury*. It's only a region. I could go to the ballpark with my father and see not a single pennant flying from the South. The North, the New York Yankees, had so crushed it militarily.

Yet something odd was beginning to happen. All my life it's been the North, the "real" United States of my youth, which is becoming the region. And it's the South or New South that is becoming the . . .

United States.

Go to the ballpark. See their flags.

And maybe one day it will be F. Scott Fitzgerald who's the regional writer. (Kids will read him in libraries and wonder, "What was that like?") And Faulkner, and the rotting orchids—that will be the *United States*.

Even I was heading South, to Washington anyway, and the whole country was. And it still is.

It's getting worse every month. Each year Florida (1.4 percent a year) and Texas (1.4 percent a year) widen the population lead over "our" best States, like New York (0.2 percent a year) and Illinois (0.5 percent a year), which are barely growing. And while the South's gain seems small in any year, it's like the "red shift" effect noted by the astronomer Hubble, i.e., the South each year moves a little further beyond our reach.

Now read this, from the U.S. Census Bureau, and think about it: "The South and West regions combined are projected to account for 82 percent of the 18 million persons added to the Nation's population between 1993 and 2000. States in those two regions accounted for 84 percent of growth during the 1980s."

What about us in the North and Midwest?

We get a laughable 16 percent.

What's it mean?

It means our great grandchildren will be speaking in Southern accents. Even now—have you noticed this—guys from Harvard and Yale, Gore, Clinton, etc., to get in power, have to go around disguised as Southerners!

Laugh. But how do you know that you yourself, without knowing it, aren't speaking more and more with a Southern accent? If everyone else around you was, you would not necessarily know.

And what does this mean, this red shift effect? We become more and more redneck; more:

> Chain gangs
> Prisoners
> Female capital punishment

Here's more: Texas has just replaced New York as the second most populous state, and Florida keeps moving up. Soon there will no longer be even one state from the North or Midwest in the top three states.

I know a few demographers now at the Census Bureau, especially Paul and Krista. Paul changes the South's projected growth almost every year—to increase it. What are the reasons? Migration of course, internal and international.

1. Internal. Even the black middle class is moving back to the South. By the way, it's the South that is a big net gainer from internal migration. California? It's losing people now. Anyway, I asked Krista why black professionals are moving back. "Oh, they're attracted by Atlanta."

God help us. There's a book, *Call To Home: African Americans Reclaim the Rural South*. On the cover a black middle-class family, nicely dressed, holding hands, walking down a dirt road.

A dirt road!

Every time I see this cover in my mind, I shiver.

2. International. OK, it's true California still gets a third of foreign immigrants, but the South gets roughly a quarter.

Now here's a puzzle: why do the lowest-wage parts of the country now attract so many immigrants? Oh, I know the reasons the demographers give me: "They have family, contacts." "They like the weather."

Yes, sure, I and my friends, we'll all lose the chance to govern, and why? "They like the weather."

If I were a mayor in a Northern ice city, I'd send out recruiting agents around the world, to Shanghai, and Mexico City, and Bangkok, and Islamabad and try to get people to come North. Our cities are too empty! Fill them up.

Because unless we in the North fill up the cities, we, up here, the party of social democracy, we as social democrats, we'll never get back in power!

Never.

And I'm sorry for the long digression, but the first moment I became scared, just a little, was when I was writing about "New Federalism" in 1972. Why were we building up the Southern states?

I knew nothing about demography then. I did not know then that demography was destiny. But I knew in some vague way the South was becoming bigger and bigger.

I could go down to the Potomac River, along Ohio Drive, on a hot August night, and hear it growing in the dark.

And that's why Nixon was talking New Federalism. This was a much bigger event, though no one cared much, than the opening to China. This was power-sharing with the South!

And now of course it has the power. Now the South does not have to "power-share" with us.

Look—in the House—how the respective strength of the North (Midwest) and South (West) have flipped in my own lifetime.

NORTH VS. SOUTH (NUMBER OF HOUSE SEATS)

	1950	1990	2030 (projected)
North and Midwest	244	195	165
South and West	191	242	272

Can you imagine—272 of them and only 165 of us? Demography is destiny.

And it isn't going to be pretty. Will, in 2030, will there even be a central government then? How can there be a National Idea, when the North is just a "region"?

But back in 1972 hardly anyone saw this, and I was against New Federalism for a different reason: "Why should we build up, out of nothing, fifty huge new state governments?" And why let them do the *things* the central government had been doing? I *liked* the idea of a strong central government. I *wanted* D.C. to have all the power. We were building up the states, nuttily, with the kind of money it took to build the Pyramids.

So I wrote a little series—well, OK, two parts, but to me it seemed like a series—and the title of the first one was "Big Brother's Little Spoons."

Oh, how I hated seeing that money go even to northern places like Columbus, Ohio.

My friends and I had just shown up in town . . . my God, was this any time to be handing power back to Columbus? So I really meant these articles for my friends—twenty-two, twenty-three, twenty-four—to shake them awake as they stood in line at the Inner Circle.

But they missed the whole thing, and who can blame them, when there was Watergate, Vietnam, etc. My own nightmare was revenue sharing, and here's the thing that still haunts me:

In my family's neighborhood, there was a civics club, which gave baseballs to kids. And when revenue sharing began my brother told me: "Did you know even the civics club has gotten a little of this?"

"They didn't know what to do with it, so they bought coffee cups." (My brother, who was an auditor, made them give it back.)

But this is what scared me: that the whole New Deal would collapse into a cascade of coffee cups.

THE RISE OF THE EMPTY BOXES

As a child in Cincinatti I barely knew what a state was. I knew I was in Ohio. And Ohio had a state bird, and a tree, which was the buckeye, a little mahogany knob-type thing that kids whizzed at each other like little rocks. But beyond that, what was it? Nothing. An empty box.

Now each box is bigger:

States do "policy."
States have "income tax."
States have "new ideas."

I listen to the Right denounce Washington, while state and local governments unnoticed move up the constitutional food chain. I could pick so many numbers, but here's one:

	EMPLOYMENT	
	Federal	*State/Local*
1950	1.9 million	4 million
1995	2.8 million	16.5 million

Apart from defense, the federal government is lightly garrisoned. Or look at the growth in spending:

	NONDEFENSE NONENTITLEMENT SPENDING	
	Federal	*State/Excludes local*
1950	16%	28%
1995	12%	34%

Worse, the state and local budgets come from sales taxes and even income taxes directly levied on the poor.

And as each state budget grows, it impinges, it poaches on the federal power to tax. There's only so much of a tax burden the majority can handle.

So as state and local grew, people in D.C. accepted that our nation, the central government, just has to do less.

And I think people *wanted* to assume this. It's as if there was a loss of nerve.

Or maybe some of us lined up at the Inner Circle knew D.C. too well. It was nice, when making our points, to think that out in the Real

World, there were state and local officials, 16.5 million, who really knew better than we what to do.

Of course now that I'm out here, I know, like everyone else, this is a fantasy.

THE OTHER DAY I had lunch with Steve, a lawyer friend. Now what sensible lawyer, Steve said, with a choice between state and federal court, or a state and federal agency, would ever go to state? "No one," I said. "Right! Why?" "Because at least the federal guys don't lose the files." "Right," he said. "You know, I know. Why don't they know in D.C.?"

You mean at the Cato Institute, the think tanks? At some level I think they do know. That's why they're living in D.C. and not in one of the fifty states.

The odd thing is, in real life, day-to-day business: the feds are much more flexible, responsive, than any state official.

A state bureaucrat? As Steve says, it's malpractice to go to one when there's a federal official available.

A more serious point: At least the fed isn't paid off. No one brings this up; it's impolite. As I write this, we are devolving welfare et al. to the states. Our Illinois Department of Public Aid was on trial all summer (1997). A company which contributed thousands to the governor now seems to have compromised the department's staff.

When the state officials go on trial, who prosecutes? (Worse, who judges?)

All the prosecutions have to be done by the U.S. Attorney, because even the state prosecutors are out seeking to raise the same kind of money.

The U.S. attorney offices around the country could exist simply to prosecute the states. And where would you even begin? Jim Burns, the former U.S. attorney in Chicago, said he could go in at random, not just Illinois, but anywhere, any state, and bring dozens and dozens of prosecutions. The cost to the U.S. is staggering, every time we "devolve" anything to the states. I once compared it to Mexico, and a friend of mine said, "Well, really, aren't you going too far?"

But in terms of billions, the savings and loan scandal, which came when the Feds simply turned over all the regulation to the states, is at least on a scale with the sums stolen by the Salinas brothers. In 1996 U.S. attorneys indicted 219 state and local officials on corruption charges. Look, I understand the feeling of Ben and Jerry for Vermont; or of backpackers for Oregon; or of all people who have to live in Mayberry RFD; or of city people who have state capitals in their own cities where they can watch them. But for the rest of us, devolution is a way of avoiding accountability.

But the weaker all government becomes, the more the states get built up in Washington, D.C.

"Oh, they're so flexible."

"They have ideas."

"Did you see they have no welfare in Wisconsin, blah, blah . . . ?"

When the states *do* look good, which is hardly ever, it's always because of something Washington, D.C., is really doing, e.g., if unemployment drops due to national policies, the states end up with budget surpluses and say, "Look, state government works!"

But people my age floating around D.C. were always moaning, "Maybe we should try the states, maybe they have ideas, etc."

We didn't have ideas.

When Clinton was elected, I was in an argument with J., who was saying, "You know what bothers me about Clinton?"

"What?"

"He doesn't have any ideas."

"So?"

"'So'? What do you mean?"

"So, he's the president. He's not supposed to have any ideas. What about you and me? What ideas do we have?"

"You're right. What's the matter with us?" But then he asked (this was early 1993), "You know what's scary?"

"What?"

"The number of people *you and I know* who would love to see Clinton fail."

Right then I knew: in this it seems to be like the Carter era. All over again.

Now even under the Democrats, the states get all the marbles.

But why did we lose our nerve?

It was the sense all around us that we were getting outnumbered, as

Florida, Texas, the South, were building up. Or that's what I think. Wallace had been scary, and then all the talk of a Southern strategy. And Kevin Phillips had written *The Emerging Republican Majority*, and it was emerging, but mainly because the South was getting bigger, and bigger.

And more conservative.

"It wasn't so bad," a Texas lawyer told me, "until all these Northerners began moving down."

Well, OK, maybe we did make it worse.

Anyway, I felt this unease all through the Carter era, the late Antonine period. Reagan barbarians invading the perimeters. More and more people I knew were being mugged or murdered.

The white marble began to seem funereal, and it occurred to me for the first time that life could be short. Think of poor Nixon weeping as he left office. Of course I'm not looking for pity. Arlington Cemetery, after all, was full of the bodies not just of the Kennedys but of kids my age who weren't able to sneak out of Vietnam. They were just lying there across the river. All the time we went back and forth moaning, "What's the matter with us? We don't have any ideas!"

Anyway, from the moment I came, I could feel, in some strange way, power slipping out of the city.

But maybe I was a little strange, with my interest in revenue sharing. One day the managing editor came down (this was 1972) and in a friendly way pulled up a chair: "Have you thought, maybe, of trying a new subject?"

I frowned. "New subject?"

"Something other than revenue sharing."

"Like . . . what?"

"Well, look," he said, more excited, "two weeks ago . . . you know, the break-in over at Watergate? Why not drop all your other duties here, and simply follow *that*! Just that one story, just follow it, see where it goes."

I gasped. "You really . . . you really think, this break-in . . . is more important than revenue sharing?"

He shrugged and walked away.

Years later I told S. what I had said that day, i.e., did he, the managing editor, think that was more important than revenue sharing? "Ah," he said, "a man's subject!"

CROLY WARNED US

I myself didn't know what the New Deal had done.

Every day I used to come into the *New Republic* and pass the photo of Herbert Croly, our founder. By then the "new" in *New Republic* was like the "new" in New York.

Poor Croly in his high starched collar. Sad little mouth, wire glasses. A sissy who became a "Bull Mooser." By then no one ever read his book, *The Promise of American Life*. "Ever read it?" I'd ask people there. No one had.

Yet once he'd been so famous, and in every good American history there's a page or so on Croly. Why? "That was the book!" S. said. "In the 1920s everyone read it. My teachers said, 'Read Croly.'"

Indeed, in 1910, Theodore Roosevelt read it, and was so excited he ran for president in 1912.

"My God, it's dreadfully written though," S. said.

That wonderful title, though! And what was the "Promise of American Life"? It seemed to me that Croly, in his collar, choking, was trying each morning to tell me—what?

But I was young and blithe, and eager to eat my almond crescent rolls. And I know now, "Poor Croly! He was trying to warn us." If the states got stronger and Washington became weaker, we would have the old evils back, the evils of 1909.

Inequality. Stagnant wages. Big Business running the country.

Who could have known, when I was twenty-two, the standard of living would stop rising for so many, as it had in Croly's time?

I know now that it is the purpose of our central government, in Croly's view, to raise *continuously* the standard of living. This was the point of having a federal government, a nation. As my teacher said, "You don't have federalism just to have federalism. There has to be an idea."

Croly's was social improvement. Pushing up the standard of living.

Now even Democrats, certainly Clinton in his State of the Union, have trouble saying it. Now we say, equal opportunity. College loans. Clinton begs people, "Don't give up hope."

How dreadful. A Democrat, begging like that. "Don't give up! Maybe your child will do well on his SATs!"

It's the president's job, Croly would say, to raise up the standard of living now. But alas, I ignored this.

But one editor knew my obsession with the New Deal. He said: "Why don't you go and pay a visit to Ben Cohen?"

Cohen, when he was young, even about my age, was writing up the New Deal laws, setting up the agencies for securities, for utilities. He lived a golden life, building the . . . well, "new republic." A real one!

Now that was the time to be young in D.C. Many of them gathered around Felix Frankfurter, and they were known in those days as Frankfurter's Hot Dogs.

The kids who wrote up the New Deal, though they were about the same age as Hamilton and Madison, the Hot Dogs of Philadelphia.

But it's chilling how fast people become old, and Cohen, a bachelor, lived in an apartment and all alone.

Anyway, I came to find out what he had never written down, but I learned nothing. Or I didn't know enough to ask the right things. Or I hadn't read, before I came, *The Promise of American Life.* What a fool I was, to miss that chance.

I was too dumb to be enlightened by the master.

Of course I have now read *The Promise,* and I have a sense of what the New Deal did: it raised wages, and barked at businessmen, and it set national standards, national minimums.

Back then they had lots of nerve.

But here's what took me years to find out, and it's the terrible thing Cohen and all of them did as young men. How bitterly he must have rued it, too, when he had reached his old age. And what they did, the terrible thing, was . . . they made a deal.

The "Deal" in the New Deal was that it never applied in the South. That's how Roosevelt was able to get so much of it through Congress. The South had no labor unions or wage bargaining. The sharecroppers down there did not even get a federal minimum wage.

While we got prosperity, the *"affluent society,"* they had to go barefoot. While I read *Sartoris,* they had dirt roads.

I suppose if there hadn't been a "Deal" we couldn't have raised wages in the North. And for a while it didn't matter. But then came air conditioning. Then came the opening of the South and West. Business could go down there, to get away from unions. And the labor laws by the 1960s were much different from, and harsher than, those in the New Deal, and unions couldn't organize, i.e., do the secondary boycotts, mass picketing, running wild in the streets, as they'd been able to do then. And it was as if a hole had been punched in the bottom of the New Deal. The wages, the jobs could leak slowly into the South . . .

Drip, drip, at first.

Then gushing, in a flood.

Yes, we kept them barefoot, we cut them out, and they came back in my lifetime out of the South for their revenge.

And wages began to drop nationally, as the South, in population, in GNP share, grew and grew. Now many of my friends argue about this: "No, no you have this all wrong."

Fine writers I admire say that the great story of our time is that the South became like the North, i.e., the country was leveled *up*.

"You think they're all barefoot down there," said a journalist friend. "You should go to Tennessee, Alabama—they have fourteen-, fifteen-dollar-an-hour jobs."

As well I know, since I have represented people living down there. It's just a partial truth that "their" wages came up. It's also that "our" wages went down.

It is one country more and more. Whether or not the economy is global (which one can debate), it certainly became national. Business flits, in my experience, not from country to country but from state to state. Sprint one day has a big office in Chicago. Next month it has folded its office in Columbus. People say "It's the global economy" when they really mean it's now national. Just as Europe is Europeanized—Holland, France, Germany all together—so the U.S. is now Americanized, with Massachusetts and California really in the same market.

And when this happened, did we bring the South up? Or did we pull the North down?

Are they more like us? Or are we, now, more like them?

Voting is a good example, since the North and South now vote at closer to the same rate. With the end of poll taxes and literacy tests, people in the South voted more.

But just as important, people in the North, where the voting rate in some places would be up to 75 or 80 percent (i.e., Sweden-type levels), began voting less and less. So who became more like whom?

That's worth emphasis: In presidential elections, it may seem the national voting rate has declined a moderate amount. But in the North and Midwest, which, for GNP purposes, was once the real America, the falloff is much sharper. It was we in the North who really lost our republic.

Anyway, the more I lived in D.C., the more I wanted to head north. I came up with so many reasons.

"I should see the real world."

"I should see a real city."

But now, years later, I think it was an innate, Democratic instinct: "Get out of this city. Head to the North."

Something was wrong. What? Some emanation from Croly's photo, that I'd live here in the ruins of "the National Idea"?

Oh, I told people I wanted to see the real world.

One day I went to see my editor. "I'm quitting."

"Too bad," he said. "You could have had a career here."

"Yeah," I said, "but I'm twenty-three, and I don't know anything!" He shrugged. He didn't really disagree.

Of course if I had known there were going to be talk shows, I never would have left journalism.

Anyway, I did leave. It's too late to go on them now.

At the time people said, "Oh see the real world."

Instead they should have told me, "Never leave the city where you have your best friends." Never leave such a city . . . even if it's D.C.!

I left. I left the capital undefended. The Reagan Republicans were on the way, and I was not going to be there. This is a shameful thing. And the two things are tangled now in my mind, in a dark way.

"I left the capital undefended."

"I left my good friends."

Never betray your country.

Never leave any place you have your friends.

I SHOULD HAVE DEFENDED THE UNION

When I think of D.C., I still feel ghastly, like I betrayed it. I should have stayed on over the years and fought to save it. Why didn't I? Maybe by instinct I was scared of the South.

One thing I like about Southerners—they have courage. I remember Jody Powell's line about Jimmy Carter: "If I were in a fight in a bar, he's the guy I'd want on my side." (And not simply because, at the time, he was commander in chief of the armed forces. Powell meant something else.)

But of all the times in our history to "decentralize"! What could be dumber now, when the whole economy has been nationalized and firms can flit from state to state.

It's at least arguable that in this highly mobile U.S. economy, it is harder now for states to handle even their traditional programs, like worker's comp. This is precisely the time when we should centralize, in Washington, the programs the states used to run well.

Incredibly, public policy is headed precisely the wrong way.

But that's the least of it. As I write this (1997), the Supreme Court is "playing" with the "idea," the National Idea, handed down to us from the time of Lincoln and the Civil War.

It's not FDR who's under attack now; it's Lincoln.

I know this sounds hard to believe, but have you read the *Term Limits* dissent?

S. had mentioned it to me. "Look, you ought to read this, they're quoting Calhoun . . ." In *U.S. Term Limits, Inc., v. Thornton* (1995), four justices in dissent said that a state can limit the terms of U.S. Congress members from that state. That is, the state can regulate, in a sense, Congress. And sure enough the justices quote, though indirectly, John Calhoun.

Remember Calhoun, gnarled and old, and rival of Daniel Webster and Henry Clay? Calhoun who argued that a state had the right to nullify a law of Congress?

Well, Calhoun is hot now, and read a lot by Ayn Rand types on college campuses, and they are known in some law schools now as "neo-

Calhounians." And it's startling to read the opinion by Clarence Thomas, though it is important to stress: a total of four justices signed.

First, they say: There is no such thing as "the American people." They adopt Calhoun's famous argument as to why "We the People" in the Constitution really does not mean "We the People." Or rather, to Calhoun, it means "We the People of Georgia, the People of South Carolina, etc."

Well, if that's what it means, why didn't the Founders say it?

"So?" you say. "Who cares, and what's the point?" But the point is, you and I are no longer "Americans," or that is not our true and first *name*. What Lincoln said—"of the People, by the People, for the People"—this is not just a legal fiction, but the neo-Calhounians say it's a legal mischief.

When you are in Paris and say "*Je suis américain,*" you are spreading error. It is better to say: "*Je suis illinoisian . . .*"

Or Virginian, or Georgian, etc.

Second, they say, in passing: Even the term "the United States," in the singular, is incorrect, really. "The United States," in a sentence, is really plural.

So a lawyer like me who says "The United States is of the view . . ." is speaking nonsense. The lawyer is better advised to say, "The United States *are* of the view . . ."

Likewise in the Olympic Games, people commonly say, "The United States is number one."

The justices will indulge this, but really it's "The United States *are* number one!"

But still, what difference does this make? This: if there is no American people, if there are only as Calhoun and four justices claim, only the peoples of South Carolina, Georgia, and so on, virtually everything that Washington does should be subject to strict scrutiny. Have they gone so far? Not yet. But last year, in *Prinzt v. United States* (1997), the Supreme Court by a vote of 5 to 4 held that the United States Congress cannot compel a sheriff, for example, to perform any function for the federal government.

In certain ways, Officer Friendly in his sphere is sovereign over the Joint Chiefs of Staff.

And the cops who sexually assault people with broom handles? Yes, they can still be sued for the moment under federal law. But the neo-Calhounian logic may soon, one day, put even that certainty "into play."

Indeed, in the minds of many in D.C., and on the Supreme Court, there is no such thing as the American people. It is, in their world, always 1787. Washington has not taken office. Lincoln has not even been born. There never was a Civil War.

And the majority on the Supreme Court, in the *Term Limits* case, even they seemed to lose their nerve. As a friend said, "Even their opinion was weak. It doesn't even go as far as Lincoln, who said in effect, 'It's not the states that created the nation; it's the nation that created the states.'"

If the justices are right, if the neo-Calhounians are right, how do we justify the Civil War? How do we justify abolishing slavery, for example? I don't recall the people of Georgia, of South Carolina, signing off on that.

And when I read the *Term Limits* case, I felt a chill, and not just because I live in a Northern city.

This is what comes from letting the South grow and grow. Of course, what could we have done? No, the real shame is, we kept them out of the New Deal. Maybe that's what I sensed when I was in D.C. in the 1970s: one day we, the children and grandchildren of the New Deal, would have to pay, drop by drop, for what they did.

And now we debate, hotly debate, too, up on the Court, not just the legacy of Roosevelt, but of Lincoln, too. And wait till—2030. What will it be like *then*, when the South is much bigger than it is now?

"I am an American!"

That's what I'll shout when they come for me.

No, they'll probably just laugh and leave me alone, if I'm still alive. To me now it seems an omen that my apartment was next to the statue (on horseback) of General George McClellan, who as commander of the Union Army, was famous for retreating North. Poor McClellan! They stuck his statue far away from the tourists. Yet in a way he is and always will be the hero of the city.

How often do we think, "Oh, be careful! Don't commit!"

It's not Lincoln, but McClellan, outside my apartment, whom I secretly followed on most days.

I retreated, too. As the South became stronger, I drifted farther and farther North.

Now I never go back to D.C.. And what about my friends? Oh yes, I miss them. I wish I could go to the Inner Circle tonight and see someone, anyone, I knew.

It serves me right for drifting out of the city. How stupid it was to do it and leave all my friends behind.

THREE

When They Burned
the "White House"

BEFORE I COULD LEAVE D.C., I HAD TO TRY, AT LEAST ONCE, being a "National Planner."

A New Dealer.

As if Satan had taken me up to the rooftop: "I'll make you a special assistant, and you can start planning all this below . . ."

Let me plan, I thought. An industry or something. I would plan in the French style, centrally. To me, in a way, it would be like living in Paris.

And is that so odd, to like the central government? Look at the most ardent Ayn Rander, free-marketer. What does that person dream of?

To work at the Fed. The Big Bank. The central government at its extreme. If laissez-faire types can go to Washington and set the price of capital through central planning, why can't I think big too? Say, set the price of labor. Or any other price? It's strange, but the only people who can feel the thrill of central government now are those who believe most fervidly in laissez-faire.

Back then I had my heroes—not Ayn Rand or Alan Greenspan, but Rexford Tugwell and Harold Ickes. I wanted to stand, like them, wind blowing in my hair, "on the commanding heights of the economy."

I'd be a civil servant and meet with labor and business. Once I met a Dutch official who said, "Oh yes, we meet every day!" Every day, imagine: they meet and *talk*! Business. Labor. Government. Up on the heights.

This, I think, is what Clinton wanted, too—yes, really. When I first saw him, I thought so. I'd slipped in the back of an early fundraiser (1992).

A lot of empty tables. K. and I sat at one with twenty salads uneaten. As Clinton rose to talk, I was gulping salad after salad—but there was one other at our table, and he was African American. In the whole room, the only black. "So," I whispered to him "what attracts you to this guy Clinton?"

He looked away, flipped open his wallet: Chicago Police.

Just then Clinton was saying: "And I see in this room tonight people of *all races*." And then he went on to say: "And America needs a New Covenant. And it has to be a covenant . . . between government . . . and business . . . and . . ."

I said, excited, "He's going to say 'Labor'!"

No, he bit his lip and wandered off to a new thought, but he came back to it later like a pilot looking for a place to land . . .

"And so . . . America needs . . . a New Covenant . . . and this has to be a covenant between . . . government . . . and business . . . and . . ."

But kept circling and circling and could never find a place to land.

Still, when he was elected—oh! He seemed to beckon us, I mean people my age, who were now so careful of our diet, how we jog . . . to go to D.C., come pull an all-nighter and do some great deed, and then eat at McDonald's and die.

Yes, friends, but we would have lived!

Now when I think of the words "special assistant," I see a dinner party years ago and sitting next to S., and she was purring how she worked on the National Security Council.

She was gorgeous. And she tracked Soviet subs.

"Oh, and where are those subs exactly? I've always wanted to know."

"I could tell you," she whispered. "But I'd have to kill you."

Oh, but for that one night—I would have lived!

AT THE CREATION OF DEREGULATION

Being at the Energy Department was a much cooler thing (I thought) than being at OMB now. I could plan and balance imports and exports of oil barrels the way people might balance the budget now. I'd dream of oil barrels of staves as I went to sleep after work. Wasn't this, in my time, the crisis of the West? Yes, it's what André Malraux would have been doing, I used to think.

Carl W. first told me to join up: "This is where Carter will make his mark."

"But I know nothing about energy!"

"Take any job! Sweep the floor!"

And he added, rightly, "Because how often in your life will you see the federal government really pick out a problem and go after it?"

So at age twenty-eight, I was the lowliest special assistant there. So lowly that the civil service kept saying, to my various bosses, "His job really belongs to a second lieutenant in the Alaskan Naval Petroleum Reserve."

It's awful to think now of that poor bastard freezing up there in northern Alaska while I played around in Washington, D.C.

I wanted above all to work for James Schlesinger, who was the energy czar. A few friends were shocked, "But he's a Republican!" Good!

I wanted to walk on the dark side.

And I remember how all we did was work. I never saw Schlesinger. No one did. He was in his cabin.

All the time. *Was* he in the cabin, though? Yes. No.

The men told stories. How in the last days of the Nixon administration, he, the secretary of defense, said to the Pentagon generals, "You will take no orders from the White House without clearing them with me."

He was our captain, but we never saw him.

In those stormy years, we changed course and tacked many times. Sometimes . . .

We were to convert industry boilers from oil to coal.

(This would save oil.)

No, wait: now we had to convert back. (This would clean the air.)

Or hold it; maybe we'd press the button for NUCLEAR (but not after the accident at Three Mile Island).

So then we'd press the button for SOLAR (but nothing would come on).

But the main goal at all times was to save oil. If we ran out . . .

Well, there'd be inflation and unemployment, and Reagan would storm in.

So people worked, and worked, and worked. Once I even worked 23 hours straight, and yet always, with a sense that we were listing, while Schlesinger, whom we worshiped, because he was a Republican, in part, was up there in his cabin alone.

I gradually made my way up a bit, though for no reason I understand. I thought natural gas, for example, meant some kind of unleaded fuel. So once at a staff meeting I asked, boldly, "What *is,* exactly, natural gas?"

Several people stared.

But then some thought: "He's right—what *is* natural gas?"

Let's start with the basics, like Heraclitus. What is, etc., etc.? So a few people (not many), thought I was asking the most piercing of questions.

But I loved the National Energy Plan. We called it NEP to give it a little Soviet buzz. I loved its ingenious solution to our biggest problem: That problem was, we had put a ceiling on the price of our own U.S. oil, so that it was much lower, artificially lower, than the world price. It made our gasoline too cheap. We drove too fast—1975, 1976, 1977—the years racing past faster and faster; we were using too much oil.

But what if we lifted the ceiling? Then Big Oil would get a windfall. There'd be inflation. Lost purchasing power. So cleverly, the NEP said, in effect:

"Tax the U.S. oil up to the world oil price, then with the extra 'tax,' send it *back* to consumers in little envelopes."

So it was a mix, a little New Deal, a bit of market; we had to carry it, carefully, like a glass of oil and water, first through the House, then on through the Senate.

And meanwhile, there were other bills to draft. Subsidies to hand out. Treaties to sign with Canada.

God knows we worked late. It still annoys me that once I worked twenty-three hours straight. Why?

Talk to the Canadians. So help me, that was the reason.

Even now when I pass the EOB, I shiver. That's where I had to stay up all night with Canadians!

Sometimes I'd get a Coke, in the Coke machine way down next to the cell where they kept the Princess Anastasia. We could always hear her screaming through the building from 3 to 4 A.M.

(They say Carter was sick about it.)

The Old EOB was, we told each other, part of the White House. In real life that's where they track Soviet subs. Of course, it was not the White House at all. It was a big wedding-cake kind of building, and the icing was the color of the Confederacy, and if you worked there, you'd get to hang on the wall a big map of the world.

Even if your job was to feed the bears at Yellowstone, somewhere in the room you had a coffee table with a book like *Security in the Balkans*.

But what I remember most was the smell; it was even stronger in the White House. It was the smell of rosewood mixed with gold paint, and by the end of the day, the smell—well, it would ink its way as if by needle into my skin.

I'd sniff my hand as I went home as if it were cologne.

I'd pass people all day, and they were sniffing their hands. I could often hear people sniffing by late afternoon.

And everyone was crashing. That meant, "Hold my calls, I'm working on a project."

So:

"Joe is crashing!"

"Schles is crashing!" Though who had ever seen him?

All day long, a kind of keening, one would hear, "I am crashing!"

Or, "I'm burning out!"

With a shiver I can still hear the screaming of Yalies who thought they were on fire.

And it did seem the world was about to explode. How to regulate our way out?

In a sense, we wrestled with the problem liberals have had ever since the New Deal: we wanted "the market," and something else. Alan Brinkley in *The End of Reform* argues that as early as 1937, and 1938, the New Dealers became divided as to what the "something else" was. In this case of oil, I *thought* we had an answer: "national security." And of course "equity." We wanted a market solution that would (1) ensure the nation's security, the special goal of the hawks, and (2) fairness, which was our concern for the little people.

But how did you number crunch fairness? Or anything that's not efficiency?

How often did I sit through meetings—and with people smarter than me, which is always annoying—and someone would say, "Should we leave it to the market?"

Do I say "no"? Yet sometimes, I knew, that's why I had been brought into the meeting. (I was even told this once.) "What's the problem?" someone would turn and say. Oh, I wanted the market, yes, and something more. But how do I say that at a staff meeting?

Some of the staff sympathized. They didn't want big deregulatory shocks. After all, why did we come here, except to insulate against OPEC, the biggest market shock of all?

No, we were right to deregulate, but once you get a taste for it, how do you know where to stop?

Oh I can pick apart a regulation. "Let's ditch that one." "And that." "And that."

But what happens, in the long run, to the sense of citizenship, if we knock down all the laws, inefficient as they may be?

What if we make the majority run faster, like little lab rats? Pretty soon, with enough little shocks, people run around, frightened, won't come out of their houses.

TOO MANY OF THESE little shocks, they stop coming out to vote! I believe in the market, a lot.

Once I asked a professor at the Kennedy School: "Why teach all this microeconomics?"

He made clear it wasn't *his* idea. "But when we set up the school, we felt we had to teach them something. So . . . why not give them this, microeconomics, to sharpen their minds?"

Well, why not Greek and Latin, like at Oxford and Cambridge? If they wanted a jungle gym for their youthful minds to play on, why not that?

God knows it worked for the British: they got India. When they won battles, they'd send back the news in Latin, e.g., one-word telegrams like PECCAVI, which means "I have sinned," i.e., Sind.

But soon, it seemed, it was all microeconomics. Cost benefit. Deregulation. Getting prices right—which usually implies, I have found, getting wages wrong.

But what about the other, nobler aspirations of public service?

Anyway, it's now become a kind of scandal. Kids sign up, because they want to do good. I met a young woman recently who goes to the school, and she began crying: "I came here," she sobbed, "because I wanted to help people, and now, now . . . now they say . . . I *can't do anything!*" ("And," she went on, "I have all these student loans . . . !!")

And the terrible thing was, these Kennedy School people were the best I knew. They *did* care. They were the kind who, in the 1930s, would have been at the cusp of "Yes, it's the market and something else!"

Without their help, what can you and I do?

I became very morose. All we did was deregulate.

And work.

I was used to the *New Republic,* and the Old EOB was entirely different—no almond crescent rolls, no leisurely reading of the *Post* and the *Times,* just people running, and inhaling clouds of rosewood, and ululating all day long,

"I'm crashing!"

My God, this wasn't how I wanted to live.

It's odd, but in college I had read Keynes's "The Economic Possibilities for Our Grandchildren." He wrote that the time would come, my time, since I was the age of putative grandchild, when none of us would have to work.

We'd just have our investments. We'd clip coupons. We'd read Bloomsbury. We'd garden. We'd dabble a little in public policy.

Associate general counsel of the Smithsonian. Director of development for oceanography.

I thought in college I could go down to D.C., and I'd never have to work.

And now I would walk around and see people so exhausted they would be crashing into walls. It was a sight I'd see again, in 1980, in fishing villages in the west of Ireland. When a man drinks too much and falls down, or crashes into a wall, the people would shake their heads and say, "He's lost his self-respect."

In the same way, I, and some of my friends, exhausted, would crash into walls. We had lost our self-respect.

There was a poster at the Tabard Inn: WHAT DOES IT MEAN TO BE AN AMERICAN? HARD WORK, AND PLENTY OF IT."

In theory we deregulated to become more productive, but just as we began to deregulate, our productivity growth rate began to drop. Oh, there may be no connection. I can't prove any. But it's odd how when I deregulate in my own life, work late, stop putting up boundaries, my own productivity begins to drop. (It would only pop up again fifteen years later.) Maybe some of us, in our own lives as civil servants, and people, could have used a little more "regulation."

When I look back now it seems like we hardly worked. No fax machines. No voice mail. Not even computers. All these "labor-saving" devices, which, all day, have us constantly under their surveillance.

Exhausted, we'd fantasize as to what we'd do "later."

I had muesli the other day with a man who was a Clinton staffer, and he said, "You know what the difference is between Carter's and Clinton's time?"

"No."

"Under Carter, remember how everyone said, 'When I get out of here, I'll go up to New York and be an investment banker'?"

"Yes."

"Now they say, 'I'll go out to Hollywood and do a picture.'"

OK, laugh at this, but *Jurassic Park* is as formulaic as writing testimony for the Hill.

This always bothered me. What did I really think of what I was writing up for "DOE"? It was a little worry, worming away inside: "Well, what if I didn't agree?" I couldn't write a letter to the editor. Now it's strange for me to think that way. Never in my life have I written a letter to the editor, about anything, but what if I wanted to? I couldn't. In an eerie way I had given up my right to speak under the First Amendment.

I didn't have the right to vote either.

At least not for Congress, but I could vote for the D.C. City Council. Wow, was that bleak. One day at a poll in an Episcopal church, I thought, "I'm all alone," but over in the dark, a solitary man was voting. As my eyes adjusted, I could see a shape, a face . . .

"Good Lord," I thought. "Robert McNamara!"

Never have I seen a sight as poignant as Robert McNamara voting for City Council.

To me it seemed we were citizens of D.C., and in charge of the Keys to the Kingdom, but in our own personal civic lives, we were like the castrati in the papal court.

Anyway I kept thinking, oh, one day I'll be out in the midwest, and just wait, wait, I'll really write a letter to the editor then.

But the horror would be: to go out there, start on my letter to the editor and find out at last, "I don't have anything to say."

GOODBYE TO CALL CARL

I loved the White House, and never wanted to leave. Of course I was not really in the White House. But my secretary, in another building, would tell friends who called, "Oh, he's not here. He's over at the White House."

Indeed, all of us hangers-on at the Old EOB would have secretaries elsewhere, saying, "They're at the White House!"

Well, this was wrong, so I told Lisa my secretary to stop. "You can't say that."

"All the other secretaries do!"

This was true. ("Oh, let her say it!" the angels sang.) But one day we had a fight, and I began shouting, "Look! We're at the Old EOB!"

Lisa ran off to cry.

Oh sure, I was wrong, but I felt like a fraud every time I saw, on a coffee table, these books like *Security in the Balkans*.

And were any of us planning? Nothing could get through the Hill. The NEP had turned to ashes. I told people at the time, "The U.S. is too big to plan. Maybe they can do it in these small countries, like Holland, but all we can do is deregulate."

Geography is destiny.

But the real truth was, we couldn't get anything through the Senate. The country laughed at us. "Some plan! Where is it?"

Everyone laughed. Carter for a while began to back away from the energy issue. (Iran had not cut off the oil yet.)

The natural gas bill? Hung up in the Senate. Like everything else.

As the energy bills were mangled, I could see my friends, the Rhodes Scholars, the others, we clenched our fists and said, "Oh, they'll never humiliate us like this again."

From now on, we would deregulate everything.

I remember my shame when, for a while, we had a new message: there *wasn't* an energy crisis anymore.

"Well," I asked my boss, "can I say there's an 'energy problem'?"

Hm. "No, too strong."

"What do I say then?"

"Oh . . . let's say we have . . . an energy concern."

And then came May 1979. The Ayatollah. The embargo.

And the country sort of ran out of gasoline.

Inflation, like Latin America. Awful. Oil prices went up 100 percent. Since "energy" was 10 percent of the GNP, that by itself was an inflation rate of 10 percent. It was 11.3 percent in 1979, 13.5 percent in 1980, 10.3 percent in 1981.

Poor Alfred Kahn, whom Carter put in charge of inflation. He tried to be a czar, but was just an advisor.

Then came a real czar. Paul Volcker became the head of the Federal Reserve. Carter, a Democrat, put in a Republican, and Volcker now did the central planning of the economy, by the control of interest, the money supply.

It's hard to grasp the constitutional shift: Once, the White House planned. From now on it would be the Central Bank.

And it started with the oil blowing up. And that was to be the end of my career as a "New Dealer."

Kids fled out of the Old EOB, and they went north by night along the road to New York, where they all became investment bankers. Things were so bad, well, Schlesinger began to appear. I went up to the Hill with him once or twice. I was way in the back behind the other special assistants. Each S.A. handed his attaché case to the one lower, and I, being the lowest, ended up with two. But as we came out of the committee room, there was such a crowd, press, the aides, I was lifted off my feet like at a rock concert and seemed to float on air until I was right next to Schlesinger—and to my everlasting horror, on national TV.

People called for days (there were no answering machines back then). "I saw you on CBS next to Schlesinger!"

It was virtually the first time I had seen him.

"I'm sorry!" I told everyone. For weeks I kept apologizing.

Slowly I turned bitter. They, the American people, didn't want our plan?

Fine. Deregulate. Let the oil companies have their way.

We weren't going to try all this equity stuff. Equity was—well, all of that was for losers.

Let the price rise, damn it. Let the Fed fight the inflation now. And it has seemed, ever since, that the only way to control inflation was the Fed's way.

What does that mean?

Raise the dollar, slow down the economy, get rid of the steel mills, until people were too scared, and intimidated, to ask for a raise. And that's what Volcker (and others) did for the years to come.

And when they were done, the poor were even poorer, and the unions had collapsed. It was the Time of Deregulation. It's funny, after all this, we're supposed to be the envy of the world. But the overall median wage is still, now, 15 percent below the level when I *left* D.C. Entry-level wages? For high school grads (male) they're 30 percent (says the Economic Policy Institute). That's not after Carter, but Reagan, Bush, Clinton, up till now. Why, why would any country "envy" that?

But we solved the oil crisis, right?

Yes, that's what people would taunt: we never had to plan at all. That's why it's so hard for people to take global warming seriously. But is it true that "deregulating" solved the problem at OPEC? No, no! It wasn't the market! No, it was luck!

Luck, there was enough oil in the ground.

Luck, that about half was in desert kingdoms, like Saudi Arabia.

Luck, that these kingdoms could never diversify or develop a real economy, not dependent on oil. (Then they could have cut back supply).

But so what? It didn't happen. Planning was discredited.

For hours I'd brood. Usually up on the rooftop bar of the Hotel Washington.

At night, I'd go up there with C., and we'd watch the sun set. I carry the memory around like a ten-dollar bill, literally. Yes, the other night in Chicago I took out a ten, flipped it over, and saw the Treasury, just as it looked from that bar.

I'd go up, have a Campari, and see the Treasury . . . and as dusk fell, I could see the Jefferson, Lincoln Memorials . . . see the marble, white as human bone, sticking out of the green, the dark green North American forest that Francis Parkman wrote the history of . . .

They set up tents, glowing—one for Jefferson, our First Founder, and Lincoln, our Second—but where was the one for FDR?

Nothing for him. It made me depressed.

What did it matter? I thought. We all have to die.

Across the river. Into the trees.

I'd pause. Sip the Campari. And sometimes late at night the idea of it—dying . . . going out to Arlington, the Flame, and all . . . it didn't seem so bad.

So long as I could get coffee in the morning and still read the *Times.*

Well, I'd think later, nothing I could have done about it. The standard of living, the growing poverty, etc.

For years I'd defend the Europeans, because they did regulate. It was easy when their unemployment was lower than ours, but now . . .

See? People say, look at Europe. There's nothing you can do. You can't plan, can't do anything.

But even in the 1990s, much of "regulated" Western Europe has raised its standard of living twice as fast as we have: as measured in the rate of increasing its productivity and per capita CNP. I could also cite the work of Professor Stephen Nickell of Oxford, and others, who attack this idea that the European labor market, the high-wage Europe I love, is "overregulated."

Some of the regulation is good, they argue. Some is bad. It depends. About a third of the European economies, after all, have unemployment even lower than the U.S.

Oh, we can *think* of regulating tobacco now, because it affects little children. But we don't dare to regulate, as we once did, the wages of adults.

Ah! Back then. "What was it like?" I asked a man whose father once worked in FDR's D.C.

"Oh," he said, "my father used to argue politics with the cab drivers." See? They'd debate with cabbies about the Promise of American Life.

And in our time? It's hard for us to believe we can help the high school grads: no, it's too late for *them*. Is it?

I ran into a man, Eli, several years ago on the streets of Chicago. He's a lawyer and he told me how he knew a vice president at Montgomery Ward: "'Eli,' he said to me. 'Why do you think we rich people hated FDR? Because he raised taxes . . . ? Pfftz! *No,* because after FDR you couldn't get any help! *Before* FDR, you gave your maid like a dress, but *after* FDR, there was the minimum wage! And before FDR, if you wanted your kid to go to Harvard, *go*, but after FDR, there was a middle class and they had to take all these tests!'"

And in the 1990s? We have the maids and waiters and busboys back.

It was sad, the end of the Carter period, not just the end of planning, but even the idea of public service. Once, even Republicans believed in it. Indeed, the old civil servants told me, when I was a cub at DOE, how they used to welcome Republican presidents. "The Democrats," Nick T. once said to me as he perfumed the air with his pipe, "come up with the ideas, with the new programs, then you need the Republican presidents to really manage them."

But the new Reagan Republicans did not come in to make government work, but to trash it, harass the talented people, demoralize them, push them out: the idea, from now on, was to manage even worse than the Democrats and say, "See? Government doesn't work."

ANYWAY, I DID HAVE one good experience as a civil servant. It was when I dropped off my car at Call Carl, the auto repair empire. Of course when I drove in (with a Vega!), I was treated, well, like an intern at the *New Republic*.

Maybe. Maybe he'd fix it.

Later in the day Lisa phoned me over at the Old EOB and said, "Call Carl called. You better call."

I ran to the phone, and the guy who was so haughty had a new tone of voice.

"Your secretary, she said"—he paused—"she said *you were at the White House*!"

Huh?

Well . . .

"When will my car be ready?" I said. Slowly.

It was in a voice I would never get to use in the private sector. Ah, if I could be young, and be a civil servant, and just Call Carl again.

FOUR

In the Gridlock
Archipelago

THE CARTEL THAT REALLY SMASHED US WAS NOT OPEC BUT
our own U.S. Senate. One night during a filibuster, I was trying to
sneak out of work.

"Come in here," said an aide who scared me.

I did.

"Shut the door."

Uh-oh.

I thought I was going to be fired.

He stared, then said, very wearily, "The president doesn't understand
the Hill."

I gulped. Why tell me? I knew that the Energy Plan was dying,
but . . .

It was dark outside. And no one understood the Hill.

By now filibusters had been rumbling through the city for weeks.

I knew there was something evil in the dark out there, and I began to
know its name: the *Senate*.

Look at Carter, even Clinton: everything they wanted, everything,
Carter's oil plan, the labor issues, Clinton's early program, before health
care I mean, everything would pass the House. But nothing, nothing
would emerge from the Senate. It was the Senate back then that beat
down the Energy Plan. It was the Senate that blocked labor law reform,
so that unions died off. It was the Senate, as any historian of the time

makes clear, that ended the New Deal in 1938–39. It was, and is, the Senate that denies the promise of American life.

How?

"It denies us one person, one vote."

"What?" said a friend, an academic. "What do you mean? We have one person, one vote."

"No, it's like South Africa." (We were talking in the time of apartheid.)

"South Africa—are you nuts?"

"Don't you know? There are two senators from each state!"

"So?"

"So? Two! Don't you get it? Wyoming, New York . . . they aren't the same size."

"Oh, that!" he said.

Oh, that! Yes, we tell children once in the fourth grade and they nod, and no one tells them ever again that they don't live in a democracy like almost every other country . . . except China, I suppose.

I didn't "know" either until I got to D.C., and went up to the Hill. My God! Do others know that there are twenty-four states, two senators each, west of the Mississippi? I should have read, before I came, *The Journals of Lewis and Clark,* but until I came to the capital, and went up to the Russell and Hart Office Buildings on the Senate side . . . well:

I really saw the country, what it really is: it's a Louisiana Purchase of "rotten boroughs," empty states, with two senators. Two of them!

The academic laughed nervously. "You aren't serious about this, are you? I mean, you wouldn't get rid of the Senate?"

I was still.

"Come on!" he laughed. Then after a pause: "I mean, you aren't serious about this, are you?"

ONCE DOE BECAME A CABINET AGENCY, I had to leave the Old EOB, and we trekked to our new home in the Forrestal Building. It was hard. At night there was no rosewood to sniff on my hand anymore. Instead, there was the stench of ammonia, so strong it would ruin the taste of the cappuccino.

My job now was to lobby up on the Hill—not the big bills, which were for Schlesinger and top staff, but little bills. These would be on coal slurries, hot slurries, and the routes of pipelines, and things no one else had time for except lower staff like me. Yet these "little bills" showed me the dark side of the Hill.

That's why I went to "hearings." One of my bosses said, "The world's most inefficient way, ever, to collect information."

Riding back we'd talk about this.

"How can anyone be a congressman?" he'd marvel, "and sit there."

"What do you mean?" I still thought it was a great job.

"Oh," he'd say, ". . . is that any life for an adult?"

That's what my friend thought of me when I'd go up there. "He's not doing real work."

Bald men reading aloud; it was like being back in fourth grade, and the children would pass around the reader: "John, you continue where Mary stopped."

As it was then, the unbearable part would be the dumb little questions on the "reading."

Then it was over, and I went up at other times to cut the deals.

Of course, the adult work is to lobby and cut deals. But at times this was more demeaning than just to sit through the "reading."

An example: Let's say we had a bill for a new pipeline. First we had to talk to the chairman's staff. Now often the chairman was a rancher, or cowboy, or veterinarian (in fact, the "vets" were my favorites; at least they were kind). This could mean we'd have to spend an hour comparing him to Churchill.

Quietly, while our side talked, one of us would push—quietly, though—a copy of the bill we wanted introduced. Everyone at the table would pretend not to see. Then a week later the chairman would introduce it, the one we (I!) drafted. Then—here's what stunned me—the Senator would attack us!

"I begged the president to act on the pipeline issue . . ."

Or, "When I saw the administration was taking no action . . ."

Or, "I know, while others hesitate, the time to act is now. . . ."

Meanwhile, back at DOE, my superiors would pop open beers, cheer, buy us McDonald's all around. "He introduced our bill!"

This meant the following:

Dear Senator X,

    For years people in government have puzzled over the pipeline issue. But you were the one to act. You saw the importance of pipelines. I thank you, and Mrs. Carter thanks you, and the American people personally asked me to thank you for introducing such a farsighted, pathbreaking pipeline bill . . .

The first time I had to do this was the hardest. I came to see my boss—not the one I loved, but the other one.

"I can't do this," I said.

"Why?"

"Why? Did you read his press release!"

"Yes."

"He's attacking us!"

"You don't understand the Hill."

"No, I do understand it, it's all a lot of . . . Ah!"

I understood it all right when I read *Democracy,* the novel by Henry Adams, who says somewhere, "When it comes to flattering a Senator, you can never go too far." Now that's hard to believe, right? To get in the Senate it takes some intelligence. But I learned to keep a copy of *Democracy* with me. It was like the way Senator Taft of Ohio would keep a copy of the Constitution, and if he was troubled, he'd take it out and see if he was doing the right thing. Likewise, when I was troubled, I'd take out *Democracy* by Adams and read where he says you can *never* go too far.

The thing about the Hill is, don't try to be in control. Look at Clinton. As long as he tried to pass things like health care, he looked awful. He "didn't understand the Hill." But once he gave up, he looked good. He "did understand the Hill." He did what FDR did, just signed whatever it was. Whatever came out, sign it. Even if one lost. Pop open a beer. What's in it? It doesn't matter. Then one understands the Hill.

No one knows what's in it, out in the country. And when you know that, then the insiders marvel: "Now *he* understands the Hill."

When Washington was brand-new, in 1802, it was said a rider could sink in a swamp while going from the White House to Capitol Hill. It was daring to try. By 1980, it was even more daring to go on foot: at night someone could blow your head off. So "understand the Hill" had a second meaning, as in "understand where to walk."

It was chilling what happened to Steve R., who was locked by carjackers in the trunk of his car. How many interns were shot or raped? I remember S., and other women; when they were held up, they'd move in with a friend and stay for weeks.

Great city, right? How I hated it. Even then I had a sense it was Congress's fault, though I didn't know why. By Carter's time D.C. was supposed to have home rule. Now in 1997 it's been taken back by Congress, and the mayor, Marion Barry, busted for drugs, has been busted now as mayor. And it is often said, "Well, 'they,'" meaning blacks, "couldn't run the city." When I go to D.C., even friends on the left are bitter: "Don't try to defend him. You don't live here."

"I did."

"You don't know what Barry's done!"

Who put Barry in charge?

Congress.

It blocked D.C. from saving itself, e.g., with residency laws to keep the middle class. Mayor Barry was unable even to pass a law keeping the cops and civil servants, his own, in the city. So they fled, out to the burbs, just like the members of the House. Who but the poor were left? No wonder Barry was mayor. The Congress ensured it.

Then they tut-tut, "See? You can't give those people 'home rule.'"

BACK THEN I BEGAN TO THINK: "Why didn't I think of this as 'home'?" I decided to be a volunteer. Do something for my . . . city. I couldn't do anything for my country.

So I signed up with the Red Cross to visit old people in "D.C. Village." It was the biggest nursing home I ever saw, a red brick archipelago of old people, many all alone in their little cubicles like bureaucrats.

I was to go room to room like a lobbyist. I was one of the few males; most visitors were girls in their twenties. We were all under the charge of Miss D., proper, Southern.

I mention her because she was tougher on me than anyone at DOE. She put me to a test right away. Her idea was, I could visit "the men." So she took me to see her good friend Mr. S., who had Lou Gehrig's disease, the very horrifying last stage when one can't talk, the body shaking, the eyes just staring, in fright. And Miss D. would drag me in and chat as if we were at tea. I put my head in my hands. I was woozy. She finally gave up on me.

"You don't have to do this, dear."

All week in Forrestal I'd tell myself, "Next time I'll do it."

But she gave up on me, and sent me to see Mr. W. Finally, it was decided I could spend my whole time with him.

"Oh, you can visit the men!" Oh, the poor men, like Mr. W.! All they wanted to see was a girl.

But Mr. W., near 100, became my last mentor in Washington. He talked me into staying on, really. On Schlesinger, he had strong views, and might say of him, or some Senator: A scoundrel! A rascal!

In short a good man to work for. Heh, heh. Mr. W. approved of these men highly, especially for a young person.

So on his advice I resolved, "I should stay to understand the Hill!"

UNDERSTAND THE HILL

By the Carter era the Hill was changing.

Now by the time I came, the Senate was changing, and wasn't. I mean, senators began to look like Warren Beatty in *Shampoo*. But they now acted like Charles Laughton in *Spartacus*.

Now when I was in high school, I liked the House better than the Senate. Its commonness. Very appealing in Ohio.

But when I was in college, I came to like the Senate much more, because, in my mind, it had glamour, and was more royal and purple, and it alone might stop the war, but also it slowed things down. It stood for the principle of delay, of hesitation, which was appealing, at that time, to a generation of student princes. When, as an intern, I came to D.C., I was in awe of great senators like Warren Magnuson or Philip Hart, whom no one in the country knew but who in the city were known as "the Whales," who would rise and spout and crash along in the seas.

But most of all I liked Iowa's Harold Hughes, who'd been a truckdriver. Once, while at the *New Republic,* I met him when I'd been taken to meet another senator in the Senate dining room.

The senator we were sitting with asked me, kindly, who would I like as president?

"Harold Hughes."

To my horror, he called, across the room: "Harold! There's a young man here who thinks you should be president!" Hughes looked up, rose, and in the slow way of a big man began to walk over—step, step, step. I wanted to bolt. He stood over me, and looked down.

"President?" he said. He looked at the other senator, not me. "Well, if I were nominated, you know, I'd want to level with people, I'd have to say: 'Look, if the Russians launch all their missiles at us, while they're in the air, coming our way, I'm going to get on TV as your president and say, "My fellow Americans . . . we aren't firing back!"'"

Then he shrugged. "If they still want to elect me, OK."

"God," I said as Hughes walked away.

Years later I realized: Hughes was going to take a much bigger risk than run for president. He would just disappear into the streets of the city.

Hughes was about to quit the senate: to work with the poor, with alcoholics. It was his way of going off, for real, to D.C. village.

Maybe he was sick of the Senate, the whole conceit of it: that senators and their staffs that were from "Ohio" or "Iowa" or "Alabama," when it was all a lie, and everyone lived, really, right here, in D.C. But instead one says: "I'm from Idaho." "I'm from Utah." "I'm from Alaska."

They should chisel on the capital rotunda: is anyone here really from out-of-state?

Now let me say why people from the real Idaho and the real Utah to me seemed to own vast tracts of the Senate.

It was a shock to me at twenty-eight. It had never occurred to me there was really anyone out there—Wyoming, Utah, Nevada, empty, empty, empty. Who wants to live out among the rocks alone. But the pay-back is . . . they get a piece of the rock in D.C. A man who might own a gas station in Idaho might have more say in foreign policy than the whole Trilateral Commission. "Good," one may snicker. But is it? Because energy was our issue, I came to know the voters in the West.

Really, what babies.

Oh, some of the Senators I liked, like the veterinarian. But most . . .

The Senate, then and now, overrepresents:

1. Small states
2. Deserts
3. Republicans
4. Babies

The biggest of what Michael Kinsley calls the Big Babies.

Now what some of them want is their gold. My friend David tipped me off to this years ago. "It's the Mining Act of 1872." And he told me how it fixed the price the mining interests pay for gold taken from federal land at a scandalously low price.

And all of this gold belongs to us, in New York, Chicago, East St. Louis, but the way the Senate is set up, we can't get anything through, until we "throw down the gold." It's like Frank and Jesse James holding up every train.

And gold is just the start: they want the timber, the oil, the minerals, and it seems in D.C., two senators from every state have a gun to the head of every non-West American.

"Throw down the gold." Or they'll shoot.

And then! They get on TV and all they do is whine and whine, how "Washington" is interfering, etc. We, or "Washington," or the nation, I should say: "we" *own* the states, literally in the case of the public lands. "Own" them?" We started the states! Who do they think paid for General Custer?

One would think, over the years, in return for the gold, they would have let us have higher wages. They would have let us have labor law reform. They would have let us have, at that time, the Energy Plan. The majority of the country being so nice to these privileged few, the princes of the West, one might think, They'll cut us a little slack.

Never.

Not for all the gold in the world.

The country went dark. They laughed.

Wages dropped. They laughed.
The poor flooded into the cities. They laughed.
"Throw down the gold!"
They're laughing at us now.

THE COUNT

Years later, after the 1980s were over, after the fall in wages, after the Democrats lost both the Senate and the House, I woke up one night and thought, How badly was the Senate skewed away from one person, one vote? Had anyone ever calculated? It was hot and sticky. I couldn't sleep. I did the numbers in front of a fan.

I just took the fifty states, and on the back of an envelope I wrote down each state's share of the total U.S. population. It went like this:

Alabama	1.6
Alaska	0.2
etc., etc.	

By 1 A.M., I knew how bad it was:

Let's recall a filibuster takes three-fifths of the Senate to stop. That means two-fifths of the Senate, or forty-one senators, can block any bill.

Health. Tobacco. Oil.

The forty senators from the twenty smallest states represent 10 percent of the population.

That is, 90 percent of the population base as represented in the Senate could vote yes, and the bill would still lose.

Even without a filibuster, the fifty Senators from the twenty-five smallest states represent 16 percent of the population.

But consider this: in the example above, I say 16 percent or fifty senators can block a bill. That also means, conversely, 16 percent and a bit more can pass a bill.

And sixty senators, and that's a landslide, from the thirty smallest states, represent a population, still, of only 24 percent.

My God! The fan was blowing. But I felt a chill for other reasons.

I mean, no one in the country knew this, and I was here alone. OK, so maybe I was acting a bit like Julia Roberts in *The Pelican Brief.*

Now I gave extreme cases (the smallest states all on one side), but it shows the coefficient of the tilt away, in the U.S., from one person, one vote. Even a country like Germany, which has an upper chamber representing the Länder, has nothing remotely as skewed as this. (Indeed, the German states have weighted votes, as should ours.)

WHAT'S SO BAD about this? It's that in this arrangement, even liberals stop being, well, "liberals." They morph into something else, because they come from a different country. A white, Republican, conservative one, much more than the real United States. A Carter, or a Tip O'Neill, they'd represent the real America. But the Senate Democrats as a group, by definition represent a different America, one in which Nevada and California have the same number of people. But of course no such country exists.

Really, the ethnic skew is a small part of this, but it's worth mention. One day, for example, the U.S. will become minority white. The white population could drop to 72 percent in the year 2000, and 61 percent by 2030, and barely above 50 percent by 2050. But how does this register in the Senate? It doesn't.

The Hispanic population, or 75 percent of it, is in just five states. Two-thirds of the American-Asian population is found in just five states.

So each year, in this sense, the Senate is becoming more and more unrepresentative. That is: things are getting worse.

HOW COULD MADISON HAVE ALLOWED THIS?

How could the Founders have allowed this? Well, it wasn't so bad at first. Consider the Republic when it got up to eighteen states. Well, the eighteen senators from the nine smallest states (if I can continue the example) represented a population base of 33 percent. And remember, it was partly skewed, because the new states, like Kentucky, were still filling up. (And there were no filibusters in the early years.)

So that's one answer to those who say, "Well isn't this what the

Founders wanted?" But there's a better answer still: "The Founders never wanted two senators from each state."

As Seymour Martin Lipset writes in his book *The First New Nation* (1963), all the young lawyers in Philadelphia were nationalists, centralizers. They wanted a Senate that represented people, and not states. Indeed, Lipset claims that even the delegates who put forward the "New Jersey Plan," which provided for two senators from each state, thought it was a bad idea.

Whether they all thought so, it's clear enough that Madison said yes, and Hamilton did. Especially Madison. He was appalled. In despair. This is clear from the Convention debates (reported in the Mentor paperback I have at home).

He stood on the Convention floor and pleaded with the other delegates not to do this. How then, he said, sick at heart, can we then say we'll have a *republic*?

Now why was Madison so upset? No one is today. No one even thinks of this.

The reason is, he had very careful ideas of the nature of representation. He did not take the idea of representation for granted, but argued, and believed, it was a highly tricky thing, which absolutely required one person, one vote. The New Jersey Plan was not just a "bad idea." It wrecked his idea of what republican government was.

And what's the final, bitter irony?

From that day on, if anyone questions the Senate, the first thing even some of the academics say is, "Oh, but this is what the Founders wanted."

"What? Are you against Madison, who wanted checks and balances?"

Of course he wanted checks and balances. I want them in my own life. I certainly want them in my government. (What could be worse than to be an Englishman under the unchecked, unbalanced rule of Margaret Thatcher?) But that has nothing to do with two senators from each state.

My old college teacher once said, "Just about every disaster in American history is the result of the Senate." Two senators per state: that's been our secret combination for gridlock.

The Civil War, for example, was the result of having a Senate. For each "slave" state (two senators), there had to be a "free" state (two senators). In time, with majority rule, the problem of slavery might have gone away: Think of the northern congressmen denouncing it in the House.

And it was the same with Jim Crow. With majority rule it would have gone away eventually. But the Senate, once again, was able to lock it in.

Later, when I went to law school, we spent much of the time discussing how to justify judicial review in a democracy, and especially the famous case of *Brown v. Board of Education* (1954), which declared segregation unconstitutional. In class after class we'd agonize: How to justify this in a democracy? How? How?

Hours and hours—how can we have *Brown* in light of majority rule?

Not once, in any of these hours, in any of the classes, did anyone ever say, "Well, there *isn't* majority rule, is there?"

Brown v. Board, Supreme Court activism—maybe none of it is *legitimate* in a democracy, or a republic, but we don't have a democracy or a republic (I use the term "republic" in Madison's sense). So how does the issue even arise?

Indeed, we can't even say it's a "democracy" in the sense that the Senate system is the kind of government we as a democracy choose to have. There is no way to change it by majority rule. There is no way to change it even by a supermajority of two-thirds. There would be no way to change it even if 90 percent of the population base, as represented by the larger states, wanted to change it.

It's true the Constitution provides explicitly that no amendment to the Constitution can deprive any state of its two senators, or "equal suffrage." But that's a mere technicality. (It's like a contract clause that says "The two parties can't change the contract." But of course the two parties can change that clause saying it can't be changed.)

No, the problem is simply that there is no conceivable way that two-thirds of the States would ratify a provision that gave to the vast majority of state populations a heavily weighted vote.

The U.S. Constitution is not like other constitutions. There's no way out, for the majority, or even a supermajority. We're trapped forever in a crypt under Capitol Hill.

Now this one-person, one-vote thing . . . well it's taken over my life. I can use it to explain everything. It's like the addiction of playing "Six Degrees of Separation," because it seems to work on any issue. Race. Labor. Energy. It works as an explanation even when it doesn't seem to work; e.g., why is there now (1998) a Republican majority in the House? Because the Democrats, the majority party, cannot enact a "majority program." So there's gridlock. Stalemate. The voting rate declines. If there's a Senate, why vote for Democrats? Sooner or later, with one label or other, Republicans win.

No "majority program" to stop falling wages, or the other things that lead to White Male Rage.

When the public thinks Democrats are in, but they aren't really, many voters simply give up.

If a lab rat presses A and A and A again, and only gets an electric shock, pretty soon it stops pressing A.

Some stopped voting, others began to vote Republican.

But in the mid-1970s, the Senate, as an evil, came into its own—just in time for our Energy Plan, when the filibuster, rarely used, became a matter of course.

MR. DOLE'S COUP

The filibuster was unknown to the Founders. It appeared only when the debates on slavery began in the early 1800s, and even then it was used rarely, and considered extreme. But by the time of Jim Crow, after the Civil War, it did become serious, though still rare, and it took two-thirds to cut off debate. During the 1950s it was being used by the South to stop anti-lynching bills. Indeed, it was used mainly on the race issue and it became somewhat discredited.

So in 1976 the Senate set out not to end the filibuster but to "reform" it, and now it took only three-fifths of the members, not two-thirds, to end debate. And once it had been "improved" and "reformed" and "pruned," the filibuster became, if anything, worse than before, since now it was routinely used on any bill that came to the floor. Because now, in its new form, the filibuster was OK.

Should a president push campaign reform? Should Public Citizen lobby for a certain bill? How do you know, in advance, if it will take 50 votes or 60?

HERE'S JUST ONE OF its many evils: How do you know in advance how many votes it takes to pass a bill?

A Senate leader, a leader of a bloc, could decide, on a whim, at the last minute, right on the floor, to raise the bar to 60 votes, or not. Imagine if one of the new republics in Eastern Europe had such a constitution and went to the World Bank for a loan, and the intake officer said, "Ah, under your system, how many votes does it take to pass a bill?"

"We don't know."

"Wait—how could you not know? Isn't it written somewhere?"

"No, no, not really . . ."

If we weren't the only superpower, our republic would be a joke, like Belarus.

As minority leader, Bob Dole used the sixty-vote rule so often it was like a constitutional coup. The Democrats were, in effect, the minority. At the rate Dole was going, said the Congressional Research Service, there would have been two hundred filibusters in Clinton's first term. But who noticed? When the *New Yorker* published the CRS estimate, Dole's reply was that in most cases, *some* bill got through. Yes: stripped like a car in downtown Boston!

No one cares any more if it's a republic or not. That's archaic, nineteenth-century stuff, Madisonian "car talk." It's not that my friend the academic would approve if the Senate raised the bar from sixty to seventy votes: he wouldn't care enough to *know.*

It would be news to the country that we don't have majority rule. When I saw this dimly with the Energy Plan, I thought, What's the point of being a public servant? But what of FDR? How'd he do it back in the New Deal?

"Get out!" The green statues said urgently. "It's not a republic—flee!"

But now when I go back to D.C., and see the statues, I'd love to ask: "Didn't it work once?" I understood how Lincoln did it. There was no South in the Senate to filibuster the Civil War.

THE SECRET LIFE OF THE NEW DEAL SENATE

The way it worked, once, was faction. It's all set out in Madison, in something we all have to read: *The Federalist*, No. 10, his theory of faction.

Why did Madison support the Constitution anyway? It was in the way he thought there would be "a balance of faction."

By "faction," Madison meant something different from "interest group." A faction to Madison was not the gun lobby or Mothers Against Drunk Driving. A faction was, well, it was the way people organized themselves as producers. We now, in our time, think of the middle class as "consumers," or maybe "taxpayers," but Madison thought of them as "producers."

A "faction" could be the "have-not" producers, i.e., the farmers rioting in Rhode Island. Or it could be the "have" producers, i.e., the sea captains and merchants in New York. But factions represented people's interests as "producers," i.e., farmers, workers.

It was important for Madison for "faction" to exist, because the government did not have one person, one vote. There could be "virtual representation" through what Madison called the "creditor class" and "debtor class." Back then the debtors were not people with VISAs but farmers with pitchforks.

But what if the "creditor class," which was the minority faction, became too strong? Not to worry, Madison said. "If faction consists of less than a majority, relief is supplied by the republican principle."

He meant debtors being more numerous could use majority vote. Even the Senate was somewhat based on one person, one vote.

But the question Madison did not answer was this: what if the minority faction became too strong, and the republican principle became too weak, because the Senate departed too much from one person, one vote?

A Madisonian would say, "Uh, well let's just hope that never happens."

But it has! That's the constitutional crisis now.

So how did it ever work in the 1930s? Ah, it worked then because the majority factions were organized as they never were before. There were farmers and unions, both strong, all at the same time.

Even in the West, the Senate seemed to work for once. After all, back then the old West really *was* wild—even radical. There were majority factions that represented people's interests as producers. In Nebraska, in Kansas, in the Dakotas, there were the granges, the farmers with pitchforks, who were able to *organize*. Think of the senators from the West, George Norris, or Burton Wheeler, and the free-silver Populists.

And in both East and West, a new kind of faction, the labor union, arose, and this, too, represented the interests of people as producers, i.e., as steelworkers and autoworkers. Just as granges would stand up for farmers.

Indeed, for a lucky moment in the New Deal, there were two types of "majority" factions to represent people's interests as producers. First, the granges. Second, the new CIO unions. It may have been the one time in U.S. history when not one but two types of factions represented the interests of the "majority."

And what happened in our time?

The majority factions have disappeared. The granges no longer exist. The labor unions have collapsed. Out West, there are still plenty of have-nots, but no factions for them to join.

But by the way, the Senate didn't even really work in the New Deal. Even then, the balance wasn't enough on the little people's side to get through Roosevelt's program.

That's why people were always accusing Roosevelt of selling out.

But at least, and this is the miracle, he could enact things, pass bills, that did *something* for the majority faction. By the time of Carter, it was silly to think bills would ever pass to help people form unions, i.e., to organize as majorities again.

BUT MY LAST MONTHS IN D.C., I wasn't worried about "republican theory." I was worried about being shot. On New Year's Eve, December 31, 1978, I was at a party at Tom Southwick's, and I told myself, this year, 1979, I'm going to get out. I hated going on like this, and feeling helpless, and always getting down on my knees to some staffer on the Hill.

Nope: I raised my glass, "I'm out of here."

And back at my building, as I was fumbling for my key, he stepped out, with a shotgun, two barrels at my head.

This . . . it's . . . I can't believe . . . I'm going to die like this . . . right now . . .

It was in my head in some way that this was silly, and . . . Can I go back and walk down the street again? I was going to die. I couldn't believe it. I couldn't believe it.

"When they don't wear a mask," someone had said to me once, "it means they're going to shoot."

Like at the Omega—two people, behind the Omega restaurant, had been shot to death, just like I'd be.

But I wasn't. Why?

By dumb luck three drunken Inner Circle types stumbled, babbling, down the block.

He fled. I'm sure the babblers didn't even see us.

I dialed 911, and in ten minutes the cops rang, and had a guy who had the same T-shirt, Keds, jeans, height. But it wasn't him. "Huh?" said an ex-P.D. friend of mine. "You must be the only white guy who'd have said, 'It wasn't him'!"

"It wasn't."

And when B. came by on New Year's morning and said, "Oh, you're so brave" . . . so brave, so brave . . . she did not know how I begged for my life in the City of Fabulous Jobs.

FIVE

Knock Down the Door

Was i afraid of a shotgun? i could have moved to Maryland. No, it's not that I was afraid of dying.

Oh, I was afraid to fail: fail, in front of my friends.

That's the truth: It wasn't Madison. Who makes a life decision based on *The Federalist,* No. 10?

By now I knew the 1980s wouldn't be going my way. Soon the old New Deal agencies like the FCC would have Gap stores in the lobbies.

So I wanted to head north. Didn't Madison himself do so, when he ran and left his capital undefended in the War of 1812? More and more, by the way, I have become annoyed with him, even as a thinker.

One day groveling to Thomas Jefferson, his mentor: "We've got to help the small farmer!"

The next week, to Hamilton or others: "We've got to stop small farmers!"

I CAME FOR THE MAJORITY RULE

Anyway, I did leave D.C. and ended up in Chicago. When people used to ask, "Why'd you come here?" I'd say: "Because of the weather."

You know how Humphrey Bogart in *Casablanca* says it: "Why'd you come?" "Because of the waters."

"But," people would say, "the weather's terrible in Chicago!"

"I was misinformed." (Like Bogart says it.)

But it never worked like in the movies because they'd say, "What do you mean, 'misinformed'? How could you be 'misinformed' about that?"

But I did come north in a way because of the cold. I thought the cold might preserve these old cities of the New Deal.

Chicago was, in a way, the truest New Deal City. It was the city where people could always get a job, or at least thought they could.

Even if one failed in New York, or L.A., or even Florida, even now, there's still a belief one can come here and Get a Job. Blue-, pink-, or white-collar.

Even TV writers, movie producers, ad copy people who can't cut it in New York or L.A. can come here.

They show up at O'Hare, to move in with their mothers. "Ah! The Midwest! I'm here because I want to be!"

They're here because they have to be. It's the last chance in America for a W-2.

It's what you got from the old mayors, like Daley, who was still alive in 1976 when I first came.

The new Daley, Richie, is more like a city manager: he dreams of cutting payroll. But the old mayors were different. Even when Harold Washington, the first black mayor (1983–87) was elected, his voters, the blacks, must have been thinking, "Jobs!"

An organizer who in the 1940s worked with Saul Alinsky, the great radical, told me how it used to be: "Now even with Daley, the Old Man, the Mayor, he used to sit right in the middle . . ." He stopped. "Give me a piece of paper, I'll show you how it worked." Then he drew this:

Cardinal

Mayor

Labor   *Business*

"Now see the immigrants were Catholics"—he drew a line from the Cardinal—"and . . . this line goes to the Mayor, see . . . then the Mayor would take them down here to Labor, the hiring halls . . . and . . ."

He paused, "And the job of the Mayor was to go from the Cardinal box, then to the Labor box, then go over here to the Business box, make sure they all got along. . . . But it's dead," he said.

"What killed it?"

"Race."

For one thing, the blacks who were the new "immigrants" didn't come through the Cardinal. And by 1970 there wasn't much of a "Labor" anymore, though many failed to notice.

It's true, the city patronage became illegal. But often writers make too much of this, and these were more than "city jobs" that Ed the organizer was discussing.

"Now," E. was saying, "I read where Richie Daley was saying the other day, 'Chicago's greatest asset is its business community!'"

He paused, "His old man would have strangled him for saying that! Old Daley would never have said that. He'd have said, 'The city's greatest asset is its neighborhoods, its working people!'"

Though what mayor now, even a Democrat, would talk that old way?

I'd be curious how Harold Washington, the first black mayor, would have answered this. "City's greatest asset?" Well, for him it was "the poor," or the fact that they voted.

For the poor, Harold Washington would play the roles: he was the "Mayor" and he was the "Cardinal."

Anyway, when I came, it was, still, the City of Fabulous Mayors.

Showing up in bars, I'd see photos of the mayor up on the wall. In the bar!

Once, it was O'Sullivan's, I saw photos of not only the mayor, but other pols, and one especially. . . . As I drank, I kept thinking, "Who is that guy? I know I've seen him!"

Then I knew: "It's this guy drinking next to me."

A state rep could get his face up on the wall!

In some bars there was Old Daley when he was young, 1955, just elected—he's young, with hair like a movie star's.

All these old photos, and where are they now? In the basement of the Met in New York? There's the famous photo *The Four Mayors*. Do you know that? It's in 1933, and customers would say, "See the three men, see, two will be mayor, and . . ."

Then: "So now. Where's the *fourth* mayor?"

"Don't know."

"It's Cermak! He's in the casket!"

Poor Cermak: shot by a guy aiming at FDR. A lesson for us all: keep your distance, even from Roosevelt.

What's so great now about a Daley or Cermak, or an FDR, is that they *used* power. "Now," as Ed says, "someone like Clinton just wants to *have* power, not use it." A mayor really did broker. He really did move, like a big bee, from the Cardinal box, Labor box, Business box.

Maybe Daley I overdid it; he had to approve *everything*.

That's why all the teams were in last place.

As a developer once told me, "It was only after Daley died the city could have a winning team!"

Michael Jordan, soaring? You'd have to have had the mayor's approval.

So customers would look up at O'Sullivan's and *think*, "Oh, the mayor got me my job," even when he didn't.

But then a black man became mayor, and that broke the spell, and now people don't know how they got their jobs at all.

Go into Piano Man? Stop and Go? I suppose it's Paul Volcker, Alan Greenspan, and the central bankers who should have their photos up on the wall.

Not that I spent a lot of time in bars. Indeed, when I came here, I despaired of being a citizen: for one thing, I did not drink. Except for two beers a day. Two cans of Old Style. Then at night I'd walk down to the Farwell Pier, and look at the city, twinkling.

M., who was my date and from the East, said once, "I think you have a drinking problem." But the problem was, I didn't drink enough. I had to force it down.

The city's motto, Urbs in Horto—the City in the Garden—should have been Urbs in Vino—the City Is Pickled. At least the white part, up on the North Side back then.

They say that voting is the *least* important thing you do as a citizen. I should say. Drinking in bars was much more important.

The journalists, the lawyers: it seemed worse than D.C., though there was less drinking at lunch. If you were for Daley, you were in the bars, and if you were against Daley, you were in the bars.

And there were some bars with pictures of Daley, where they weren't the right pictures, and you knew people didn't like him.

The whole opposition to Daley seemed to be centered around Mike Royko, who wrote columns, five or six a week (he was in a bar).

Ah, Royko.

The short paragraphs.

"The sense," Eric Zorn wrote, "that you were reading and not knowing it."

Why he was in a bar, dark, instead of out looking at the landscapes at the Art Institute, I have no idea. And where *was* this bar he was in, anyway?

But there were so many things I heard stories of but never saw:

> Midget bars
> Dog shootings
> Fights breaking out at weddings

Did I see them? No, because I'd stop after two beers.

Even now I just heard, jealous, a story of a famous journalist, in a cop bar at 3 A.M.

Now a "cop bar" is mean, and two cops were brawling, and my friend's pal said, "Come now, gentlemen, take your guns and let's go out and settle this like gentlemen."

"Come on!" he hissed to my friend. "They're going to let us be the 'seconds'!"

They stumbled out and the two cops raising guns suddenly realized, "We're not that drunk!"

This was the opposition to Daley. Sometimes people would be reclining on the floor in inebriated discourse on the nature of the City and the Street.

MEANWHILE, OUT IN THE REAL CITY, something bad was happening to the poor. In the 1980s the poorest families in the bottom fifth had an income drop of 15 percent.

Not single-parent: two parents. And this drop was really because:

1. For the poor the cost of living rose faster than the consumer price index. Yes, a fax machine got cheaper. But what about the monthly phone service? Or taking the bus?
2. The collapse of public schools, etc. Didn't the poor pay in lower living standards?
3. The rise of the states. Who pays a greater share of income in sales taxes?

And they were unemployed. In Chicago an economist at the Urban Institute explained to me: Maybe 250,000 in the city are unemployed when times are bad, as times were in much of the 1980s. Many of the unemployed were never counted.

In the inner burbs, income didn't drop *as* much. That would come later, during the recession of 1987–92. But I note incomes of working people, even now, 1997, still aren't back up to 1989 levels.

It's in the boom that I realized just how very poor so many did become in the bad fifteen years. Even in the rich wards I still can walk to a stunning number of places like

> Currency Exchange
> Gold Star Jeweler's
> Western Union

The auto repair shops have gone, but pawnshops hang on like cockroaches.

Anyway, after the Old Daley died, the poor became even poorer: even the whites did. Chicago's greatest asset? That people of the city accepted this so passively.

IT STILL SEEMED A WHITE CITY. Yes, whites left in the 1960s and 1970s, but even after this exodus, blacks were just a bit over a third of the city. It was, always, and seemed like it would be, always, the City of Fabulous *White* Mayors.

That was the city's cachet, in the nation, in the Democratic party. There was no reason, demographically, why a black should ever have been the mayor.

Yet it was the blacks who often decided who would be the white mayor. It was the blacks, in 1955, who gave Daley his margin of victory. At first, he *was* the black mayor, their mayor.

Though they asked for nothing. And as Royko said, nothing is what they got.

Civil rights came (1960s): they asked for nothing.

Then came Martin Luther King, in Marquette Park (1966).

They did nothing.

Then King was killed, and, well, they burned some of the West Side, and Daley said, "Shoot to kill."

But even then, they did nothing. Daley in his last election, 1975, won by an even bigger margin than in 1971.

Most of all, the black politicians did nothing. For years my law partner Leon Despres was one of the few aldermen denouncing the racism, how Daley kept the blacks from being cops and firemen. Timuel Black, a black activist recalled, "The only black alderman, we used to say, was a white alderman."

Racism?

Harold Washington, being part of the Machine, kept quiet.

King came? The West Side burning? It's eerie to think of him being quiet.

Now little of this was discussed in the bars, at least by me. I thought we'd sit and make fun of the white mayors forever.

Only something was changing.

It wasn't the collapse of the Machine, but the collapse of wages—even the central government, far away, getting slowly weaker.

Of course I know this now, because I can see the numbers.

At the time, though, who knew? Who knew what people were feeling when they, well, lived so far away?

It's hard to explain how far away they were.

Once I was trying to explain this to I., a young German woman, on the balcony of a German official: "What a beautiful city," she said nervously, "if only people weren't shooting each other."

"Oh, you're safe. You'd have to go to Robert Taylor Homes."

"Oh! With my luck I'll end up there on my motor scooter."

"Well, you can't get there on your motor scooter!"

"Why not?" she said.

"I don't know, you just can't."

She was going to say, "Why not?"

Look! It's Chicago, you can't get there on a scooter, so let's just drop the subject!

The white machine always wanted to drop the subject.

A million blacks live in Chicago and 50,000 of them in high rises like Robert Taylor.

And so restive that in 1979 they elected a woman, Jane Byrne, as mayor! It happened because of a blizzard, when City Hall decided to run the Els only in the white wards.

So on TV there were scenes of El trains roaring past old black ladies, shivering. Well, Jane Byrne happened to be running against the Machine that year, even though she was a Daley protégé.

She was famous for being in charge of taxicabs and trying to get the drivers to wear uniforms.

So Byrne was elected. But again it turned out badly. She made a deal with the Machine, i.e., the Evil Cabal, and she seemed as disdainful of blacks as any mayor before.

In the bars we made fun of her: "Crazy Jane." But in a way she was one of us. Her husband was even a journalist.

She was one of us in the way she liked a cocktail.

Sometimes she was too much like us. Sleepless, chain-smoking. She'd call up all-night talk shows at 3 A.M. when even the cops who were in the cop bars were starting to go home.

A tsarina, many hated her. But she did have a touch for symbols. Once she moved into public housing, Cabrini-Green. She was living there! It loomed dark and gloomy over the dark little bars we drank in. We laughed at her, but did we have her guts? *Cabrini*: yet this white woman had moved in! Though Cabrini, an old reporter once told me, had seemed so "nice" at first. It was all "white" then, though remember: white can be the color of terror. At first, he said, white men with knives would follow him around.

Then the men were black and had knives.

Then they were black and had guns.

When Robert Taylor Homes opened, he said, "Anyone knew by then they should stop."

Now a white mayor was in Cabrini; the city gasped. The cops waited on her like angels, as they do with all mayors. It's one of the city's legends, and it's *true,* there's a cop who pulls a shift, in 1997, in front of Old Mayor Daley's house, as if he's still whispering, laughing, running from room to room. It is one of the city's two fantasy jobs, first, to guard the Old Man's house, and second, to be the guard out in the lighthouse in the Lake. (Though some people say, "It's automated!")

Now Byrne did this to fend off the challenge of Daley's son, Richie. No one expected a black, like Harold Washington, who was in the U.S. Congress—not even a city job—to be, well, a serious candidate.

I didn't. No one did. A black, for mayor? By the way, this one had been in prison.

When I look back, I think I was uneasy about a black mayor. Am I for civil rights? I do civil rights *law.* I'm wildly for it.

But I wanted to feel, oh, like a citizen of the city. How could I feel this if the city had a black mayor, and became, well, like Detroit, a black majority, and *I* was a minority?

I wanted it to be white, though exotically white: full of Poles, in scarves, who had been to the University of Krakow. Of course, I only had to go two or three times to the Taste of Polonia festival and see all the Elvis imitators to change my mind about that.

One day I thought this, then I thought that. But I still felt much more cut off from blacks.

I still do even on the Saturday in 1997 when I go to a brunch at Wishbone, near the Loop, and it is a crowd that is actually half, and *just* half, African American. "This is wonderful," I think. And I look at the black loop professionals, men and women, specks of grey hair, with wire-rimmed glasses like mine. Sitting there, eating salmon and eggs.

Ordinary brunch-type couples, in a way.

But to me, of course, they're as unapproachable as the French.

But back then, why didn't I want a black mayor? Well, other cities had them.

"Isn't it good," said a friend then, "there's at least *one* white Democratic mayor?"

Yes. Even when she seemed nuts.

It was a shameful thing to think, but I did. And in my case—see, I'd come all this way to feel like a citizen, and . . .

I know, that's not a reason, i.e., "I'd-picked-out-a, etc., and didn't want it to change." As it turned out, I would be much better off in a black city. At last, I wouldn't have to go into those little bars! The African Americans, I came to realize, didn't care if I drank the two beers or not.

Of course I only knew this much later. I was wary at first.

It's funny how the black percentage of the U.S. population is so much lower than most of us think. Most people, black and white, guess it's about a third. Indeed, it's twelve percent. But maybe for most of us, at least the whites, it comes from our seeing so many African Americans up on "center stage," in the middle of our major cities.

But I do live here, so why don't I have black friends? "Oh, I didn't go to high school here." Sure. It's chilling to talk with North Side whites who seem to know as little as I.

HERE'S A STORY:

I was reading *Beyond Good and Evil* by Nietzsche on the El racing through the black wards. The thesis is, every philosophy is disguised autobiography, and since I'm the one and only white on this train, I feel, oh, special, inviolate, alone.

Then I hear a black woman's voice, wry: "Lara, you ever have to read in college *Beyond Good and Evil?*"

"Oh, yes." Soft drawl.

Don't look up. No, go ahead, look up!

But the two women have gotten off, and later when I tell this to T., he laughs: "Well, they were putting you on!"

"But maybe they weren't."

"Oh yes," he's now angry, "they're putting you on! 'Whitey'! 'The White Boy'!"

Soon, though we're friends, we're shouting, furious at each other.

And what about the public school teachers? I represented many who were black. Then one day someone says, "Did you know that your clients Mr. ——— and Mrs. ——— are black nationalists?"

"No, I don't think so."

"Well, they wouldn't tell you."

Even Mrs. ———, who when I had a cold gave me that tea, made from tree bark? But still I didn't really know.

I FIRST SAW HAROLD WASHINGTON in a union hall.

He was a U.S. congressman, not much of a job, and he'd just said he'd run for mayor. Until this night, I figured, vaguely, I'd support Rich Daley.

Harold talked too much, I thought.

Anyway, I'm at the hall, and talking about a case, when . . .

Bam! Doors slam open. He's here as a guest speaker.

I saw four blacks in London Fogs; he was the shortest of the four. Up they came; not bow ties like Black Muslims, but suits like Loop lawyers.

He walked up. I had been talking and stepped back. He looked out, all workers, but a mix of white and black and Latino. He reminded them how Jane Byrne, and Ed Vrdolyak, her City Council leader, had come to this hall many times and said—well, lied—that the mills would reopen, and especially before an election, they would come here and lie.

Well, he wasn't going to kid them.

The first thing to do . . . is stop the lying.

The workers gasped. No one dared to stand up and talk like this! Who was he?

He turned. Big grin. "What's your name?"

I was the only other guy up there in a coat and tie.

"Oh," he said, "that's an Irish name, isn't it?"

I was pleased, since most people hearing it, don't know. Later, I found out, he thought most white people's names were Irish names.

Then poof, he was gone.

Then another man in a London Fog (I had met him once before) whispered, "You should work for us." In a voice like he was placing, with a tweezers, each word in my ear.

Well . . . yes! I think!

After all, someone had used my name! So I went home that night and wrote a long letter, which no one answered.

A few weeks later I walked into an office and became part of the campaign. Though of course I was certain he was going to lose. The race was between Byrne and young Daley. So I had to explain why I was, well, sitting it out, so to speak, by being for Harold.

"Oh, I understand," said a friend who was for Daley, "you, like, 'know' him now."

"Yes," he said. "Chicago's a small town."

But that's not it.

But maybe it is it: I had come out here to be a citizen, and someone had used my name.

Here was my real civic thrill: I was both "in" the city now, and "outside" it, with arms folded, and my younger friends even said, "You're for Harold Washington? Cool."

Cool. He was an ex-con. He had been to federal (not state) prison for failing to file his tax returns. Failed for four years! How can I defend that? I couldn't, but no one thought he would win.

It was just a stance, I think, my friends could admire—provided he didn't win.

Now really, was I so childish as to be for the guy because he had been to prison? No. But I did look into this life a little, and the more I knew, the more I felt . . . because hadn't I almost done these very things?

There's a chilling book—*Churchill: A Study in Failure,* by R. R. James—telling how Churchill managed to make himself, before being great, "a total failure." All his life, Harold had done that.

He didn't file his tax returns—why? "A mental thing," he'd mumble. He wouldn't talk about it.

He took money for divorces, small nonsense cases, and didn't file, why? Not to make money. He had none, and was indifferent to it.

So why not file? It would be so easy. Just go over and file the cases.

As my friend J. said, "That's what bothers me. He took fees for divorces and didn't file them." OK, but what about me, and J. himself, who's a lawyer? I go into the office. I've got to file this case, and it's such a little thing, and yet somehow . . . it could be *me.*

Once I represented a Greek waiter. He had come over from a village, and he saved, and saved, and then he sent back to the village for his wife. She was nineteen, and he was forty-two by the time he had saved enough. In a year, she had a child, and then one day she had fled, with the baby, back to the village. Probably to her true love.

I was sitting up on the fourteenth floor where the divorces are. It was ex parte. Me. Him.

I took carbon paper and started writing up the decree . . .

This is what Harold Washington did. Outside, all the women walking up and down. The swish-swish of the silk stockings—the scratch of carbon paper . . .

Why am I doing this?

I stumbled back from this ex parte case and I knew why I was for Harold Washington. It's when I'm up there in agony in domestic relations.

WHY, AS I LOOK BACK LATER, did the poor pour out of the high-rises and vote for a black candidate?

I could give the wage data, i.e., concerning unemployment and the working poor, with my friend Nick's remark: "Harold Washington, in the 1980s, was all these people had." Back then we didn't know why the "underclass" was going down so fast. The *Chicago Tribune,* puzzling over it, did a fine series, "American Millstone," all about Lawndale, where it was hard to find people standing and walking around.

But now many economists suspect: the high-school grad middle class just above was dropping down, too. Indeed, some think even college grads were dropping. "It's just, the fall was relatively slower," said an economist to me once at the Bureau of Labor Statistics. "You know, how can you tell? It's like measuring a 'gap' between two falling objects."

Only the bottom quintile was falling really fast, at least 2 percent in real income a year. Does "2" sound like small change? Do it ten years, and it starts to be a lot of money.

Not to mention: Reagan, a huge crunching halt in aid for housing, taxes, etc.

As Nick says, maybe it didn't matter who collected the garbage, but what else did people have?

Nor was it just having someone "black" in office, but it was Harold's exquisite gift to tell the poor who to hate. Now in a way, the white local pols, like Byrne and Vrdolyak, had nothing to do with the poor being poor. They were just picking up the garbage, in a way.

But though as local pols they did not have enough real power (even the power of the Old Mayor) to do anything really bad, they were so lovably bad.

Of late I have been reading about the famous antiliberal thinker Carl Schmitt, who wrote *The Concept of the Political* (1927). To be political, Schmitt says, is to define ourselves by our enemies. To be "moral"? It's to look for the good. To be "political"? It's to look for our enemy.

Harold said: The enemy is Byrne and the Machine.

Now we all said this in the bars, too. But we were whites and lawyers.

This was a black man telling the poor, and telling them to *hate*. All I really knew up until then was how to make jokes about Byrne and the Machine. I began to sound like a Royko column.

Harold was utterly different, since he introduced a whole new idea, which was, to *hate* them.

And of course some of us did, or I did, because he was so charming. The big grin. I started working on the campaign. And each day I liked him more. And this was something unhealthy, and maybe it was akin to the "Salzburg bough," which the miners drop into salt mines and which Stendhal writes about in *Love*. The miners drop in a bough and after three months in the salt it's covered with crystals, and it's the same way with one's political hero.

I was starting to endow this man with all sorts of perfections. I know it's nuts.

I became fascinated with every detail. He was a bachelor. He lived alone. He had an apartment in Hyde Park down by the U. of C. ("I wanted one!") And his friends would complain: "You go in the apartment, and what is there? Nothing! It's nothing but books."

Most of all, by far, it was Harold's talk that drew me. There's now a library with his name slapped on it. And what are the quotes all around the top floor of Harold's library?

They're from Kafka. Long quotes on people feeling powerless. Then you're supposed to remember Harold, and how once you didn't feel that.

OK, but Harold was as good as Kafka, and I like the quote picked by John Kass, at the *Trib:* "This is America, and in America, we don't have to bow, and scrape . . . You want something in this country? Knock down the damn door."

Kass says: Why not engrave that?

What candidate would show up and say, "God! I love every inch of this *ugly* town!"

Or making up words. His brother complained about this.

"Yeah, what's wrong with that?" Harold said. "People know that words are made by man—God doesn't create words."

But should you elect a guy who says that? Maybe someone should have said, "Look, you're not from here. You didn't go to high school here. Think: is it *wise* in this town to 'knock down the damn door'?"

BEYOND PLUS OR MINUS

But Harold had no chance, did he? Hopeless. He actually gave one of his first speeches in the County Jail! True, the inmates could vote. But how crazy? Even the pro-Harold whites groaned. How could he? The County Jail!

In addition, Byrne had a cash horde of $10 million, thanks to the "new urban progressives." This was the era when progressives and liberals were killing off the old patronage, *and* subcontracting out government. It's known as "reinventing government," and quite a lot of it was sensible. But it had a mean, vicious side in an America that was deunionizing, and paying poverty wages. It became common, in Chicago and other cities, to "contract out" to yuppies, who would hire nonunion low-wage labor, and in return, though this was not illegal, "kick back" into the mayor's campaign.

And this was supposed to be, in my time, the great Progressive idea. Kickbacks. Everything the Progressives fought against in 1916 was now looked on as good. So long as the kickbacks were coming not from inside—i.e., the civil service—but from outside, from developers.

I once asked a friend in the city, "Aren't you contracting this stuff out because it's nonunion wage?"

I braced for a denial, and I was disarmed, and admired him for shrugging and saying: "Well, of course it's because it's lower-wage!"

Thanks to the lower wages, the mayors had huge campaign chests. Now maybe I overstate this, and there's not a dollar-for-dollar matchup between the money a mayor has for television and the difference in a living wage.

OK, I don't want to make Byrne or (later) Daley monsters.

But some of the machine pols did take up prioritizing and themes like "reinventing government" with an eye on the bottom lines: the city budgets, the campaign coffers.

Of course, Harold had none of this money. So our side had to do it the old-fashioned Chicago way and canvass door-to-door. Fast disappearing, this is the "old way," the Machine way. But the anti-Machine people used it too: Knock on each door.

Stand and deliver.

Are you, the voter, a plus or a minus or a zero?

It was the old Machine way. Except the Machine naturally, with $10 million, was already into television.

(Oh, some of the Machine people went door-to-door, but it was like attending, by then, a Latin mass, a kind of liturgical silliness.)

Door-to-door. Slowly. Chanting in Latin.

Are you a plus or a minus?

A plus meant you were voting for us. A minus—you were voting against us.

A zero—you were still thinking.

I had never done this. I was stunned. "I have to go to every house?"

SINCE I WAS NEW, and hadn't gone to high school here, and didn't know anything, the others began to whisper: "Give him the high-rises."

OK, I said. So? What are the high-rises?

These were the huge lake fronts, a wall-like bank of buildings, full of widows and secretaries in studios, that blocked the rest from seeing the sun come out of the Lake. Just like New Yorkers, some in Chicago have never seen the water.

If I had a diagram, I could show you the problem that I or a mining engineer had getting into one. Each is heavily guarded. No loitering. Locked doors.

And once inside, no one answered the door. It seemed to be all widows. Open up! A black ex-con wants your vote.

By 1983, in all America, no one outside Chicago even dreamed of going door-to-door. My friend Larry moved to Boston, and when he asked in a campaign there, "When do we go door-to-door?" they gasped, like he was a burglar.

In Chicago, too, it was dying out. Standard reasons:

Race
TV

In the 1950s in Chicago, whites actually went door-to-door in black wards. (Though blacks, of course, could not go door-to-door in the white ones.)

In the 1950s, women actually went door-to-door.

In what block, however elegant, would a woman go door-to-door in the city now? None. They only do this in outer suburbia, where there are no elections.

This killed off Chicago-style campaigns, because as the old hands say, the women in the 1950s ran the campaign.

Women love campaigns, while men hate them. Men love running for office, but they hate the detail work, the infinite patience, but what they really hate is:

In campaigning, you're always having to consult these maps.

Men hate, hate, hate, hate this. I used to tell them, "Hey, just knock on *any* door. Don't look at the maps."

So when women were afraid, that was it for door-to-door. Maybe that's why the voting rate dropped.

Anyway, I had to break into the high-rises. I tried everything. I read books. I went to see *The Guns of Navarone*.

The best advice was from Professor S., a longtime Chicago independent, who also taught political science. He says, for example: (1) Take the guard in your confidence, or (2) When the guard looks away, ring forty doorbells, fast, and see if someone opens up.

I forget the others. Anyway, he says that each of these ideas will work "one out of ten times."

The other nine times? Someone calls the cops.

It was supposed to be a two-way race—Jane Byrne and young Daley. But when Harold got on TV with them—neither, I guess, had ever met a real trial lawyer. Wow. Harold destroyed them.

Arguing motions in Divorce Court finally paid off.

Then came a huge rally at the University of Illinois—a black mob, cheering. How many were there? Fewer than Sox Park, late September. But electorally, I guess, that's enough to change history

So here was my problem. The whites had stopped laughing, and what were we to say when they screamed at the door?

It was scary. OK, these were high-rises, not bungalows, but it was still a white neighborhood and he was still a *Black Man*. What to say? I just didn't want anyone to get hurt.

Indeed, I thought the "plus" and "minus" system was absurd. Why do it? In theory, in the old Machine days, one would sit at the poll sheet and mark off each plus.

Plus and minus is not a survey technique. It is a list of literally which bodies have to be hauled over physically to mark the ballots.

Oh yes. Mr. Jones has voted. But where is Mrs. Jones? You snap your fingers. "Larry! Run over to Mrs. Jones's house and bring back Mrs. Jones. And say you'll shop for her while she's voting."

That's the theory. But in this election everyone was coming anyway. The old way (e.g., send out "runners," get the "pluses") was ridiculous in an election where it seemed if you didn't fly, heart pumping, the voters were going to run you down.

OK, I'd been promoted, I didn't have to go door-to-door, but who was I going to send? I went in and talked to my boss, J., a woman. "I can't find anyone to knock on doors. I can't find any white person. Look around this office! We're the only whites for Harold."

I couldn't get any volunteers, except . . .

S., who was blind.

A., who was black.

And a white male who was, even then, a computer geek. Also, my friend Tony.

I had to report to a chain of women, and there was nothing to report. Each week on "Report Night," i.e., Thursday, my volunteers would say how many doors they knocked on, and how many were "pluses" and "minuses."

Oh. "Is that all you could get?" I'd ask. "Of course, it's better to be honest!" (I wanted them to lie.)

Then I'd have to report my "pluses and minuses."

"Is that all you could get?" the women would ask. "Of course it's better to be honest!"

So I lied.

I now understand how they got the body counts in Vietnam.

Before each Report Night I'd think all day, "Gee, tonight I could have gone to the symphony." This was strange, since I never went to the symphony, much less on Thursday night, Report Night, but it was hard to keep it out of my head. I felt sick about sending out R., who was blind. One day I decided maybe I should knock on a door and see what it was like. So I went to a house down the street, and the door cracked open, and a very frail old woman opened the door, maybe for the first time in days.

The air was very stale, like no air.

"Oh," she said. "My husband's name . . ." She became upset. "Is it on the sheet? No? *Why not?* Oh, let me see . . ."

Now I was upset. Why wasn't it on? I told her I'd try to do something.

"Well," she said, "he's been dead for six years."

Then she opened the door wider, because there was something inside she wanted me to see.

As I ran, I knew: I can't ask people to go out! Not the blind woman, or A. herself, who was now a wreck.

Or the geek who never went out of his room.

"Let's just call up people, phone them," said Tony.

"Like a telemarketer?"

"No," he said, "like an adult!"

So we did. If the voter had an Irish name, we'd make up Irish names. If Jewish, then Jewish. If Polish, then Polish. "Mr. ———, Harold is one of us!"

In fact, I was called once, by the Daley campaign. "Can I ask who you're for?" said the woman.

"Well, I'm Irish, and I'm a lawyer. Who do you *think* I'm for?"

"Oh! Thank you!" she chirped.

Anyway, I felt guilt about Daley. I'd come out here . . . well, to be a citizen of the city. I didn't want to ruin it for . . . who? The whites? What was I thinking? Lovable? Ethnics? My God, the hatred, the spitting, choking way people who hated Harold talked—it gave me the creeps. And I left D.C. to avoid the—what, people from Heritage Foundation? The whites here were about to kill me.

Meanwhile, I was probably scaring people away from Harold. If I saw a "Washington" button, blue and white, I'd go up, not even to the person's face, but to the button, right on the chest, and say to the button, "Will you work for us?"

One day, in the Loop, I did this, and the man said: "Tom, Tom. Look up, it's me—Dan Swanson, your old friend from college."

And it was true, he'd just come into town.

I'd have left town. But as an "area chair" (what a title!), I had responsibilities. Thank God, on Election Day I got out of some of them. I was sent out "into the field" to be a troubleshooter. It's awful to be in the office. Exhausted, we ate Dunkin' Donuts, doughnut after doughnut, and then: hyperactivity, screaming.

They should close, by law, the Dunkin' Donuts on Election Day.

My first job was to open a poll, i.e., be there by 5:45 A.M., and J. was worried I would sleep late. "Can you get up at four-thirty?"

"Yes."

"You can? Are you sure? You want a wake-up call? 'No'? Are you sure?"

I remember lying in bed: "Why didn't I say yes."

Of course by 3 A.M. I'm awake. "I'll get up, eat a doughnut . . ." No! Try to sleep.

My God, why are we getting up this early? Because "they" might steal.

This was nonsense. If they want to steal, they'll steal. But I bet at that moment there were a thousand people lying awake thinking "How are they going to steal this?" The day before, Ed Vrdolyak had called a meeting of his precinct captains. That weekend he was quoted as saying, "It's a racial thing, don't kid yourself."

Shocking. To say it.

Of course, what the hell was it?

I dozed, and in my dream Ed Vrdolyak was putting his hand on my shoulder: "It's a racial thing, don't kid yourself."

I had an extra worker, a lovely young woman to stand at the poll on Election Day. When she went to her poll, which was in a high-rise, all the election judges (male, bald) fussed over her.

"Sit here, Miss."

"No, here!"

"Can you see, Miss?"

One smiled at her: "Think anyone will be showing up for that nigger?"

She nodded her head prettily.

After that—nothing, not even a doughnut. But the doorman, who was black, slipped her lunch when no one was looking: "Don't worry, Miss," he said, very low, "I'm not going to let you starve."

Meanwhile I was about to go to jail. I went to troubleshoot a nursing home. The trouble was that the white precinct captain was asking each voter, "How you gonna vote?" (He meant, he said, Republican or Democratic primary?) Frightened, each patient told him, "Oh, of course, I'll vote for Mayor Byrne!"

Had to stop that, so I protested, until the poll judge said, "If you protest one more time, I'll have you arrested!"

She looked over at the cop: there was a cop in every poll.

So when I protested once more, she said, *"Arrest him!"*

She stared at the cop.

I did, too.

Poor cop! He looked around . . . (Who's going to win the election anyway?)

"Arrest him!" she said again.

"Uh, uh," the cop stuttered, "maybe . . . could you call downtown about this?"

I grinned. But it's true the state's attorney, aghast, came out, and though the captain was kicked out, well, I had to be, too. I guess, to show they were evenhanded.

A reporter was there by chance, and the next day there were two stories on the front page:

WASHINGTON ELECTED! With a smaller story: TWO MEN KICKED OUT OF POLLS. It was a little human-interest thing.

"Clip it and send it to your family," said Lew at the office, "to show them how well you're doing in Chicago."

But we had *won*! But I was sick, nibbling pizza that night. "Why didn't I do more?"

I was miserable, until it hit me: Harold Washington still wasn't mayor—far, far from it. He'd only won a primary! There was, still a general election. It's true, the Republican candidate, Bernard Epton, was a joke: he had a goatee; he even looked like a goat.

He led a goat mob, too, of whites, spitting and punching people. One ran into a clothes store and punched Rich Daley, for dividing the white vote. When Mondale came to town, they ran after him, too.

Republicans gloated, and back in 1983 this looked like the Democratic party to come—with a white mob chasing, punching even the Daleys, even in the stores.

Now Epton was a liberal, or had been, but seeing this mob, he took on a new life, a kind of goat life. His slogan was "Epton: Before It's Too Late."

Unsigned pamphlets floated everywhere: "Your cars will be stoned. You will be robbed or killed, white women will be raped."

Still, it was the signed pamphlets, letters to the editor, and ads that I found more upsetting. But I was mad at my own side, too.

Why wasn't Harold reaching out to whites? To reassure them? "It is so easy," I prayed to him each morning. "Just say something nice."

But he hardly gave us anything! I guess it was "strategy." Expand your base, expand your base, expand your base. But the whites were expanding *their* base! Didn't he know that?

Why don't you say something? I kept begging. And the less he gave me, the more I seemed to be caught up with him.

And . . . oh, liberals who said nothing!

Well, laughably, I was now the big captain in my ward. The Byrne regulars of course had fled. (Some were working for Epton.)

I was still too young to be a . . . captain, a boss. That's what I kept thinking on Election Day as I walked from poll to poll and stared at voters. I'm too young! But it was blue and sunny, and I loved how I could walk around.

I felt good. Knowing I was the boss, for a day. Harold was running spots now denying he was a child molester.

That night, by less than 4 percent, the city had a black mayor.

SIX

"Now Do You See Me, Mr. Mayor?"

O H," CRIED L., WHEN SHE MOVED BACK IN 1996, "I DON'T even know who the Recorder of Deeds is!"

"Oh, L.," I said, "no one knows who it is now!"

When Harold fought with the City Council, we knew that name, the names of the aldermen, as any kid can recite the names of the Bulls. It was a time, 1983 to 1985, when everyone watched, talked about the "Council Wars," which was the feud between Harold and the City Council's white majority. Harold Washington had twenty-one aldermen who voted with him as a bloc. Vrdolyak, on the other side, had a majority, twenty-nine. Who would win, the twenty-one or the twenty-nine?

It is said too much, "the personal is the political." Once, under Harold Washington . . . even the public was the political. We even knew the name of the Recorder of Deeds.

SHUT THE GATES OF THE CITY

From the day Harold was sworn, it was "Council Wars." Gridlock. Deadlock, twenty-nine to twenty-one. Nothing could pass. "Beirut on the Lake." People around the country laughed. The twenty-nine white aldermen who hung with Vrdolyak met in secret, and voted as a bloc. As a bloc: to block everything this black mayor tried to do. Every budget. Every ordinance. Every nominee he put up for the Park Board.

It was like the GOP's brief attempt in 1995 to shut down the government. Except city services did go on. But the idea was to show that a black mayor, this ex-con, for God's sake, couldn't even sweep the streets.

So what was my duty as a citizen?

Well ... protect my government. What an idea for an American!

There's a great book about this standoff: Gary Rivlin, *Fire on the Prairie* (1992). It explains how the two factions tore at each other. "What a time," I think now. "I really did live, once, in Madison's republic." But was this a case of the evil of factions? It was not like Madison's factions, since at first it seemed to be not "creditor v. debtor" but "black v. white." But it was not even clearly race. Some of Harold's twenty-one, also a bloc, after all, were white liberals, like David Orr.

If not race, what was the war over? And what does a mere citizen, me, you, do in time of war?

Here's the moment it started.

THE INAUGURATION, 1983, was at the end of Navy Pier. It was still undeveloped then. It jutted way, way out into the Lake. I was a two-bit precinct worker, with no right to be there. But someone had sneaked me in, to listen, sip white wine.

Watch the white city, far off, slip away.

Then ...

"Here they come!" people shout. Police boats, the City's navy scudding over the whitecaps. Out steps the mayor. Ah! An amphibious landing. He came to us by sea.

People put down canapés and applaud. What a sight: black mayor. White cops. Green lake, setting off the blue jackets of the cops.

He walks through, more applause. The cardinal, the Greek patriarch, we all let him through.

I look around, there's Jane Byrne, looking haggard without a cigarette. What will the black mayor say? Something nice about whites?

He takes the oath, turns, and ... then he thunders, biblically, *"I'm going to destroy the Grey Wolves!"*

The cardinal, the patriarch, we all turn pale. "Grey wolves?" He means the white aldermen, the Machine guys, who hunted with Vrdolyak in a pack.

Wow. We put down our crosiers. Canapés.

People ran back to the wards.

And that's what it was like for the next two years.

It was said Harold blundered: He had tried to organize the city council, with "his" floor leader and chairmen, though he only had twenty-one votes and the other side, the Vrdolyak side, had twenty-nine. Why not cut a deal?

That's what some friends would say later: What's the matter? It's twenty-nine to twenty-one, can't he count?

"Yeah, can't he add?"

Of course, if he had made a deal, then they'd scoff, "Oh see? He made a deal! He's just like the rest, etc."

That was the great thing. Harold would never compromise. Never. Not like Clinton and Gingrich: "Oh, OK, we'll compromise, cut off food stamps for half the immigrants." Never.

The whole point was: This was not to end happily like *Federalist* No. 10. Someone would be smashed completely.

So, I ran back to my ward. And never, never was the city more fun to live in. Of course I had to moan how awful it was because that's what the world outside told us:

"Beirut on the Lake." "Gridlock on the Lake."

The *Wall Street Journal* did stories, "The City doesn't work." We'd soon be like Newark.

It did work in one way, like no other city: It gave L., and me, and a few others a sense we lived in a republic that was un-checked, un-balanced: just straight on majority rule.

POW!

People voted. Marched.

In the wards we formed little militia. We drilled.

It was kind of like the Spanish Civil War, in that we fought with the allegiance of the Latinos who spoke Spanish!

But to me the unheard-of thing was: simply to be in it, as I was. Personally. I didn't have a city job. The voting was over. But as one of Harold's people, I was, at least potentially, ready to come back "on" as part of a crowd. What an odd idea, that a crowd (or is public a better word?) might come down to City Hall at any time. Be an assembly. Be there at all. Watch the cops, let the cops watch us back.

Harold would get on TV. "We won't be pushed around or . . ."

Then Vrdolyak: "We're willing to work with the mayor, etc. etc., but . . ."

Our side, even the poor, could watch this and think, "Well, you know, I'm really part of this."

Now Madison and the Founders knew about this thing, the public assembly. In the old Greek cities, in Boston in the 1700s, even in cities like New York, San Francisco in the last century, there was not just "majority rule" but "public assembly."

Now in theory we like this: it's right in the First Amendment. But newspaper editorials hate it: "The scene at City Hall was a disgrace." "People, shamefully, hooted at the aldermen."

Of course only columnists for newspapers should hoot at the aldermen.

Until Harold I assumed public assembly was dead. It was archaic. People had ten kilometer runs on the lakefront, but we didn't have public assembly, like the old nineteenth-century cities.

How can we since we don't even have cities? I often thought, "What would it be like to live in another small Midwest city, like Cincinnati, or St. Louis?"

They're not like Chicago: a big, rich city, still intact, helplessly being plundered by state government. No, these little cities, being under half a million, disappeared long ago into unofficial, de facto "regional governments." It's odd, when I was younger, and lived in D.C., I argued for regional government. It seemed the civic thing to do. What would Madison have made of such government? It's now even written up, on paper. These little asteroid bits of government float around, with no clear boundaries.

These regional governments always seem to meet in secret, in Hyatt hotels, where they decide things like where to put the runway or tollway. Who are they accountable to? This is not just a problem of one person, one vote.

No one knows how the tollway gets routed. One day, people drive along and suddenly, "Hey, the tollway's there."

Now the odd thing about Harold versus the twenty-nine was that everyone knew, physically, where it was going on. City Hall smelled like a boxing gym. The poor could walk in: it didn't feel like a Hyatt. The interesting but galling thing to many was this Harold (a machine guy!) saying he was a reformer. He said his goals were the goals of the old independents, the white liberals, who'd fought Old Mayor Daley. A neutral civil service. No reprisals.

Now when the poor, or a new immigrant group, took power, it's supposed to be the opposite. In other cities, when blacks took power, it was simply: it's our turn.

With Harold it was more complex, word and deed. It was "our turn," and it wasn't.

Maybe this snippet of "Harold talk" gives a sense of this:

"We've been through the crucible. We've been pushed around, shoved around, beat, murdered, emasculated, literally destroyed. There's been an unfair distribution of the goodies . . ."

But . . . our turn to do what?

If Harold wanted to redistribute the goodies, why bring in unions, collective bargaining, extend the federal court *Shakman* decree limiting political hiring. Of course he wanted his own court, but that's not the same as the Daley Machine.

But, it's true, Machine versus Reform is misleading: If it had been just that, somebody would have to compromise. "Let's stop fighting!" That's what Vrdolyak kept crying.

To me, the war was really about the need of Harold Washington to destroy the Machine that had silenced him, made him crawl. What did the poor get out of this? Not goodies. That never happened, in any serious way. With many of Harold's reforms, like collective bargaining, it seemed to be the whites who got more. The blacks got revenge. What Harold got. Revenge for the years they had to crawl.

What stake did they have in a neutral civil service? An ethics ordinance for aldermen? Simple. They got the chance to look down on white people as vulgar.

They got what only white liberals like me were supposed to get; the pleasure of condescending, in the City of White Mayors.

RUN BACK TO YOUR WARDS

But here's what I got out of it: though I was just a citizen, *Harold gave me something to do.*

First, I could be part of a network. There was a Network 43 for the 43rd ward and a Network 44 for my own. Up and down the lakefront.

The network's purpose was to be a presence for Harold. In my ward, the alderman was on the Vrdolyak side. "You don't have to go through him," we'd tell the neighbors. "You can go to Harold directly."

Go through me, my friends. We in the networks will get the cat out of your tree!

I didn't know Harold Washington, but I felt, wearing my button, going to meetings, that I was . . . a part, an extension really of Harold's government. See? I didn't have to be a special assistant to feel like I was part of it.

A few years ago I met a professor who'd been to South Africa and she said, "Under Mandela, you can be, oh, a public health nurse, and feel like you're really part of his administration." I knew vaguely what she meant, since I'd had that feeling in the 1980s: just going to the Loop, coming back to a network meeting.

OK, I rarely did it.

I have often thought how Democratic presidents used to give us things to do.

Under FDR? I could start a union. Under JFK? I could join the Peace Corps. Under LBJ? Go to the inner city and teach a child.

But under Carter and Clinton, the two Democrats of my adult life? They didn't give us anything to do.

I mean there must be others like me in St. Louis, Detroit. We'd like to come to D.C., but we can't. So? How do we come into the story? And by the way, what is the story? I listen to NPR and I'm not always sure.

Clinton, it's true, says, "volunteer."

But volunteer for what? Join a militia in rural Michigan? He doesn't say. He's not really giving us anything to do.

So what did we do in Harold's networks?

First, spread the "true" story. We began by telling each other in our meetings Harold's side of the standoff.

In a way, the papers were helpless to tell our "true" story, ours or Vrdolyak's, because it's hard to tell objectively.

Because modern journalism's objective, the reporters are . . . well, they can't even be citizens and go to fundraisers.

Yet they want to write about politics! I've never really been able to grasp this. I'd invite friends, i.e., reporters, to come to coffees. "Oh, no, I can't, I'm neutral."

"Neutral?" How can you be neutral?

"My paper . . ."

"Oh come on, it'll be our secret."

By the way, since it was a white press, Harold's people were suspicious (though, I think, unreasonably). That's why they started "All City News." I saw a copy in the Public Library. How weird to be reading: BE STRONG! SUPPORT THE MAYOR'S TEN POINT PROGRAM. What is this Moscow, 1922? Of course "All City News" is no more. But, in a way, it's still around spiritually, as the homeless paper, *Streetwise*.

But Harold's Chicago really was cut off, news wise, from the other one. Here's a story as to how bad it could get.

Right after Harold died, it turned out a man named Steve Cokely, a top aide to the new Mayor (Sawyer), had been giving a horrid, sick speech: "Jewish doctors are spreading AIDS."

But what was weirder still was that Cokely had been giving this speech in public. Over and over. Yet no one in "my world" knew. How could we know when no black person in *that* city was willing to tell us?

So, OK, we "put out the word." What else did people in the Networks do?

We swept the streets. Oh, not literally. But if a street was dirty, or had slop, maybe we'd arrange a meeting. Now in one case there was chicken slop all over a street. There were chicken factories at George Street.

Necks

Gizzards

Little chicken phalluses, or that's what I was told. Pulsating in the sun, and smelling horribly.

One might laugh, "That's what you mean about chicken shit?"

Well, that's what real citizens do. We called up the City, and to my shock, we snared Harold's best man, the commissioner of streets and sanitation. Yes, he'd meet with us.

The commissioner! His name was Halpin. Irish, with a brogue. It was said he drove around all hours patrolling the city blocks, and whites hated him, thought him a Judas, for keeping the city so clean, under a black mayor. "Judas!"

You know how the Irish treat each other.

Anyway, on the big night, Halpin came and said, "Yes, we'll clean this up. But you! You keep the pressure up. Call a second meeting. Keep after us!"

I think of Halpin when people say now: "Come on, how can you defend that gridlock, deadlock? Nothing could get done."

But in a way everything was much easier. There was the Mayor's party. Then the Vrdolyak twenty-nine. It was like two teams, rivals, racing each other to see who-can-get-the-cat-out-of-the-tree first.

Now we have Daley II, he's Manager. After Daley came in, many thought: "Not like Harold. A manager. No more brawling." But is that good? It is at least arguable that services are better when two parties are brawling. Then anyone with a gripe can run to the other side.

Now that might lead to more competition than "contracting out." Besides, it was under Daley the manager that the famous city disasters occurred. Take the flooding of the Loop. A city inspector warned about the contractor dredging in the river. After Harold one inspector could be ignored. So the contractor punched a hole in the bottom of the river. The water gushed down, into a system of tunnels, it gushed into the basements in the Loop. People like me, lawyers with all our briefs and worldly goods, had to leave and walk out, out of the Loop. Like a fire drill for the apocalypse.

What would have happened under Harold? One inspector, if ignored, could run screaming to the other side. Nothing is more responsive than the two-party system.

Or take the time that private contractors tore up Clark Street. Opened up big holes, then walked away, seemingly for months. But what could anyone do? Some friends of mine went to an alderman. "We turned it over to a private contractor," he shrugged. He could have yelled at a city worker, but . . .

OK, WE CLEANED UP. What else did we do in the Networks?

Now remember we were on the Left. It's hard to know where the Left should be on some neighborhood issues like night baseball. For example, the Cubs played in my ward. So . . . what did Network 44 think? Should there be night baseball at Wrigley Field?

Lights? Or no lights?

People used to scoff at Network 44: "Oh, they're more interested in what's going on in Nicaragua than in lights at Wrigley Field!"

We used to grumble at this: was it a cheap shot! But once our leader, calling us, said: "Yes, it is a cheap shot. But look, if the day ever comes when we really think that lights in Wrigley Field is more important than what's going on in Nicaragua . . . then, you know, maybe we should all disband."

What else did we do? Well, I wore my old campaign button. Many of us did, while the council wars went on.

Now I'd hate to pin that Harold button on a Brooks Brothers suit. But it was important for whites to see, right?

Yes. And for blacks to see, too.

And I learned something: for years, I, too, had been a kind of "Invisible Man." Or at least for the first time I'd see blacks staring at me. People would actually stop and turn around on the street. And I now know how women can catch guys trying not to look. There was a night at a Bulls game when I'd thrown my coat over a chair, and had turned to my friend Jim . . .

In the far, far corner of my eye, for a nanosecond, I saw a man, black, nudging his son's gaze ever so slightly to the button on my London Fog.

Did he see me seeing him? I wonder.

Of course for weeks I'd take off the button and go on "break." The deadlock, after all, lasted years.

But then a day would come when I'd think, "Oh, I want people to see me, right?" I'd pick up the button, turn it over . . .

No, it's vanity. No, it isn't. Big decision, every morning, for two whole years.

Finally, the best thing I did was: I worked for Ron, who ran for alderman. I even gave a speech.

Aristotle in *The Rhetoric* says: the first duty of a citizen is to give a speech. What Aristotle really means is: Have a good speech ready, in case someone in the assembly wants to put you to death.

Anyway, I did one. Ron, who was Network 44's candidate for alderman, was a doctor and a gay activist. I had a coffee, which is an open house: I invited my neighbors, etc. Well, I still didn't know the neighbors (I'd only lived here eight years) so I invited a lot of paralegals.

I can see Ron by the mantel. He would soon be dead of AIDS. But no one knew that then. Lori was up serving coffee. Ron stood up and said:

"Oh, I just wish the election were over!" There was so much joy in his saying this, his happiness was eerie. Did he think he would really win? He wouldn't. He must have known, but this night he kept saying, "I just want to be in there, in the job, JUST DOING IT! I don't even want to talk about the race, my rival . . . I just want to be in there doing it!"

Then I rumbled up to pitch for money. And I knew I'd be downbeat, as I always am. So how can this doctor, of all people, who's seen so many of his friends die . . . How can he be so joyful? Full of gloom, I thought about all this, and stared at these kids . . . God, don't I know any real people?

I'll tell you the problem with kid citizens: no money. I sometimes pass the plate at our local parish. Now, remember, the kids are at the Mass, there's no one forcing them. But what's in the plate?

The kids look away, not a buck! But remember this. Here's a shocking fact: of the white working poor in Chicago, over 45 percent are college graduates or have some college.

Once I heard a priest say, "Come on, just pay what you'd pay to see a movie."

But what kid in church has seven bucks?

They walk around with nose rings, some with turbans, so Belmont Avenue feels like India. Of course those kids in the turbans don't go to Mass. I kept thinking of Ron's joy, so this is what I told the kids:

"I've known Ron as a doctor. I can tell you his stands on things. I don't even know if I agree with all of them. But here's the reason, the real reason we need him in our city council . . . so you and I will have someone down there, who, just by his life the way he lives it . . . I mean, this guy's a doctor for the poor, at County . . . will set us a good example!"

And now, years later it looks so dull on a page. But that night, it felt like a burnt offering to Aristotle, and as the smoke rose up to some civic heaven . . .

Of course, I personally had to give, that night, half the money.

I suppose a civics class today would have to teach a child to raise money. The consultant stands there, in huge Magic Marker:

1. Identify. List your twenty-five wealthiest friends.
2. Cultivate. Take them to lunch.
3. Solicit. Ask. Give a dollar amount

STILL, WHAT I MISS about Harold, and also Ron, is that to feel part of it, I didn't have to raise money. A few years ago a woman I knew ran for governor. I wanted to help. So . . . what could I do? Nothing. And it was no one's fault, there was nothing I could do, if I couldn't do fundraising.

I write the names of my twenty-five wealthiest friends. After twelve, I'm down to the names of Dominican nuns.

THE BIG BANG

Oddly enough, it was under Harold, a black left-wing mayor, that whites and the wealthy kept coming back to the city. How do I explain this?

Once I was struck by the Jane Jacobs's book *Cities and the Wealth of Nations* (1984). It was her thesis that the city, not the region or the nation, but the city was the fundamental economic unit.

It convinced me, reading her book. But just as I was caught up with Jane Jacobs, there were economists, economic geographers, who began to argue, it's not the city, but the region.

Factories in the Midwest were not huge, and self-contained, like little cities, but they were small and specialized, and linked across the states. As one economic geographer explained it to me, "A governor can now bring fifty jobs to Michigan, and by doing it, creates a hundred jobs in Illinois." By this he means: each plant is a feeder to other plants. And all the plants are dependent on each other, and on new techniques like "just in time inventory" and outsourcing. The geographers would say: what we think of as the global economy is the regional economy becoming more regional.

Somehow, in ways I admit I don't fully grasp, Chicago was destined to become the center of all this. Harold Washington becoming mayor was simply brushed aside. This was to be the City where the regional economy would shop, and have lunch, and the poor and the homeless had better get out of the way. The city was back again.

It's as if the city were a series of big bangs.

Our First Big Bang

In the beginning, as in Genesis, there was a North and a South Side. The South Side was Protestant, millenarian, and made of wood. It had a habit of blowing up. The Great Fire, 1871. Pullman strike. It would blow up like a movie set. Indeed, it really had a precursor of a movie set: the Columbian Exposition of 1893. It was the famous World's Fair, what was called the White City. Marvelous buildings of wood and canvas. Put up by the city's great businessmen, dreamers, sons of millenarians from upstate New York.

Then they tore it down! But that's our history. It's as if a few children of millenarians trekked across, stopped in the middle, and threw up the South Side. Saw it as a rough draft for Hollywood, and kept moving on.

Slapped it up. Burned it down. Kept moving west to the Disneyland to come.

But in the 1960s, it seemed torn down for good. During the riots it seemed both the South Side and West Side had been burned down.

Once again, by millenarians, one could say.

This was the fate of many American cities. But the North Side? It was always different. The North Side was Catholic, and German, and made of brick. It was impossible to burn down. Nearby me was that Schlitz beer hall they turned into a rock club. "It was the old brick German housing stock," a demographer told me, "that really saved Chicago."

So when boomers and singles were ready to move back into the city, Chicago had all this brick that hadn't burned.

Not just brick, but German, Catholic brick that no one knew how to burn.

The Bangless 1970s

Even so, by the 1970s the city seemed doomed. De-industrializing. Mills closing.

Unlike L.A., we'd been stupid, and had stayed out of defense and aerospace. No one wanted it. There's a story, I guess untrue, about a meeting of the Chicago Machine after World War II. The question was: should Chicago try to get a piece of the defense work? Would the cold war go on?

"Look," said an alderman, "that defense stuff doesn't last. Besides, we'd have all of these engineers, college grads, coming in here voting!"

"And we all know," he said, "that college grad's don't make good Machine voters!"

So Chicago took a pass. Now, for a while it looked dumb. But then the cold war ended, and then we looked smart.

But the main thing is that civilian industry (auto, capital goods) kept creating more and more jobs back in the city. True, the people of the city were no longer in the factories and "tending the machines." The new machines didn't need anyone to tend them.

Still, the machines generated jobs in law, advertising, etc. And we needed valets to park the cars. So in a way, the people of the city were still ... well, tending the machines. It's just that now we were standing way, way in back of the machines. Some of us were back, all the way to the Loop.

Our New Big Bang

Actually the North Side was coming back by the time of Mayor Byrne. I have a friend who was there the night it happened.

"It was the night they reopened the Biograph Theater," he told me. "I was there. I was hired to take photos, you know, of the interior. The bathrooms. They were showing this movie, Visconti's *The Damned.*"

"With Dirk Bogarde?"

"Right. And there's a huge mob trying to get in. You know, people shouting, and they're drunk, and yelling, even as the film's going. Then the owners . . . these guys had shirts open to their navels . . . they come storming out, and they're shouting at people, 'You! You, you're all Philistines!'"

They had never shown a Visconti movie on the North Side.

Actually, they don't show them now either, but it's for different reasons. At any rate, the night marked a turning point.

"You know what my wife and I used to do for dinner in the 1970s?" my friend said. "We'd go to the Seminary. At Clark and Fullerton. And you know what the big thing was? It was to order the caramel custard for dessert."

He paused, and we remembered when Lincoln Park was still, in 1975, so raw, so dangerous that couples only went out on Saturday night to have caramel custard for dessert.

THE DEATH OF HAROLD

It was in court that Harold's forces won the standoff. The ward map was thrown out, and some of Vrdolyak's twenty-nine had to run again. And after a victory in the 26th ward, Harold finally had a majority, barely, twenty-six to twenty-four.

He'd done it. Even whites were impressed. No deals. He had just smashed the other guy, Vrdolyak, so completely, so utterly, he ended up on Talk Radio.

Then at the moment of victory, Harold died, rather mythologically. He simply disappeared from the earth.

It was eerie. I saw him in the last election. He hugged Katy, an election worker, and shrank back in horror: "Baby, you are cold!" And then I saw him on TV, in a last debate with Byrne (yes, she ran again), and he was sweating, horribly.

As it was, he barely won. But as racial as the voting was, it was much less bitter.

The voters, the poor, still had to come out in droves. I say this, but I look at the percentage: it's only 75 percent of registered voters. It did seem like a revolution, a mass upheaval, and I think it was. But in the end, if I'm honest, and look at the turnout, this mass upheaval was really nothing more than a routine turnout in a European country.

But for us, it was drama enough.

And there was another turnout, a bigger one, a true public assembly the week he died, November 1987.

It was a grey, rainy, horrible day. A friend, R., a paramedic, got the call to go to City Hall, and it dawned, bit by bit, as he pushed through, where he was going. I was sick that evening when I had dinner with friends in one of the trattorias where there will never be a black waiter, and everyone was laughing, and it was packed—after all, why did these people care?—and I thought, "half the city is keening, is mourning, what am I doing here?" Now I know how to many it seems overwrought. Well, I was overwrought. I turned to my friends. "He was a great man," I said.

"Oh, yes, 'a great man'!" scoffed B., who was for Daley.

"He was!"

"Look at what he did!" she said.

"What?"

"What!!?"she said. "What about appointing Rebecca Sive to the Park Board?"

"What's wrong with her?"

"Oh! And that pimp! Clarence McClain, his friend!"

I didn't want to get into that.

"It's *not* the night to get into this, *is it?*"

You know, like ... he died today! I blew up at her in a way I now regret—but he had just died, damn it! We were surrounded by happy whites, North Side bubbleheads.

"Oh," I wanted to shout, "how can you all keep eating like this when half the city is outside weeping?"

Of course from where we were, no one could hear weeping.

"It's not worth arguing with her." But no, the devil said, it was; and I let him ravish me.

. . .

THE MAYOR'S BODY LAY IN STATE in City Hall. Up to half a million walked by. Half a million! Isn't that just a notch below a Lenin or Mother Teresa? The wait was up to three hours: I had friends who went down at 1 A.M. on Saturday night. They waited, with the date crowd. Ed and Marlene went at 5 A.M. and slipped right in.

My wait was two hours. In the dark with the poor. (Of course, it was so dark, how did I know they were poor?)

Reminded me of a polling place . . . I had the same sense of my socks filling up with ice, and moving north, up the river . . . and the cold is expressible only on the Kelvin scale. This is what had killed Harold, too, the Machine setting primaries in the middle of winter.

One last time, I scanned the crowd: "Is it too black? Not enough white? Latino? There's a white couple farther up. Wonder if I know them."

Goodness. What a thought. How could I not think it, though?

We were moving closer. I chatted with a couple behind me. The crowd *was* black, but not poor, or so it seemed to me. A lot were wearing a kind of muted grape, like one saw at the Gap.

God, this was taking forever.

Then: I was in!

Only because of the wait in the dark could inside the hall be such a shock. First, the shock was just to *see*. Second, to see light, and then flowers. The final shock: to hear the singing. A woman in a gown, a sleeping child at her feet, a child by her, was singing to us, a capella.

Outside, it was dark, November waves, beating on the Drake Hotel.

But inside City Hall—light. Flowers. A man ahead of me was holding an envelope. As he moved closer to the body, he looked at a cop as if to say, "Can I put this here?"

The cop nodded.

Everywhere people had tossed buttons: NO DEALS. This meant: no deals, with the old Machine alderman, to pick one of their hacks as Harold's successor. Harold, in death, was still teaching us not to beg.

I was before him.

I looked down at his face, to see . . .

"Well, is there an afterlife?"

No answer.

Then we were outside and all of us were clucking, "Oh, they made him too blue," or "Too purple," or "Couldn't they have put a smile on him?"

How happy I was, at least, they didn't put a smile on him. And for the first time it hit me, "What's my reason for living in this city now?"

I mean, Harold gave me something to do. Anything to do now, I'd have to think up on my own.

FINAL ASSEMBLY

After Harold was buried, the City Council met all night. It was put on TV, people gathered in bars and drank, and it went on till 5 A.M.—"the Night of the Living Aldermen" it's now called. The white aldermen were smart enough to put up a black to succeed Harold. He was Eugene Sawyer, a regular, who was friendly with Harold's enemies.

But he was not Harold's guy, and a mob gathered outside.

Some of the black aldermen crossed over, to join with the other side. I'm staring at an old handbill:

Now you know that Alderman Anna Langford has crossed over Mayor Washington's grave . . .

It goes on to give the details.

Vernon Jarrett of The Sun Times *was so hurt he broke down and cried at the UICC Pavilion last night . . .*

And the last line of this handbill:

We must not allow a few greedy negro aldermen to take us back into patronage slavery . . .

Then it gives Anna Langford's home phone number. I wonder if it still works.

The white aldermen wanted Sawyer. Once Sawyer tried to back out. But a minister came over to pray with him. Then the white aldermen demanded a vote. Harold's party tried to postpone.

Up in the galleries people waved dollar bills. "How much, Sawyer? How much?"

I had stood outside with friends earlier, and we had picked out favorite signs, like "Sawyer's in a Cadillac waiting for Vrdolyak."

The cops did nothing as the crowd surged. They still weren't sure which side would win. Even when the kids on the windowsills began to dance, the cops just looked on benignly.

It's eerie to think how they just watched the kids dancing.

But here's something eerier: my roommate was the mayor of Chicago! Well, he was a former roommate.

Years later I'd say this at parties: "I once roomed with the mayor of Chicago." And people next to me would gasp.

But it's true. When I first came to the city, I shared an apartment with a young professor, David Orr. He went on to be vice mayor, and after Harold died, for a few days, he was the mayor of the city.

He ran the council that night as I stood outside. He did a fine job, slamming the gavel. But the bad guys had the votes. The white aldermen screamed to be recognized. They said David was ignoring them and kept waving their hands. One, Dick Mell, climbed on his desk, waved his arms, "Now do you see me, Mr. Mayor?"

It chills me to think, what if it had been me? Imagine, to wake up one morning and be, oh, the mayor. The old mayor dead. A huge alderman screaming over me as I wake up, *"Now* do you see me, Mr. Mayor?"

Of course later Rich Daley, the "manager," replaced Sawyer and I thought little about the city for several years.

SEVEN

City of Fabulous Plagues

THEN ONE NIGHT I SAW THE CITY FOR THE FIRST TIME again, the way Hemingway saw the war—by ambulance.

My friend Marc, who was a medic for the Fire Department, said, "It's a hot night, let's go." We met at a small firehouse near the Hyatt Hotel, on the new "East Side" of the Loop. The Hyatt and the other hotels are up on stilts, hundreds of feet in the air, because they only own the air rights. The railroad, I am told, owns the land underneath, and by virtue of a bribe paid long ago, the land is still tax exempt, so long as it's for railroad purposes.

So why is there a golf course under there? No one can explain this.

Anyway, we got in the van, and it's as if we drove past the hotels, and crashed down off the stilts, and bumped along the streets full of potholes till we hit what is called West Town.

West Town is where Latinos are being pushed out. Our first stop was at a drugstore.

There was a young mother, a girl, really, and she was crying: her baby was in convulsions.

Marc got out. I stayed in, looking. The child, mouth open, like an angel's.

"Febrile seizure," said Marc when he came back.

It had to do with asthma: same frightened look, like the people in ads I saw on the El.

"Oh," I said, "I read an article about this." I had. In *USA Today*.

"They say what's causing it?"

"They can't explain it," I said. Except to say, it was big in Chicago.

"I think it's prenatal care. Or the lack of it."

We now turned south, and headed to the old black wards, and I had my biggest shock: they were gone!

My God, when had they done this? But block after block—nothing.

Well now, wait, how long had it been since Harold died? Four years. This was the summer of 1991, right before the Gulf War, I remember.

Block after block. Empty. Empty. We kept sailing through tall grass. Big vans that said c.f.d., or CHICAGO FIRE DEPARTMENT. Sailing through the savannahs.

Sometimes the vans stop, and pick up people, as if they had fallen down here in the field of battle.

Had there been a city down here once, or not? If there was, and there must have been, like the lost city of Harold's People, where had they gone now?

This was the first night I noticed, the first night I began to ask people. Over the years I've had different answers: "No, there was never a city down there."

Or, "There was—but they moved to the south suburbs."

Or, "They blew it up, in the sixties, like a movie set, remember?"

Or, "They tore it down, under Richie, it was all crack houses."

But it's still weird. As we drove, I thought, "What have I been doing with my life, that a whole city around me could disappear and I wouldn't *know it?*"

I had lunch with a black lawyer, a friend I see once every year or so. "Yeah, it is incredible, isn't it? They'll make it a theme park one day, Blues World, and bring in tourists, yes, over here, this is where the black people used to be . . ."

Anyway, he was kidding.

But I drove that night and thought, "It doesn't matter who's mayor, and if there's no such thing anymore as being a 'citizen of a city,' but my God, I should keep a little better tab of things."

Once my eyes adjusted to the light, I began to see people. Well, I could see them being put on stretchers. It's partly that the dust is so thick.

It was a shock to find that the Fire Department was giving out the city's primary medical care. In a country with 40 million uninsured (and climbing), this should not be a shock. But it was.

Marc talked about the epidemics he was seeing. "About a fifth we pick up are HIV."

"And what else?"

"STDs."

"You mean, syphilis?"

Yes, like in the *Lives of the Poets.* And speaking of that:

"TB."

"TB?" Actually, I guess I knew that: there was a story in the *New York Times,* but I didn't know it was here.

Marc passed no judgment on my stupid questions, but really, where had I been? I'd been in status hearings, in federal court.

Once a British friend scolded me for not following a local story: "But, oh, you don't have to read the papers, do you?"

"Why?"

"Because you can get the local news, you can just go to court . . ."

And maybe there was a time when the federal judges really did run the city, because of all the injunctions under all the civil rights acts the city used to violate.

Judge Getzendanner had the parks.

Judge Shadur had the jail.

Judge Marshall had police.

Judge Aspen had the famous *Gautreaux case,* to scatter the black poor out into white neighborhoods.

But that era was now over, mostly, and anyway I never brought big cases to revamp the city. Oh yes, I went to court on a pension class action—a discharge case—and sat through the status calls. And there's the American eagle, like the Roman imperial eagle, over the judge's head, and he sits there, like the proconsul from the Empire, as he calls each case.

Civus Romanus sum. It means, "I am a lawyer in federal court."

Anyway, for years this is all I would do. Go over each morning and wait for my turn.

Then I'd rise.

"Good morning, counsel."

"Good morning, Judge." (The other lawyer says this.)

"Good morning."

"Good morning."

"When should we have the next status?"

We check our calendars.

"Thank you, Your Honor."

"Thank you, counsel."

"Thank you, Judge."

What did I have to know to be a citizen and lawyer? To know if it was morning, and maybe not even that.

I passed a soup kitchen where I once worked with the order of Mother Teresa. I told Marc about this.

"Ah," he growled. "Why are you doing that? You'd do people a lot more good as a lawyer."

Don't be so sure.

No, this is what I should be doing, being a medic. Was it too late? I noticed now I was caked with dust, and I began to curse myself for wearing white. I was filthy. Like Moscow when I went there a few years later. I would think of the South Side when I saw big Russian women beating down the street with brooms.

All night I was embarrassed, don't ask me why, at all the dust we were kicking up. I read that in Paris in the nineteenth century, people really did need carriages to get to parties. Otherwise, they'd be filthy: they'd look in a few minutes like Marc and me.

I found out the city actually makes money sending the ambulances around. It bills the state under Medicaid, and it actually makes a small profit. The problem back then was, the hospitals for the poor were all closing. There was no place to take people. Though now, with the middle class in HMOs, the patients on Medicaid are beginning to look better.

I was upset as Marc told me the state was shutting down hospitals and those that were still around were pulling out of the ER system. It wasn't, oddly, for the poor I felt bad. I felt bad for Marc.

These men driving around and around, like in a Mir spacecraft, looking for a place to dock.

Marc thought I should see County, which is the big public hospital. County in a way reminds me of the Old Executive Office Building, or the way the EOB would look now if it had been abandoned in the 1920s . . .

and there were 2,000 women claiming to be Princess Anastasia and screaming in the basement.

We strode like gods into the ER . . .

Bam!

The nurses looked up. This was a lot different from a status hearing.

"Want a *Coke?*" Marc shouted.

"What?"

It was summer and hot and hard to hear over the big electric fans, which were blowing like the fans in Sierra Leone.

"*Marc,*" I shouted, "why don't they have air conditioning?"

He took me outside so I could hear, and said, "They don't have any money."

Didn't I know that the hospital had just lost its accreditation?

"I thought reformers were in charge!"

"They are!"

All the fans blowing germs around—I didn't want to go in. "Why would you even bring someone here?" I asked.

"They're good at taking bullets out of you."

We got a Coke and drove on. Sometimes we'd hear a call over the radio. Marc might say, "Put me on that ticket." Or, "I'm on that ticket."

We'd be off to a project.

At each one, looming up in the dark, kids would be playing. The first time, I stayed in the van as the kids looked in.

"Are you in the fire department?" a child asked.

"No."

"Are you in . . . the police department?"

"No."

A giggle. "Are you in the fire and police department?"

Now Marc came over and put his hand on my shoulder:

"Hello, Doctor."

"Doctor!" The kids went wild.

As we pulled away, I waved weakly. "You do look like a doctor," Marc said, because of my whites.

"I look like a tennis pro, held hostage," I thought.

These kids don't see doctors, he said, because the centers down here have closed. "It's like 'Fuck it, let 'em die.'"

Goodbye, kids! We were off.

It was odd to drive through the city and see empty blocks, empty Goldblatt's, empty El tracks—then suddenly there'd be a clutch of people. Sociologists have studied it all to death. Down here, driving around, I felt what many a sociologist must have felt:

God, I love this town!

Go to a phone and call my friends and say, "I'm staying down here till I get tenure at the University of Chicago."

Not only did the poor get very poor in the 1980s they became more concentrated. Here's one measure of this: In 1970? There were only 48 census tracts where the poor were more than two-fifths of all people counted. In 1990 the number had jumped to *184*.

Yet this was the very time, in theory, that our public policy was to integrate, to pull people out of these tracts. Indeed, in law school, when I first read cases like *Gautreaux v. Chicago Housing Authority*, which ordered scattered-site housing for the black and poor, this was what I hoped to do as a lawyer. It was 1971, in Professor Leibman's class. The cases were hot off the mimeo. This was urban policy then. To pull people out of projects, to "dive into the wrecks" and somehow get them out.

And as a lawyer I never did "it," i.e., dive into the wreck; but I was doing it tonight, and I was thrilled to do it the honest way, with my hands.

That night as we drove from dark lighthouse to lighthouse, big stretches of sand between, medics went in and came out with people on stretchers. What haunted me was the way we—I say "we," what a laugh—went in with stretchers and pulled people out, and how it seemed each one, wrapped in white sheets, had a look of peace, as if, "It's over now."

It seemed we'd winch them up in white sheets and sail away.

Now we got on another "ticket" and off we drove. "Where are we going?"

"Stabbing. Thirteenth floor of ————. The guy who did the stabbing is still there." When we saw the place, Marc pulled over, a block away, and turned off the lights.

"Why turn off the lights?"

"They just called a ten-one."

"So?"

"'Policeman in trouble.' And a ten-one is not like 'Policeman may be in trouble or is facing trouble.' He's in trouble. Now."

"Oh."

Are we? I didn't ask.

"Look, two cars just pulled up."

"Cops?" I began to get out.

"No, no, Tom"—he grabbed me—"those aren't our people!"

So I had to sit, like at a status hearing.

Then two cop cars did roar up—no, three, four, five cars—no, six—wow! Big whirls of dust.

The project, dark, now went ka-boom, like at a rock club, and the little kids bounced out, and the sirens flashed like strobe lights. And (to me) this was a strange thing to see: The cops who were mostly women surrounded by little kids.

Oh well—the nurses were mostly male.

They now brought out the young man who had done the stabbing. I could see his face by flashes of heat lightning, like in *The Battle of Algiers*.

I started to wander off.

"Damn it!" said Marc, and now he was mad: "Watch where you're going around here!"

"I am!"

"You've got to watch the windows!"

I looked up. Would they really shoot in front of the cops?

Back in the van Marc said, "That's enough excitement for one night, huh?" I looked to see if he was serious: it wasn't enough for me!

But there was one more stop, and it was the worst. We were to cart an old lady, a stroke victim, up to Rush (Presbyterian/St. Luke's Medical Center). Up and down the blocks all night, I had seen beat-up houses, or no houses, but this was the saddest block of all: just one house, in a pool of dust.

Up the tiny wooden stair went the stretcher with Marc, another medic, and me. Outside, there were ten or so people—were they "neighbors"? But there weren't any houses!

We burst in the house, then up a flight, then into a bedroom—*bam!*

"You'll see," my friend Tony had predicted, "there's no privacy, is there?"

I was still spooked by the block, with one ghostly house, and it was like the moon, and the ten people outside were Moon People watching.

And each time I put down my foot, there'd be a little plume of sand going up. Hissss—like a moonwalk.

And here was the old lady, half naked.

I felt sorry for her. Then we all had to slip on our gloves (for AIDS). To pick up this lady who'd, maybe, spent half her life in church.

On the wall behind her was a storyboard explaining in pictures how to stick your hand down her trachea.

Outside, gasping as we carried her, we backed through another knot of women cops. Women: watching us nurse. What would the old mayor have said? Marc slammed the door. "That," he said, "was a good piece of work."

In the van I said, "And what will Rush do for her?"

"Oh, run some tests. Check her kidneys, see if they're working . . . then send her home."

I felt good, to have gotten her to such a fine hospital. But Marc seemed sad. "A lot of 'em," he said, "would rather die at home."

The next morning, waking: My God, had I really been down there? But there were my shoes, full of dust, on the floor. I thought about this all for weeks. I kept thinking of the time I wandered off in the tall grass and wasn't looking up at the windows. I thought how it wasn't just the land, but the city—as city—that was going back to its original, grassy state. And the last people down here? The medics, carrying us off.

Fitting, isn't it? Chicago started as a public health district (1827). Before it was a village (1833) or a city (1837), it started out as this.

And as the city down here goes back to its original grassy state, it seems to be going back, too, to its original governmental form.

And one can say that about many inner cities—the medics driving around seem, in the empty blocks, the first line of government. (Of course in 1991 mine was the common view, i.e., the city's going back to grass, and now in 1998 we say, "Oh, the city's going to be a garden!")

But I couldn't lift stretchers, so what could I do? Marc had put a challenge: "You'd help these people more as lawyer." I had laughed. And besides, there were lawyers doing housing, and *Gautreaux* and cases like that from the 1960s, and the city was no better. I had tried other things, like being a labor lawyer. But I couldn't file a suit to raise the minimum wage, could I?

It was actually Ms. H., from Hungary, who gave me the idea. She was quite taken with lawyers: "Darling, you stand up there and we listen . . . we, the jury, we listen to your every word, and we say, 'Yes! Yes! And oh God, who cares if it is right or if it's wrong!'"

Then one night she told me at dinner: "I have tuberculosis."

I wanted to say: "You? But you're a yuppie?"

"You think, 'Did I get this in Budapest?'" she said. "No! Oh, no, the United States of America, it says, 'Oh darling, you must take all these tests, we must test you for disease before we let you in our precious country . . .'" She had a theory: She'd picked it up in the Loop, in a big department store.

Of course it was not active, and she was getting treatment, up at Truman College (as I recall).

But now I began to notice more stories.

It was spreading in New York. It was spreading in the shelters.

Downtown, at Harold Washington Library, a librarian now had the disease. Why not? The library was a homeless shelter. All day, the homeless, pretending to read—and coughing, and hacking.

No parent would let a child read there now, as I used to read *Sartoris*. Especially in summer, with the fans blowing—like at County Hospital.

I could see the books, still the color of brown shoes, still with plastic cellophane covers; only now, between the covers, pressed like a flower from the high school prom—the TB bacillus.

Well, it could be.

Yes, the numbers of cases were still laughably small to a layperson. In 1992 the city was reporting about eight hundred cases.

But the rate of increase was frightening, and I thought, "The laws from the 1960s, and *Gautreaux,* aren't going to help with that."

Then one day in the county law library, as I sat with the homeless, I stumbled onto the old public health laws of the 1800s, back when the city had real epidemics: typhus, malaria, cholera, TB. One statute said: "Local authorities shall take efficient means . . . to suppress or restrict contagious or epidemic diseases. . . ."

"Why not apply this law," I thought, "in the era of antibiotics?" TB and other diseases were spreading among the poor, the homeless. Marc had told me stories the whole night. So why not bring a suit?

I spoke with a woman who knew the law in this area.

"My God, you could sue under this," she said. "Aren't the old nineteenth-century laws great?"

I had been looking for a way to be a citizen since Harold's campaign. I'd gone door-to-door: "Are you plus or minus?" I could go door-to-door now. "Are you TB positive or not?" I admit, I wanted this to be my project.

But I wasn't sure if I should bring a suit, so I met with the public health group, and some of the doctors on the board were famous in the city. I explained how the law worked, and how the city was doing nothing as TB spread. Did they think we should bring a suit?

One doctor frowned. "Why do you want to do TB? I don't mind a suit, but we have a lot of epidemics that are worse."

"Like what?"

"Congenital syphilis."

"What about lead poisoning?" a doctor said.

"That's not contagious, is it?"

"It's 'infectious.' In the way this statute reads."

Another doctor said, "We have a measles epidemic, incredibly."

"What about hepatitis?"

But I wanted to do TB. I mean, obviously, there's something romantic about it coming back. I began to imagine a huge epidemic spreading up to Lincoln Park, and then people would shake their heads: "Oh! How sorry we are we abandoned the poor!"

I had some notion that the way to stop this was to build housing for the homeless. Alas, it turns out, it does not take so much. But doctors had begun to realize, it takes more than just handing out medicine. There had to be "directly observed therapy," too, or DOT. That is, it is crucial that a person with TB be "observed," and "directly observed," taking the required pills.

Why?

If someone starts and stops, the TB can come back—and this time in a more virulent, drug-resistant form. Even Einstein, if he had TB, would have to be "observed." The poor and the homeless, even more so.

That is what the city was not doing (though Boston, New York, and other cities were). And this is what we had to get them to do.

I was so excited: I had a new way of connecting with my city! I was going to do public health.

But after my meeting with the doctors, a board member took me aside: "Ah, the poor don't have health problems really."

"They don't?"

"Look," he said, "all you're doing is starting another program. The poor in this town have too many programs!"

"I don't think so."

"I'll tell you a health problem we see—rat bites. A rat gets in a crib and bites an infant, but really, is that a *health* problem?"

OK, but did he think I could raise their wages? I couldn't, so I might as well do this.

Damn it. I didn't need to be lectured to.

But I felt guilty filing the suit, even though (in fact) an incipient epidemic was spreading. I felt guilty, because I knew he was right, and I was doing this as a form of theater, in a way. "See how much we've let inequality grow? Even TB is back."

Yes, what would Clarence Darrow and Jane Addams and the old Progressives think? All the evils they faced and did away with at the turn of the century are back—and back this time in a more virulent and drug-resistant form.

It's true as our famous sometime client Dr. Quentin Young says, the big health problems of America are public health problems: infant mortality, prenatal care, etc. One way to deal with these is just to raise the standard of living.

Indeed, that's how we used to do things in the U.S. "Yes, there are drugs to deal with TB," says Alan Shaw at the American Lung Association here, "but we eliminated TB as a scourge *before* we had the drugs, which came in the 1950s."

How?

Better housing.

Less overcrowding.

Higher incomes.

As I met doctors who were TB experts, many would repeat this. My friend Dr. C., who worked at County and stopped TB from spreading among the doctors, said this: "Why's it back? It's not AIDS—it's back for the same reason it was here before. *Poverty, overcrowding, diet.* TB is like a template of how sick a society is."

"What happens if we don't stop it?"

"Ever read the novel *The Magic Mountain*? If it starts to take drug-resistant form, then all you can do is reopen the sanatoriums."

I didn't read *The Magic Mountain*; I began to sit (at home, not the library) and read the histories of public health. I soon realized, "This is the real history of the American city."

A simple glass of water. What a miracle I can drink it and not fall down and die! Yes, I began doing things more slowly. Drinking tap water. For the first time in years, I felt the miracle of living in the city.

But some of the people who ran the homeless shelters were nervous about the suit. Oh, they were scared of TB all right. The homeless were sleeping crossways from each other: A would sleep so that his head was next to B.'s feet, and B. would sleep in the same way next to C.'s feet. It was October now, and one of the "vendors" said: "Am I nervous? When we close the windows this winter, it will be like a bomb going off."

The city wasn't ready. DOT wasn't in place. Yes, many cautious, sensible people were expecting an explosion.

But it's an odd thing: The providers who *do* care for the poor find it hard to speak because they're getting money from the city.

"But you want me to sue the city?" the woman said. "The city is funding us. I can't get involved. Go see the HIV people . . ."

Even a Franciscan priest looked at the draft complaint and backed away. "No, I can't do this."

"So," I said, "you're afraid of this city too?"

"No!" he snapped, "I'm not afraid of the city! But look what this thing calls for." He meant the draft complaint's call for . . .

"Adequate spacing in shelters . . ."

What's wrong with that?

"So? What am I supposed to do? Throw people out on the streets? The shelters in the city—even now we can only hold, maybe, about a third of the homeless. So, do I kick people out in the cold in January? There are *worse* things, you know, than getting TB!"

But I kept pushing the suit. The Legal Assistance Foundation took up the case, and had clients in Uptown, and moms with TB.

More important, LAF had one of the best lawyers in the city.

Next—pro bono, a big private firm came in to do the case. The odd thing was, with a new team of lawyers, I had nothing to do.

Maybe just as well.

But I did go to one of the meetings with public health nurses and doctors, who were debating whether to support the suit. This was in doubt, because the city's health commissioner came to blast us for doing it. Many nurses and doctors stood up and accused him: "You admit, don't you, we should be doing directly observed therapy?" "Yes, of course!" he said. "You admit, we don't have the money?" "*I am trying to get the money,*" or words to that effect.

I saw how each nurse or doctor who stood began with the words: "My name is ———, and I'm 'positive.' Each meant, "I'm positive for TB."

After a while, how ashamed I was I couldn't say it, too! But I'm only a lawyer.

Later, two or three of us went to the County Hospital and had a long session with lawyers and officials. There was a young woman doctor, very pregnant, maybe her eighth month, and sitting uncomfortably. She was in white. It took me a while to realize, "Oh, this is the doctor who's working on the county's TB problem." She was silent as we lawyers argued. Then she said to us, "Maybe I can show you some of the hospital. . . ." I ignored her. "Maybe I could show you . . ." I kept blabbing.

"Maybe . . ." She finally kicked me, I think.

When she had the co-counsel and me outside, she said, "The others can speak for themselves. I just want to say, I *welcome* your interest." That's all she said, but I was touched by her words.

"My God," I thought, "why are we suing her?"

Of course, maybe it would help her.

In the end, the city did spend more on the program. Maybe we strengthened the bargaining hand of the good guys. Still—who knows?

It was hard to dismiss our case, since the old public health law had so many "thou shalts." The judge was in agony in open court. "If I throw it out," he said, "I know what they're going to say: JUDGE TURNS BACK ON EPIDEMIC." He paused. But, oh, that's his job, it's to make the tough calls, and he has a higher duty, etc., etc. One of his points was how can a mere judge second-guess the city's public health decisions? Of course we have sixteen sitting juries second-guessing the decisions of anesthesiologists. But never mind.

As the arguing went on and on, I kept thinking, "My God, why aren't I out riding with the medics?" Maybe Marc's right, and we did some good. But I'd have done more if I'd volunteered to do "DOT," i.e., watch the sick take their pills.

I suppose at the University of Chicago there's some theory to explain why people volunteer like this.

"Yes, people volunteered, because it was in A.'s interest to volunteer, and be altruistic, to stop the spread of TB to A . . ."

The Ayn Rand types can explain "volunteering." But why do they themselves never volunteer?

ANSWER: Deep down they know that in the world there are enough decent people, so they don't have to.

Anyway, while the judge threw out the case, the city felt pressured to do more about TB. What some call the "nascent" epidemic of 1991–93 was turned back. Though a doctor told me there was a scare at Humboldt Park a few years later, when "drug-resistant" TB broke out. But the few cases were contained. All's well at the moment.

Don't worry, a doctor told me, TB will be back. There's too much of it rising around the world, and here in the U.S. the poor are still poor, and they're as concentrated as ever.

I'll have another chance to try the suit. If a recession like that of 1989–92 comes back again, the epidemic may come back again.

This time we'll win the case, I think. I have a good statistic, too: "Once," a nurse told me, "there were four hundred forty-three public health nurses in Chicago—that was in the 1940s. Now, how many are there? There are only about forty."

Only about forty! One day I'm sure we'll have four hundred nurses back.

EIGHT

A Ticket to DuPage

PUBLIC HEALTH ALWAYS REMINDS ME OF WHAT ARISTOTLE says, somewhere in the *Politics:* "The first duty of a citizen . . . is to live *forever.*"

The idea is, outlive your enemies. If I can't beat the Right, maybe I can outlast it. And it's possible, some say.

"With this gene therapy," Tony told me the other night, "in twenty years they can flip the switches, and maybe reverse the whole aging process." He paused. "So if we can just hang on twenty more years . . ."

Yes. If I can just hang on till I'm seventy, who knows?

Anyway, if I'm serious about this, I better get into a club. There are so many in Chicago. Since I came in 1979, I've spent more time in health clubs than in the bars of the old Machine.

One day, if inequality ever gets much worse, we might live in them, instead of the gated compounds. We'd retreat. Lock the doors. Taking with us, of course, our personal trainers.

Of course I don't take that grim a view.

But the truth is, living at a club has always intrigued me. As a child, I was fascinated by the old bachelors and widowers who used to take rooms at the downtown clubs. One of the former mayors did. But the old clubs were quite different. No StairMasters, just a little gym, maybe, with a few barbells on the floor, and off to the side of the dining room.

In the new clubs, how could you "take rooms" even if there were an upstairs? I can't imagine. Trying to sleep at night over the clank-clank-

clank of a StairMaster. It would give me nightmares. Marley's ghost, in little running shorts, pumping away on a Nautilus.

At any rate, there are two Loop clubs I've been thinking of joining:

1. East Bank.

The initiation, five hundred bucks, is steep. But, as they say, you pay for the view.

I have a friend who takes out-of-town people here and shows them the "Big Room," where a hundred or more people are puffing on treadmills and bikes and StairMasters, all in a single room. "This," he says, "this is Chicago now!"

He means a sea of blue spandex, undulating like Lake Michigan.

Yeah. Very erotic. Breathing in each other's faces, like in a homeless shelter.

The first time I came here, a man in the locker room went on and on about a carjacking.

But is that the real fear in this place, the inequality outside? No, that's exciting, electric. It keeps us in shape.

But the sad thing is to be in the Big Room and see people pump, and sweat, and cycle, faster, faster, and know some aren't going to make it. I mean, get through the next twenty years in time. Everyone looks thirty-five, yet I know that this one, that one, is forty-five or fifty, and they aren't going to make it.

Indeed, I'm not, am I? And I just know, five minutes after I'm dead, some guy in a white smock will stand up and say, "I've got the *answer*!"

And the Big Room? They'll seal us all up in it. Leave it as a mass grave. Anyway, that's East Bank. Impossible not to think here of the two things no one can escape:

Death . . . and liposuction.

But there is one thing I like, and that's the two little cafés in the health club. Often when I go by, there's a lawyer or someone I know calling out, "Hey, come on over."

That's why I love this club.

It's odd—my neighborhood seems to turn over every six months. But downtown in the Loop I have seen the same faces, same lawyers, for almost twenty years. It's like rural Ireland.

Anyway, I walk in, a lawyer says: "Hey, come over, meet my client." I sit down. He says, "Now I don't want you to think"—his voice drops—"I come here to pick up women." Heh, heh.

I don't. That's what's sad.

And see we just sit there for a while, over an Evian, and discuss the issues of the day. Like gene therapy.

2. Athletic Club of Illinois Center.

Now this club *is* chilling.

Instead of *looking* thirty-five, people *are* thirty-five.

Except for the ones who are twenty-eight. Anyway, I don't like this place because it's younger. Though this also means, it's cheaper. No initiation fee. Or if there is, it's being waived, just for this month.

Isn't that where they have the rock climbing, people ask? Yes. As bombastic as East Bank can be, I'll say this: there's no rock climbing.

But over here? I look straight up and see these—kids—in marketing.

They've been downsized so often, some don't even have insurance. No disability—but dangling two hundred feet over the aerobics classes. Talk about "bowling alone": they aren't even roped together, but just hanging midair, over the women in aerobics.

It's strange about these women. They are of a beauty rarely seen outside in the city: as if, to take aerobics, one must also take the veil.

But put aside the rock climbers; there is one thing about this club that I like very much.

Old black men, shooting baskets. By "old" I mean thirty-five or forty. But they're sealed off, really. On a big court, in a big glass atrium. You can drive around and look at them inside. This big court-in-a-bottle is on a street of hotels. It's one of the most interesting things an out-of-towner can see.

Where do these guys work? Marketing?

The talk in the lockers is of course about aging:

"Man, you are old."

"You see Charley anymore?"

"Not in six months."

"He's too old."

"I'm too old."

As I stand off to one side, like someone from Yale, I don't envy them being black in a white world, but I do envy one thing: that even more than a group of white golfers in the burbs, these guys can come here and *do* something together. And still, at the same time, be able to live in the city, too.

Once in a while, there's a single white guy in the game. One guy, at least, who stopped climbing rocks.

AT THESE CLUBS, after workouts, people pile into cabs. It's nice to step out and feel, well, our bodies glow the way the city glows.

Maybe we're fashioning, by StairMasters, by machines, a new kind of body. If we want to resurrect the city, we have to resurrect the body, too, don't we?

Even Mayor Daley has a new kind of body. It's sleeker, faster, for slipping away. The old bodies that the old pols use no longer really work.

It's these people with the new bodies who are taking back the city, it seems to me. They're moving into the new neighborhoods, like Dearborn Park.

The big newsworthy thing is, it's on the South Side. See, the city is coming back! Of course, some grumble, they got rid of a printing industry, and jobs, to build housing for lawyers. Whose city is coming back here?

But it still amazes me and other locals. It *is* the South Side, isn't it? It's shocking to see a bit of Lincoln Park come down here.

After all, even most of the blues clubs, Blue Chicago, etc., are still on the North Side. So if the blues is still a bit unsure about "coming back," what are these lawyers and bankers doing there?

But there they are.

I saw a story in the paper that 6,000 new households have moved in here and the South Loop since 1992. This is not just rehabbing, but new construction. Now in one sense, 6,000 is a lot; but in another sense, well, where do they go at night? Do they lock the door? Do they gather around the piano and sing "My Darling Clementine"?

The other night my good friend J. told me she was moving down. In a year, when they built her new townhouse. I was shocked. First, that she was building a townhouse. Really, a mile or less from the Sears. How odd! But second, what was she doing down there? No one lives there.

But she explained it. Her church is there. She met people in her firm, and they went there. Then more people. One day she saw that most of her friends were in the Dearborn Park area. So she had to go.

"And," I said, "the mayor's down there."

"The mayor is there."

No arguing with that. But what exactly is the mayor doing down there at night?

PUT ME ON THAT TICKET!

As the city "comes back," some public housing will come down. But it's also true that in place of the high-rises, there's new, decent stuff going up.

Thanks to the run-up of the market, the movement of people into Dearborn Park, this is a good time to be poor. Or better than it was.

There are critics: Yes there is a little housing going up on the West Side. But it's not enough, or it's put up here, near the Loop, so we don't have to see the awful stretches to the south.

While it's not enough, I guess it's a miracle there's any. After all, it's a Republican Congress. I have friends who "do" housing law, and they tell me: "Drive around, look at the West Side." Look at the low rises. Not just for the poor, but for better-off working people who will be their big brothers. I'm really glad for the poor in these units, and I've heard touching stories about their joy. But it looks a little like movie scenery.

OK, but it's something, isn't it?

And some who say, "The city is coming back," don't realize it's the government that makes it blossom. As with nice new public housing. People I know think, "Oh, it's the developers, it's the market."

"Come on," a friend of mine told me, "it's the federal government." And yes, incredible as it seems, it's the federal government, Washington, D.C., building many of these new houses that we admire.

And on a very tiny scale it's like Model Cities, it's the New Deal. Only no one knows it.

The other night I gasped when a friend rattled off what HUD is paying in the city now for "new capital development." It's well over a hundred million. Then add all the other HUD subsides, guarantees, write-offs.

My friend asked, "Did Harold Washington, in a million years, ever see this kind of money from Reagan?" Under Harold, he said, one year the city received from HUD a total of—ready?—$7 million, in capital development. No wonder the high-rises looked like crap.

But under Clinton? There's real money. And that's in part why the city is coming back! It's Washington, D.C., still working for us, though nobody gives it any credit.

BUT IT'S NOT ENOUGH.

So in 1996, over 1,100 units of public housing were demolished, and only 475 or so new units of "nice" housing were built. But as the old public housing comes down, what will happen to the poor?

At lunch, Dan, a housing lawyer, explained it this way: "They can get 'tickets.' And they can get 'bricks.'"

The tickets are the Section 8 housing vouchers, which the Right favors. These are rent vouchers, and all the poor have to do is find a landlord to take them.

The bricks, of course, are the nice new units, which the Right in Congress don't want to build.

Now there are all sorts of reasons why Dan likes bricks, and doesn't like tickets!

1. Tickets get lost. Hand out a million in one year. A few years later, there are only half a million. People die. Get lost.
2. Tickets get cut. Congress can cut the budgets, etc.

Bricks are forever; tickets aren't. But there's a much, much more chilling reason to worry about the tickets.

I learned this when I talked to W., another lawyer, who represents the poor in public housing. I was at a party to raise money for his work. It's odd how courtly he was to all of us: he kept saying "Mr." to me, and this made me uneasy.

Of course, what would I be like, standing here, gulping hard, hoping rich people would give me money?

I asked him about tickets, the rent vouchers, and he brought up a point I had not considered: Yes, the poor get these vouchers. But then they have to go door-to-door and find a landlord to take them.

Then he said softly, "About a third to a half never find anyone."

"No one?" I said. "Well, what do they do?"

"They have to turn the vouchers back."

I couldn't believe this. So I asked him again: "What do you mean, they have to give the vouchers back?"

"They have six months. Then they have to give their vouchers to the next person."

"And up to half never find . . . ?"

He nodded stiffly.

"If you like, I can send you a study from the University of Illinois."

"Yes, I would like that." And I have the study right here, and yes, up to half the poor who get the vouchers never find a landlord.

My God. There's a nice civil servant job: "Your six months are up. Sorry. You have to give your vouchers back!"

I asked W., "What happens when they have to turn the tickets, or I mean the vouchers, back in? Where do they live?"

"Oh, they move in with a relative. They 'double up.'"

Thank God for the poor. Who would house the poor but them?

Once every three years or so, I make a vow that as a lawyer I'll try to do something for the poor. The TB case, etc. Usually nothing comes of it. But after this party I had the same feeling as I had the first year of law school, when I read the *Gautreaux* cases: that the most decent thing is to save as many as we can, find safe housing for them in a suburb. A real suburb, like DuPage, not one of the new poor suburbs, full of crack and heroin. Now *Gautreaux* has gone on for thirty years, a whole lifetime for a lawyer. And yet, after thirty years of appeals, cross appeals, interventions, orders, supplementary orders, how many public housing families have been placed, actually placed, out in the suburbs?

About 7,100 families.

Yes, about the same as the number of Loop professionals that have moved to the near South Side.

Now in one sense, that's a lot. I'd be proud as a lawyer to have had a role in it.

But in another sense, it doesn't seem like much does it?

There must be some other way to get them out there—again, I mean into white Cleaver-type suburbs, not into suburban Devil's Islands. But what is it?

FOR A MONTH OR SO I was thinking, "Perhaps it's lead paint." Yes, the lead paint in the housing in which many of the poor live.

I should explain a little about the lead paint problem, because so many find it baffling. What are these little kids doing, *eating* the paint chips? But then I talked with a public health official, Jonah Deppe, with the city. No, she said, that's not it.

"No, they're just poor. So they can't keep up the housing. And look," she said, "there's no topsoil . . ."

I knew that from the moonwalk I'd taken with Marc.

"So the soil, it has lead, it just blows around."

Too much for a tiny body.

"These are just babies. And toes, fingers—something goes in their little mouths, on average, once a minute."

So each year, she said, there are five thousand new lead cases. I wonder, should we in Lincoln Park move down there, with all the dust blowing around?

Sometimes when I hear the words "Windy City," I think about the lead paint.

About this time a lawyer told me that a good way to make money was to bring suit for these kids. It is strange, he said, that no one is doing it.

I met this guy at Kevin's, which is a restaurant aldermen go to, like Burt Natarus, who wants to put diapers on the horses that pull carriages for the tourists. People laugh, but it's not so bad an idea.

Anyway, Kevin's is a good place to talk business, and I went with two friends, who were also curious. I had asked them, "Why don't we do these cases together?"

The lawyer we met told us, all we had to do was find some kids with lead. The rest was easy. Sue.

"Aren't these mom-and-pop landlords?" we asked. "How can they pay?"

"They're all insured." And, the man said, often you don't even have to file. You send a letter to the insurance company; they settle.

"This sounds too easy," S. said.

"How do we find the kids?" I asked.

"Just go over to Juvenile, talk to the P.D.s."

He means public defenders. It is a commonplace that the kids in Juvenile have very high lead levels.

The more he talked, though, the more it all offended me. How dare I make money off these poisoned children?

"This is all fine," I said. "But what about the kids? Isn't it too late for them? Isn't the damage permanent?"

"Oh no," he said. "They can clean 'em up a bit."

I thought S. winced.

"Look," he said, "they might as well get some money, right? You take your third. They get twenty or thirty thousand—put it in escrow."

He trailed off.

Yeah, put it in the market. The kid can buy a house in DuPage.

Of course the market could crash. Then they'd be stuck in the city.

I talked to my friends later. Is this what I really wanted to do as a lawyer? Besides, there must be some other way to get people out to DuPage.

Of course *Gautreaux* came at a time when the middle class was fleeing the city. But now isn't it true many people are coming back?

Chicago could build the housing for the poor. Look at Orlando, our great rival for conventions. Overnight, seemingly, it has built over 80,000 hotel rooms.

Daily maid service, too.

If Orlando can do it, why can't Chicago build 50,000 units here?

In a bookstore a year ago, I met a young man, vaguely on the left, who had come back from a housing conference in Istanbul. He told me how in the Third World they know how to build housing. Just give people saws and hammers and let them go.

Reclaim the city. Throw up anything.

I scoffed, of course. But when I think of the 80,000 new hotel rooms in Orlando.

Maybe we should forget *Gautreaux*. Maybe we should let the poor build their own Dearborn Parks.

THE CITY AS STAGE

The truth is, like the mayor, I would like to see the city bigger. I heard Daley speak about this at a lunch the other day. New York, he said, that's too big.

Mexico City? Nah. That's too big.

Los Angeles? That's not a city.

No, the mayor has been going around saying he thinks 3 million is about right.

Ah, we're under 3 million and if lucky, holding steady.

Yes, the mayor knows this. And that's why he'd like to see more people come back from places like DuPage and live (with him) in Dearborn Park.

It haunts me, in my neighborhood, how people always get married and leave. My neighborhood, Southport, which is really a Northport, is full of singles.

Most people my age left long ago. "If you're over thirty-five and still single, there's nothing to do in the city," a woman neighbor said. "It's not like New York."

No, it's just a city. It's impossible to be single and live in *any* American city. That's what my friend Larry said.

"Well, wait," I said, "what about New York?"

"New York isn't a city. It's a *metropolis*." The difference? A metropolis, he said, is for "singles."

"That's why you're ready for New York. You've outgrown this."

By outgrown he means I didn't get married. And in New York, as I understand it, even the "marrieds" have to live like singles. Go to our restaurants, our plays, etc.

And the other difference between a "city" and a "metropolis"? In a city, all day long I'm aware of the "other," suburbia. In Chicago I'm aware of DuPage, on my west, just as I'm aware, conscious or not, of Lake Michigan on the east.

But in a metropolis, like New York, it's so, so big, it blots out even the idea of suburbia, as I walk around during the day. Or this is what I believe. Nothing like "Westchester" would pop into my head. Indeed, would even "the Atlantic" pop into my head?

At any rate, if I'm single, I don't want the idea of suburbia popping into my head, do I?

In my neighborhood, Southport, on summer nights, the main drag is clogged with college grads, and they wander from faux bistro to faux bistro.

"Oh, these are the people," says my neighbor J., "I went to the University of Chicago to escape."

But there's a sadness to it, the way men and women as they approach thirty roam up and down on soft summer nights, and look shyly in each other's eyes:

"Is it you?

"Are you my way out of this?

"Are you my ticket to DuPage?"

And what's awful is to walk up and down Southport, past the Bistrot Zinc, or a Thai spot, or a noodle shop, and see the ones who are still here. They never got a ticket. A letter of transit. A lot of them are not even my age; they're late thirties or so, but they're still here, and the suburb-nesting clocks are ticking, ticking. They should be out, but they aren't. They're beginning to spoil a bit.

No, that's mean. I guess I'm thinking of a night last August. I was going past Cullens, and it was beginning to rain.

One man and three women at a table began shouting: "Sit with us! Sit with us!"

Stupid, but I did.

"Now," said a woman at our table, "if you sit with us, you have to sing a song. Right?" (She turned to the others.)

By now it was pouring.

To another she said: "You went to Western Michigan? Oh, I love their song . . ."

They began humming it.

I could have wept for all of us, the way we were sitting out the storm. They'd never get to DuPage, just as I'd never get to New York. And as we all sat, miserable, wet, I thought, "Why in American life isn't there some new, improved second act?"

Why do we still have to go out there?

To escape, I think, from being citizens. It's too hard. I remember what S., a great activist, told me when she spoke of her daughter: "I'm never going to be like the other parents I know, you know. Who are their friends? I'll tell you. It's the parents of their children's friends, you know, their little play friends. Isn't that awful? As much as I love my daughter, she's not going to decide who my friends will be."

I felt a chill when she said this.

"It's true," I thought later, "when they leave for the suburbs, they stop making their own friends." Indeed, it's creepy when I go out and visit them years later.

"How do you know so and so?"

"Our kids are good friends."

"No," I think, "I can't go out there, ever."

But I can't go to a metropolis like New York; it's too big to live out this childhood fantasy of being a lawyer in the city, and being a citizen. Yes, yes, being an old fashioned "burgher," I suppose.

Now I will get to the real reason I am still out here, though this will make no sense. I truly do think it's because of the theater.

In a way, of course, everyone says this, even the people under the awning on Southport.

QUESTION: "What do you like about living in the city?"

ANSWER: "I'm so close to work, and, there are so many things, like . . . the theater."

Yes. I'm here because of the Mamet, people imply. Now it's true the last thing they saw was *Cats,* two or three years ago. But that is what people say.

And there's something secret and astounding about Chicago, unlike any other place, really, in all of America:

There's theater, lots of it, live theater, much cheaper than New York's, *and you can drive your car.* In that sense, I don't think there's any theater town like it in the English-speaking world.

And it's not like Boston or Washington, where there's just a page or half a page of listings. In Chicago it runs for pages, or it does in the *Reader,* the free weekly. Even in the *Tribune* or *Sun-Times* on Fridays.

A woman at the League of Chicago Theaters told me, once, that there are at least two hundred theater companies in Chicago.

Think of that: two hundred!

"And how many plays put on each year?"

"At least—at least eight hundred."

And I drive around here and often think, "I'm looking, in effect, at two hundred theater companies. Why can't I live my life like one of 'them'?"

I can pretend to be a lawyer but run off with the circus.

Here, because of the two hundred companies, everyone, I suppose, is in the theater. The waiters in the restaurants.

At least two or three of our secretaries.

My law partner, Al, was an actor.

And Len himself, when I arrived here, was on the Jeff Committee and went around reviewing plays.

And I thought that somehow I could be a lawyer in the city and be part of the theater, too, because in my mind, ever since I tried a year of Greek with the Jesuits, living in the "city" and going to the "theater" are mostly the same thing. The same cause. Between Aristotle the *Politics* and Aristotle the *Poetics,* there's only the difference of one or two letters.

In both books great men suffer. And they do it in an urban space.

In both books the great mayors like Harold Washington have to die, and the whole city has to gather in a public space and weep.

And there's comedy, like Second City, and Aristophanes, and John Belushi, and much of that is political, too.

So if Chicago is the great political city, it has to be the great theatrical city, too. The city that produced Mamet, et al. (though, alas, there is no et al.).

Because of the theater I thought I could stay away from DuPage, and I wouldn't have to go to New York. In New York the directors, the actors—they're all artists and unapproachable. Even if they're driving cabs, there's a little glass window between me and them.

But in Chicago they sell humidifiers at Ace Hardware. There's no window. Are they clerks first and actors second? It's murky where the line is between "art" and "Ace Hardware."

As a lawyer, all I crave is an audience, "court watchers." Instead, the ones who watch me are these actors: the ones with day jobs in law firms. It is the strangest thing to be a lawyer and do it before paralegals, i.e., actors. I keep wanting to ask them, "How am I doing?"

AT ANY RATE, as I have lost interest in politics, I have become more interested in plays. Once I wanted to drag people to the polls.

Plus, minus, zero.

Now I want them to see plays. That's become my great cause, as a citizen.

First, I tried to be an actor. I didn't get cast.

Later, I did get on a theater board. But they want you to raise money.

Then finally, the last stage of the delirium, I tried to write, and even produce, a play.

In the beginning, I just wanted to see plays. But I had two great difficulties: (1) there was no one to go with; while you can vote by yourself, you can't go to a play by yourself; (2) and the times I did go alone, there was no one else in the theater either. Maybe five or six in the seats.

I look around in horror. Where is everyone? Often the play is the rave in the *Reader*.

"Highly recommended." But there are five to ten people in the seats!

The others? They're in the restaurants, where they're being waited on by—actors.

Many a Saturday and Sunday night I have gone past the bistros, packed, and I feel like going in and standing on a table, "Hey, don't you people have a theater duty?" What is this, Paris? Eat up and get out!"

Maybe if they were at the theater, and seeing Brecht, and Shaw, and Ibsen, maybe, just maybe, there wouldn't be this growing gap of rich and poor.

To me, it is a duty, and part of living in a city. It is the duty of each of us to be trapped with an actor who is there, alive, making us nervous, pleading.

It's like the experience of being trapped on the El, and at risk, with some poor devil who is there, alive, making us nervous.

But in the El I can change my seat, get off. In the theater, trapped, I have to listen to what they say. If people don't want to listen, they should move out to DuPage.

Now maybe you think I'm mad because they'll never come to my play. Uh, well, yes, that's true. I should explain how I came to write it, since it's "political."

I'd seen a dozen plays about Thatcher. Even more about South Africa. But I kept thinking, "Well, isn't there something equally bad happening in Chicago?"

So I wrote a play, passed it around. People said, "Look, all you need to do is raise eighty thousand dollars."

But that's for Off Loop. For Off Off Loop, I could do it for a bit less. But how to get funding? How to get Citicorp or Bank America to put in money?

I did have two "readings," to lure investors. Here's the journal that I kept:

July 1996. First reading. It's at a workshop.

The night before we do a read-through. I worry about the actor who's playing me.

Later at dinner A. says, "I had to laugh, the way you looked at the poor guy who has to play you."

"It's *not* autobiographical!" I snap.

"Oh! Sure!"

The next day people laugh, but it's not a comedy! Ah!

Discussion follows. Under anesthetic I'm winched up on

stage. "Now," says the MC to me, "when someone makes a point, you *say nothing*!"

So, any comments?

"He's no Brecht. He's no Shaw, etc."

"Well, you got a lot of good feedback!" the MC says.

But no money.

Still, the night before, I wandered in the back of the stage and opened a door and—my God, there were *two actresses,* smoking!

I shut the door. The theater!

The next day I told Al what I saw. He nodded, he understood.

December 1996. Last chance to raise money. A second reading, but no backers come. Too many office parties. People are numb.

People are jaded.

My idea was to liquor them up, have a buffet, open bar. But of course the actors show up first—to my horror, the actors start eating the food.

"Oh, aren't you sweet," says one of the actresses, munching, "to have thought of us!"

What can I say? I'm not *paying* them. "They don't expect it," someone mutters.

Anyway, at this reading no one laughs. "Ah! But it's a comedy!" I try to say.

A friend consoles: "You know why no one laughed this time? You forgot to turn out the lights. People don't laugh unless you turn out the lights."

It's tragic in a way. One tiny little mistake, and now what? My stage life is in ashes.

Yet the next day people call: "Who was she?"

"What did you think of the play?" I ask.

Pause. "*Who was she?*"

People are stunned that I didn't tape it. But isn't the whole point of theater not to have it on tape? The idea that we have an experience, a civic experience, really, and if we don't show up, then it's gone, it perishes, unrewindably, without us, every night?

CITY OF VOLUNTEERS

There may be another reason why people don't vote, or go to the theater: They're too busy being volunteers. It is an inconvenient fact for me. A lot of people even in the bistros apparently work with the poor.

And that's what I wrote back then. And I still carry a great anger when I pass the bistros, and the trattorias. They don't vote. They don't go to plays.

Yes, why don't they go out to DuPage and get it over with?

But the inconvenient fact here, which I don't know how to make sense of, is this:

A lot of them volunteer. Even, yes, work with the poor. There's the study of Father Greeley's (I read it in *The American Prospect*): in America, the rate of volunteering is roughly 40 percent. In Western Europe, it's about half that.

And the strange thing is, this makes sense from what I know.

Greeley argues, in *The American Prospect,* that much of this volunteering is church-based or religiously based. Two or three priests in the "singles" parishes would confirm this, I think.

Indeed, there are crowds even in the churches. And an old monsignor who misses the old Chicago, the parish life, the American Legion hall life, admits, freely, "There's much more volunteering now."

But in a way, so what? There should be more volunteering here than in Europe.

After all, when Florida is hit by a hurricane, don't people come out and volunteer? Walk through an American city, and walk through one in Holland or Germany. Which one needs the volunteers? Yes, the "new" Chicago is glorious. But walk west here. Walk anywhere around Cologne. Which city looks more burnt or bombed?

Sure, the rate of volunteering is higher here. Is that because we're better citizens? Or because we're worse.

We should be thankful, of course, for the opportunities we have to volunteer. Maybe that's why America is so "Christian." I mean in post-Christian Europe, it's much harder to do good works. Clothe the naked? Feed the hungry? It's not possible there. It's unfair, in a way, to live in a social contract economy. Thank God for welfare reform. Think of the corporate works of mercy in the next recession.

OK, I admit, I'd rather see the singles here volunteer than go to see a play. But here's what bothers me: When I volunteer, am I doing something useful, or acting a role?

I recall the moment I realized once, as a volunteer, I was just making everything worse. I was visiting a dying woman at Illinois Masonic. Alas, I had to miss a few weeks. I had to work on a brief, I guess. Or there was a dinner. When I came back, she was so furious, she said, "I'd rather you just didn't come here at all!"

So I stopped: she was right. Yet I'd still have been counted in Father Greeley's 40 percent.

It's a point to consider: how many volunteers should be pulled out of action.

Little random acts of kindness. Sometimes, they, too, can cut and bleed?

Still, I'm in awe of a few whom I've met by chance. The other night at a party I met a woman, I think from an ad agency of some kind. Someone was baiting her, "Tell us about your program." I had ignored her because she was in advertising. Now I saw her, as if for the first time.

"Oh," she said, "I just got into that because I was lazy." You see, as she told the story, it was too much trouble one Sunday to go up to the yuppie church, so she went to a church much closer, near a project. She was shocked how poor people were. So she asked the pastor if she could start tutoring the kids. Then she got her friends. Then it became a big deal.

Anyway, she laughed the whole thing off.

Now I had a sense about her all night: she is never going to DuPage. But she wasn't trapped here, like I was.

The problem is, each act of kindness is unstable. Oh yes, it can and does work. But people get exhausted piling sandbags. Or finally, one day, they get a ticket to DuPage. And who can blame them when they go?

Each time I read of some little civic triumph, I think, "Yes, but how long will this last?" How long before someone tires, and takes, at last, the ticket to DuPage?

IT'S HARD NOW TO HAVE a sense all at once of the whole city. Take the unemployed. There aren't supposed to be many, but there may be up to 80,000.

"Who are they?" my brother said when I mentioned this.

He paused, "You wonder about these guys who stand there at the ramps off the interstates and sell the papers . . ."

"Yeah."

"Where do they come from?"

I don't know. How can you have a sense of the "city" all at once in your head? Too hard now.

It's so sprawling—the Loop, Lincoln Park, Southport, and really I should count DuPage, too.

Lately I have been trying to find out about the poor who, yes, go out to DuPage, every day, but they have to come back to the city at night. Their tickets are only good for the day. An economist told me that the Chicago area has—just think—over two hundred companies that are contractors of day labor.

Day labor. A ticket to DuPage, but one day at a time.

NINE

I'd Be Happier in D.C.

THAT'S WHAT S.H. IN BOSTON SAYS, THAT I'D BE HAPPIER IN D.C., maybe even married.

So, she says, just get a job on the Hill. At dinner I'd have company. At least someone to talk to about the line item veto.

Think of all the other good things about Washington.

I'd get to hear the word "Congress" and not have it be in traffic, as in: "You want Dearborn, pal? Turn right off Congress."

Maybe I shouold go back there, to spend the second act of my life. In D.C. I can sit in the restaurants, and there it *is* like theater duty.

Who's up? Who's down? Which pol deserves to be offered up this week as human sacrifice? People vote, like in the *Oresteia*. In D.C. such matters really are decided in certain restaurants.

So this summer I applied for a job up on Capitol Hill. "You know," the minority staffer said, "we can only pay . . . ninety thousand dollars a year."

Oh! Well. So I know what D.C. is like now, and there are four things that gave me pause.

First, it's creepy to see my old blocks: why didn't they turn? In Chicago, they'd have budded, and bloomed six or seven times over by now.

My old apartment building on Lanier. It's still the same evil shade of flamingo pink.

OK, Union Station is nice, but what of the trattorias inside? They're holed up like in a fort.

I stopped for gas nearby at a self-serve. Not one, but two, two beggars fought me to hold the hose. I tipped them 20 percent, and looked away, up at the Capitol.

Second, prosecutors are everywhere. Or so a lawyer friend from long ago says. "Thomas," he said, as we ate outside, "*never*" (a word he held up like a sword), "*never* give *any* money to *any* political campaign."

"Why?" I gulped.

"Because the laws are so vague, and it's all, in the end, all in the hands of a federal prosecutor. Hear me? Do you know what I mean?"

Yes.

Though it was hard to hear, the bees buzzing around the syrup. "I've seen it," he muttered over the bees. "And our friends, the people you and I know? They still don't understand. 'Oh,' they'll say, 'I know so-and-so, and I'll just explain it.' The prosecutors? They aren't interested in all that. They don't care who you know. All they care about are facts. *Facts.* You know? The city, it's full of people who don't get it, who think, 'Oh, I'll go and talk to them.'"

Third, C-Span is everywhere.

And everyone is famous, not just for fifteen minutes, but fifteen weeks. The tape just keeps rolling. Like the debate over capital gains.

In our times Washington means nothing. It can't raise wages, or get health care, or stop the rise of poverty—but at least it's on TV.

It's changed the whole balance of power in the city. Once kids from the Kennedy School would make fun of you if you went up on the Hill. But now it's a place, thanks to C-Span, where you can yak to the whole city.

Lawyers in their offices watch during the day. Some—yes, I'm not kidding—some go home and watch the repeat, that night. A second time!

Why is it repeated?

Fourth, Republicans are everywhere.

Even in my beloved House. Well, you know why they took over the House: it was the Senate that caused it, i.e., no one voting.

It's pretty grim to sit in the House cafeteria now. I wonder if people in their twenties are allowed to date.

I wonder if people on the grand juries are allowed to date.

In some ways, D.C. is better.

1. Service is better. Especially at the self-serves.
2. People are nicer. Or more careful. Type As used to cut each other up, but now the one I cut off in line at the Inner Circle . . . he may remember and in a plea bargain, years from now, may decide to name *me*.
3. People are fulfilled, thanks to C-Span. It puzzles me now. Orwell's point in *1984* about the "nightmare" of TV cameras in every room. Don't people want to be on TV? If he wrote it now, it'd be about a nightmare world where people couldn't get on TV. The terrifying thing in Washington is, What if Big Brother isn't watching?

CIVIC (VIRTUAL) VIRTUE

I did get on TV once. The occasion was: Testifying before Congress in favor of government oversight of the Teamsters.

But I guess the testifying is secondary next to the really important thing: Being on C-Span.

And after years of scoffing at D.C. talk shows, "Oh, it's like pro-wrestling, isn't it?" I realized: This is how you confront the Right.

The House was investigating the election of Ron Carey as president of the Teamsters: i.e., his win over James Hoffa, Jr., and whether the government should continue supervising the Teamsters.

Now the Republicans disliked Carey, mainly for giving huge sums to Democrats. So they wouldn't mind a Hoffa victory, and the other witnesses were mainly pro-Hoffa Teamsters.

Technically the issue was: "Should the United States pay for another election, after violations by the Carey side?"

The Carey supporters of course wanted this. Did Congress want the mob to get back into Labor?

I didn't want to go. And especially I didn't want to sit and argue with the Hoffa supporters ("Mr. Chairman," one witness said, "this man is not a Teamster!"). But I'd been the lawyer for a reform group, Teamsters for a Democratic Union. Someone asked me. I said yes.

I was asked in part because I'd had nothing to do with Carey's campaign, which had committed some ghastly violations. Yes, these were bad, criminal even. And it was true, the Teamsters Union was still a long way from Swiss-type democracy. But at least it wasn't La Cosa Nostra, thanks to government supervision. Is that what the Republican House wanted: to let the mob back in?

OK, I was ready to testify.

It was on Monday, Columbus Day, so I came down a day early. Everyone was out of town.

I tried to get in the Tabard. Booked up.

"Why not try . . . ?" and the young woman named a hotel over on Sixteenth.

"Isn't that dangerous?"

"It's only a block away from here!" Her lips seemed to quiver. Don't be nervous, I thought.

I went up to Kramerbooks Café, which is, more than ever, like a lighthouse at night. At the next table were some Germans.

"Oh, Washington. Yes. Really wonderful." They all nodded. "It's our favorite city, we really like it."

"How long have you been here?" I asked one German.

She thought. "Two hours."

"Ah, well . . . be careful, you know, walking back tonight."

As I went back, nervously I kept thinking: "They're going to attack me! Ah! Why had I agreed to testify? I could be in Chicago right now . . . The Republicans want Hoffa in, and there'll be four, maybe five Hoffa witnesses up there. . . ."

Oh, don't be a baby! Think of the people who have to deal with special prosecutors! This is only a House hearing. There's no grand jury. As a friend said, "Give me a House hearing any day—*any day*—over a U.S. attorney."

But I couldn't sleep. How ashamed I was! The thought of Clinton, Gore, a few blocks away—I bet they were sleeping fine. Still two o'clock, three—damn it, I can't get to sleep, this is silly!

Anyway, I drank coffee before the hearing. I read up on the congressmen. One or two, apparently, were pretty mean.

Oh well. How could I blow this? I just had to give an *opinion*!

"Mr. Chairman, all I want is to get the mafia out of labor." Yeah, let 'em attack that. Stop worrying.

Still, I was worried. Nervous. The Hoffa people gave their statements. I saw a camera, which I scoffed at. Maybe they were videoing this, like a deposition.

"Could you sit back? You're blocking this other man," a crew member said. "It's C-Span," a voice from somewhere said.

As I saw the red light, I understood, "My God, I'm on television."

"TV! That's why there are six congressmen here."

Six! Back when I was in the Department of Energy, it was a miracle enough if even the committee chairman came. But, of course, no C-Span then.

I started writing on a yellow legal pad:

Take a deep breath.

Take a deep breath.

Take a deep breath!

Lots of underlining.

When the chairman said I was up, I, well, I couldn't get my breath. Dead air, nothing, for five, six seconds. Tick-tick-tick . . .

Even C-Span doesn't like that. Then I got my voice, or someone's voice, since it didn't sound like me, but like a small boy, ten or twelve, reciting . . .

I was too scared to look down at my text. Ah, what should I say? Look down at the paper!

But I couldn't . . . I was on TV, I couldn't think.

I needed a final line! "Give me liberty." Or what? I didn't know, so in closing, I just asked the committee . . . begged, begged the committee not to . . .

"Interfere with getting the mob out of Labor!"

That was it!

Uh oh. I said it too loud.

The chairman was calm, Oprah-like, saying, no, no, the committee wouldn't do this.

But I think this irked some of the other congressmen. Well, if you talk in a pitch as high as mine, soon everyone else is howling at the moon.

I was a bit ashamed to look at my friends later.

Someone was kind enough to say, "Well, it was impassioned . . ."

It wasn't impassioned. I was just nervous. Writing over and over, "Take a deep breath!"

IT WAS A RELIEF when the panel asked its questions. For the first time I thanked God I was a lawyer.

Somewhere Dr. Johnson tells Boswell everyone in Parliament should have legal training. Of course Boswell protests.

But now I'd go further than Johnson. Every person living in Washington, D.C., should actually *be* a lawyer.

Not have a law degree like Clinton. That's not enough any more. But be an active, practicing lawyer, doing trials, discovery, just to keep in training. Because any morning you could be subpoenaed to talk on TV.

How to answer a question, when to raise a privilege, it requires constant study.

IT'S FORTUNATE FOR ME how some of the committee were non-lawyers. I could tell by the way they asked questions.

In my case, the staff had phoned me, interrogated me, so I knew what they wanted to ask.

For example, what did I know about the Teamster locals in cities like Atlanta or Houston? Personally? First hand?

But when the congressman later asked the staffer's questions it came out badly with one fatal change of wording. Did I know "the local union" in Atlanta? In Houston?

"Which local union?" I asked. I explained, patiently, there were many local unions there. The Congressman was stumped.

Even I felt sorry for the guy's staffer. He must have been writhing. He'd worked so hard on this little grenade.

Anyway I felt I owed my escape to C-Span. Without it, six congressmen might not be there . . . I'd have had to deal with the staffers directly. It *would* have been like a deposition at Kirkland and Ellis.

PLAY IT AGAIN

Anyway, that night I was at J.'s house, and J. and his wife watched it on cable. "Oh, come down and see yourself." But I shut the door like a child. "I'll come down when it's over." It was wonderful how many books were up in J.'s library. So many I'd like to read. When it was over and I could come down, he was kind enough to say nothing. He was a lawyer. He *did* know. And the next morning I phoned my office and got my voice mail. Messages of concern, four. Voices from college days: "I saw you last night . . . *are you all right?*" Yes. Downstairs, Handel was playing, and J. was pouring coffee.

Yes, even in the Gingrich era, there are times when I think, "There can still be order. Harmony. Things like Handel."

As J. poured, he said, "You know, some of your arguments yesterday . . . about organized crime . . . you *could* present this in a way that is appealing to some of the conservatives."

"I guess."

"Why not try to publish something in one of their magazines? I mean rewrite your testimony and present that in___?"

I paused. "Well, that's a conservative publication."

As if that were an answer. "You mean," I thought, "discuss it with conservatives? I can't do *that*." Besides, they'd reject it. It would be a waste. No point.

But there was J., saying, "Why not try?"

Then I remembered the moment at the end of the hearing when the chairman came down and shook my hand and smiled. "I saw that," someone in the back said, "he was trying to disarm you."

Yes, that was my thought. But what if secretly he meant by this: "Oh, you and I! If only we could be reconciled!"

. . .

FOR WEEKS BACK IN CHICAGO, I went on saying: "Yes, I'm all right, thanks for asking."

Thanks for asking? What did they think?

Anyway the trip persuaded me: "Maybe there is a virtual republic." Which is not like "virtual representation," representing the whole society organically as Burke and Hamilton wanted.

No, I mean: interacting as citizens electronically, gathering not in a public space but in cyberspace.

Yes, I had heavy thoughts about interactivity. People leaving messages on voice mail: Are you all right?

Yes, but why did they leave them? Because it was someone they knew in real life. "I used to see him at the Inner Circle!"

Sure they cable surf but what makes them stop at a certain channel is that they knew someone in real life. "Darling, stop! Go back! I know that person!"

So maybe this virtual republic is an illusion. What it offers is a chance, in a civic dream life, to remember our real lives.

Stop. Go back, etc.

Of course even that is something. TV isolated us, it got us in this fix. Maybe TV can get us out.

Maybe one day TV will save us from . . . well, TV. It could.

And admit this about the Internet: *not* everyone uses it for pornography. Though the idea of all the people who do gives me the creeps. And who wants to discuss the *Federalist Papers* in the middle of an adult bookstore.

But how can we be citizens, truly, if we can click out of the city? I learned that under Harold Washington. How can we be at a meeting without a sense of being trapped?

There is no civic life without the sense, "If I don't end this meeting, it's simply going to go on and on."

I know what it's like to click something off. I have turned on C-Span, and I know the pleasure, the almost libidinal pleasure, of being able to click it off.

"Hey, I'm not in that hearing."

Once I wanted to move among the green statues of Stephen Decatur. Now one of my pleasures is knowing I can click it off.

. . .

THERE'S NO CIVIC LIFE if people aren't trapped like this, as I used to be trapped in meetings. That's why C-Span isn't "really a civic experience." I can stand up and turn it off. There's always the almost libidinal pleasure of knowing I can "leave D.C."

TEN

If I Could Park
in My City

IN D.C. I CAN TELL THE WEAKENING OF GOVERNMENT BY THE
buckling of city streets. In the old D.C. of 1800, people would disappear
in the swamps. Then under Carter they were likely to be murdered. Then
under Clinton, their cars dropped into potholes. Now while the potholes
are a little better, the streets still seem to buck and buckle.

Likewise I can tell the weakening of Chicago government when I
look for a place to park. The streets are paved, OK, and flat, and I can see
down them for miles. But thanks to residential parking I can't find a place
to park.

First it was the closing of the frontier. Now it's the closing off of city
streets.

But this has been the worst part: Under "residential parking," each
block decides, privately, with no city planning whether "residents only"
can park on that block. Result? No one can find a place to park. I can't
even drive to a noodle shop.

As I circle and circle, it hits me:

Bad enough to lose the New Deal.

Bad enough to lose planning.

Bad enough that even our mayor lives now in a private complex, and
we can't see him.

But my God, can't there be a place to park?

Boston, other cities have residential parking, but Chicago's form of it
is the worst. It's OK, I think, to reserve parking for the residents of the

city. But residents of each block? And worse still: each block decides. Privately. Selfishly. For years, the city refused to control it. (In theory, the City Council has to approve, but it's pro forma.)

Let's say I live, as I do, on the 3500 block of Greenview. We have *no* residential parking. There are so many kids, transients, etc., we can't even get a majority to sign a petition. But near us, the rich homeowner blocks have "flipped." They went "residential."

It's like the domino effect. As each private block flips, it dumps the nonresident cars on the next. So that block has to flip too. The cascade of nonresident cars gets bigger and bigger. Then it hits our block. Bam! Cars from everywhere come crashing down on our heads.

But do the people on the other blocks care? I imagine them on their terraces and drinking champagne from fluted glasses. Ha. So the single women here have to park their cars a mile away and walk back late at night, alone. Rape? Purse snatching?

Ha. It's not our block.

But the very worst is, I feel trapped on my own block. If I go to a noodle shop or trattoria, where can I park? See, *I'm* the nonresident—in my own city! I'm starting to go to Polish restaurants and sip cabbage soup, simply to find a place to park.

AFTER THE TB SUIT I THOUGHT: "Well, this is the public interest suit I should bring. Challenge this residential parking. Yes. That's what could unite us as a city.

Now in my suit I would not attack the city's right to have residential parking. Only the method. Block by block. Private neighbors doing it.

In law school this is called "delegation of public power to private groups." In the 1920s, the Supreme Court said this was illegal. A group of private neighbors can't impose a ban, like residential parking. Though it gets complicated: another case says that neighbors can agree to waive or lift a city ban.

Anyway, I wanted to sue, attack this as unconstitutional.

"Wait," scoffed a friend, "this is how you help the poor? Look who you'd be representing. The trattorias!"

Well, they're citizens, too.

I did meet with some restaurant owners, shrewd guys, it turns out. "You know," one said, "look at a map. See where it's in. The edges of Old Town. Uptown. It's really to keep out blacks."

It's a race thing. Blacks. The poor. But for me this was to be a suit about the collapse of the central government. First TB, now resident parking.

It's the same thing, no government. Too many little blocks making decisions: Tocqueville would have loved residential parking. Madison would have been appalled.

Anyway, the business guys backed off. How can restaurant owners, with licenses, sue the city? I don't blame them. They're like the operators of the homeless shelters.

Besides, the mayor is trying to change things. He wants a new rule: not just one block, but three continuous blocks have to decide for residential parking. As of 1998, the City Council so far opposes him.

But why let any private group decide? The Old Man, the Old Mayor Daley, *he* would have made all these decisions. Can't this mayor, who grew up in the 1960s, take back the streets?

WAITING FOR JANE JACOBS

A few months ago, I *was* at a Polish restaurant far to the west. Not only could I park, but I had a nice long dinner with friends, including one who's a planner.

"This is our moment," she said. "You know the planner Daniel Burnham, 'Make no little plans'? Well, that's what I mean. This *is* no little plan."

She was referring to one of the plans to replace a public housing project. Now the "moment" she talks about is here because Congress has ordered many of the old federal projects to be torn down by 2002.

So where will the poor live?

Well, here's the good part: Though housing will come down, the Chicago Housing Authority will still own the land. So the CHA can tell the developers: "Want to develop it? All this rich land next to the Loop? Then put in housing for the poor."

Now wouldn't it be wonderful if the Chicago that lacks the nerve to tell people where to park could tell developers what to do?

There is such a plan for Cabrini, which is the housing project near Chicago's Gold Coast. "It's wonderful," my friend said. "It's multiuse. It's got shops. Grids. It's really Jane Jacobs. This is no little plan. People have thought about this for twenty years."

A billion-dollar plan. Poor people, too, living near Michigan Avenue. Cheek-by-jowl with Henri Bendel.

I paused. This was wonderful.

But I had an objection: "How can you make the rich live right next to the poor? They won't!"

"No," said another, "that won't be a problem. Remember, these would be pretty odd rich people."

Some rich like to live like this. It's the city. They like it.

Go into the chic restaurants and look at the kinky art in the restrooms. Some of the rich are pretty odd.

But still, many of the poor don't believe the plan is "real." But why couldn't it be real? Couldn't the existing tenants' council get a 51% stake (that's what the CHA would later propose).

That night my planner friend was excited and said, "The tenants should act now. The developers are in a good mood. There's been the boom."

"What if there's a recession?" I thought. "The developers could turn nasty. Yes, the poor should act now."

It's been my habit to scoff at the "boom," because more people are going to soup kitchens; more are losing health insurance. I scoff because this boom has failed to raise in any serious way the standard of living of the bottom half. But should I scoff? Look, for example, at our conversation this night. There's a chance to build housing—low-rise, nice housing for the poor. I heard yet another story about the new units near Horner. "I walked in, it was so wonderful! Oh, it's so inspiring. It just makes you feel great."

Yes, I scoff at the boom. But at least people are employed. As my old teacher said, "Do you understand what a dreadful thing it is to be without a *job*? I'm not sure you do."

OK, I scoff too much. They have jobs. And as my friend says, here's what I really underrate: the rich are in a good mood. Why do the poor hang back? This is the moment to take advantage of the generosity. To take a risk, and believe there will be planning, just like Jane Jacobs.

I DO IT FOR DUPAGE

We had a lot of time to talk that night because Lutnia's is an elegant and Old World restaurant. The waiters expect us to spend the evening there. At any other restaurant, we'd have been hustled out, long, long before we got to anything so recondite as Jane Jacobs.

It made me feel snobbish, European. Yes, who else but me would drag his friends here? Also, I believe in planning. Order. Just like a European.

So how do I justify being a centralizer, a planner in America?

In America, without the planning at the top, there wouldn't be any "grass roots."

Back in the 1960s Washington, with each program, seemed to require a public hearing.

A new incinerator? A hearing.

Airport expansion? Had to have a public hearing.

Build a new mental health clinic? Had to have a hearing, too.

Now, thanks to the New Federalism, there are block grants and no hearings and people out in DuPage rarely get to meet at all. Indeed, as my friend Theresa says, "If it weren't for federal laws like NEPA, there'd hardly be any hearings in the burbs." Yes, at least there's still the National Environmental Policy Act (NEPA).

She works at the Citizen Advocacy Center, which was set up by Claire Nader, Ralph's sister. The purpose, in a sense, is just to teach people how to "advocate," i.e., how to stand up and speak at public meetings. It reminds me of the centers that George Soros is setting up in Eastern Europe, to teach people how to be citizens in the new democracies.

In July, I went to the center for its dedication. Claire Nader gave a stirring speech, then came the awards to people who'd been "citizens." In most cases, it was a man or woman who had gone to a meeting and was alone in the room.

These were not New England town meetings where, notoriously, very few people, 5 percent or so, ever go. No, these were official government meetings to which no one from the "outside" had ever been!

Imagine, like Sakharov, going in all by oneself!

Now it's easy for someone from Chicago to put on airs. "If in Chicago they were cutting up a park, why, there'd have been a mob," etc.! Three lawsuits. Six articles in each of the dailies.

But here? One person alone had never walked into a meeting before. Not since the federal government, in most cases, stopped requiring them. Now that we've "empowered" local government, it's too powerful for the local people to control.

I talked to T., who told me at first she mostly filed demands to get documents, basic public documents, from the village and towns. Now she wants to move from Freedom of Information suits to getting people out to meetings.

It's hard. No, it's scary.

Look at the Tollway Authority, which she fought when she started the center. (By the way, this was my connection: I had offered to review one of the handbills for libel.)

Since the 1950s, the Tollway Authority had collected tolls, i.e., road taxes, then figured out how to spend the taxes. Traffic jams, cars lined up, people cursing as they paid the tolls . . . and how did the Authority, which no one elected, get the power to raise taxes, and spend taxes, with no legislative appropriations.

It was the Cyclops that ate suburbia. No one said anything, because out there, they don't know how.

Then a lawyer, Lee Schwartz, in 1996, on his own, with no mob behind him, simply filed a suit, and argued that the whole thing was grotesquely unconstitutional, which it was. Even the judge, a conservative, agreed.

Though the Illinois Supreme Court, which is even more conservative, has put the thing back. Still, what astounds me is that suburbanites sheeplike pay tolls or taxes that no elected person appropriates . . . and no one has peeped for thirty years.

Somewhere the Founders are weeping for DuPage. Maybe a place like Dupage should go back to being a "territory." Remember the territories of the last century, like Arizona, Iowa? It was Washington, D.C., that governed the territories directly until people in them *proved* that (1) they voted, (2) attended meetings, and (3) yelled when someone raised the tolls.

In DuPage there are officials who forbid people to applaud at public meetings! That's what it's like in "Tocqueville's America" now that the central government has disappeared. At least in the 1960s, Kennedy and Johnson were still making these wild places hold meetings.

We have forgotten what Americans in the 1860s knew, what Lincoln knew. The Union came before the states, as S. said: "That was Lincoln's point. It's not the states that created the federal government, but the federal government that created the states."

Imagine what goes on in these wild places now. They're "reinventing government," people say.

What kind of "privatizing" do they do? When I point out the risk of kickbacks, bribes to my policy-wonk friends, I get patted on the head: "Well, you live in one of these old cities, like Chicago, with machines."

What machines? There are no Daley-type machines any more in the big cities. Does Rich Daley have one? Does Giuliani have a machine in New York? I don't think so.

The machines today are in the suburbs, where suburban Republican bosses like Pate Philip (Illinois) and Al D'Amato (New York) are from.

Indeed, in the suburbs they have political machines with *no* meetings. It's "Tammany" without the "Hall."

COLLECT THE GUNS

But here's something else that worries me about suburbia: the gun fairs or flea markets. That's why I want Washington, D.C., to be out there. I want someone to collect the guns that flood into the city.

I like to think that in the New Deal, if guns had flooded into the city the way they do now, FDR or somebody would have stopped them. But now it seems up to us in the cities.

At any rate, while suburbia has its flea markets, we in the city have as many handgun control groups. I have flitted from one to the other group the way suburbanites out there go from fair to fair. Here are some whose meetings I have attended: Citizens for Handgun Control (I have not been there lately). HELP for Survivors (*They* asked me for legal advice). Coalition to Stop Handguns (I now have a good friend who works there). There are other groups I could crash, if I liked.

But oddly enough I have never been to a candlelight vigil. Maybe that's what holds me in the city. An ablution I should perform. Until I've been to a vigil it would be unholy to move away from this city of dead children.

I'd have to walk with them one night around the projects before I could leave. It's strange—I can go to the meetings, but I shrink from holding candles.

At first I went to meetings of lawyers. We'd talk policy. Lawyer talk. It was 1993 when the meetings began to seem absurd.

I remember one at Sidley & Austin. The murder total that month was 93. The American Bar Association was about to meet. We decided to draft a resolution to condemn the violence.

Resolution? We're like the U.N.

Of course everyone knew it was absurd. I decided to make a joke: "Why don't we call on Mayor Daley to set up 'safe areas'?"

"He's already set up safe areas!" another lawyer snapped.

The others stared at me. Someone saved me by saying: "It's a public health issue."

Odd that the lawyers would turn to educators and say: "Oh, it's really a public health issue, isn't it?" We don't do this on tobacco, and that is a public health issue. And isn't this area a natural for a lawyer? Sue the industry. After all, lawyers don't usually change the world by fighting for civil rights. What we do best is raise the cost of accidents.

So why have lawyers given up?

1. Too many law firms to fight.

2. Our goofy federalism. Have Congress pass a law?

"No, leave it to the states."

Sue at the state level? "Sorry," the conservatives say, "federal law preempts." (Because gun dealers have to register, etc.)

3. "There aren't any cases."

This is partly because the police make little effort to trace the chain of sale.

4. "There aren't any lawyers" (who have the resources the cases need).

That's why it's a public health issue.

Still, sometimes in a dream, I'm standing at midnight in the Department of Justice. I'm on the same floor with Robert Kennedy. People are whispering: "He's phoning in the federal marshals."

Wake up.

When the murder rate hit ninety a month in 1993, I began to notice the foreign hotels around me. There was, then, the Meridien for the French, the Swissôtel for the German, the Nikko for the Japanese. Maybe one day I'd take shelter in a foreign compound. Or maybe they, the colonial powers, would have to come back. Stop the war of all against all. Maybe they'll come back and collect the guns."

YES, IT'S TRUE EACH YEAR the Chicago cops collect 15,000 to 20,000 guns. A year! There was a big photo a year ago of Daley inspecting the haul. But the strange part is, no one I know in this city is going to be shot. I think.

I just met an artist from Germany. "When I was in Germany, people told me, 'Oh, don't go to America, you'll be shot.' Seriously. Yes, this is what they said. So. I have been here four years. And have I been shot?"

"It's exaggerated," I said.

On the other hand, what if the guns really kept coming in at the current rates? Could I say this in ten or twenty years?

The other day I had lunch with M., who's an ex–Chicago cop who now works with the group HELP for Survivors.

That seems to be my handgun group of choice this year. Anyway, we met to discuss a draft of a proposal to a foundation. This is my first handgun group where I actually meet, well, victims and survivors of victims.

I walked into a HELP meeting a few weeks before. No lawyers. No activists. No liberals. No one but parents of murdered children and this guy, M., who was a cop who took eleven bullets and lived. He's disabled, of course, big time. But he's able to work with HELP.

He's very tall, holds himself in a stiff military way. This is partly because he has a bullet three centimeters away from his lower spine. He told me he once was a "replacement medic" in Vietnam. "A replacement medic was the man who replaced a medic who'd been shot. But the funny thing was, I was never shot. I always thought I would be . . ."

Back here? Eleven bullets.

"I was at a SYMBOL meeting today. Know what that is?"

No.

Single

Young

Men Living

By

Law.

"I try to teach etiquette. With police. Street etiquette. How to behave when you're stopped."

I thought of the last time I was stopped by a cop here. "Oh," the cop said, "that's an Irish name, isn't it? Welllllll . . . drive carefully!" (I suppose they don't stop kids, "Oh? That's an African American name, isn't it? Well, etc.")

How old are these SYMBOL members?

"They're eighteen, nineteen. I was just saying to them, 'Look at the Latino kids taking jobs as busboys.' 'But,' they say, 'those jobs don't pay.' 'We don't want to work at four-seventy an hour.' I said, 'I worked as a busboy.' I said, 'You have to start somewhere and work your way up.'"

Except: they won't.

On the other hand, didn't M.?

I said: "The murder rate's dropped. You were a cop. How do you explain it?"

He paused. "Say that to the parents you met."

That was two weeks before, and most were women. We had been meeting with a guy named Skip, a Chicago cop and a community rep.

Skip was a nice guy, and every time a mother told a horror story about a detective being rude, or blowing off the murder, or walking away, he'd say, "Look, I'm not going to defend every Chicago cop."

He said that a lot. Or he'd say, "I'm sorry, it's the luck of the draw." As it turns out, the detectives don't solve a lot of the killings now. "It used to be," Skip said to us, "say, in 1980, we'd solve about ninety percent of the homicides; now we solve only about sixty percent."

"So? What's the problem?" I asked.

"We don't have the detectives," Skip said.

"I thought," I said, "there were tons of cops. That's what I read in the papers. What about this Clinton bill?"

"I don't know. I just know that in 1980 the city had thirteen hundred detectives and now we're down to about eight hundred. In the old days you know a detective, he could go back to a cold case, but now . . ."

I make this sound like a seminar in the Kennedy School. Remember, as we're speaking, a mother of a dead boy is screaming right at him.

Of course the murder rate is insane, in one sense. There was a big headline this year that it hit a new low: ONLY 55 MURDERS IN THE FIRST THREE MONTHS OF 1997.

It's slow in winter, and I could say, "But the murders are going up out in Chicago Heights, Ford Heights, and Maywood." But OK, I admit it's a "new low."

Still, looked at another way, it's a huge number of mothers of murdered children. I guess that's obvious, isn't it?

But M. had to *say* it to me.

"Actually," M. said, "we don't know how many people are shot. These gangs, a lot of times they aren't going to go to the hospital, are they? And get involved with the police? I figure, there's a minimum each year in this country of a hundred thousand people who have been shot. Minimum. I'm on panels. I'm with experts. 'You prove to me,' I say, 'how possibly, possibly it can be less.' It can't be. We know that."

I thought about my dinner with the planner, and how we have jobs now. The kids, like the developers, are in a "good mood." What if there's a recession and the kids with guns are, well, *not* in a "good mood"?

Remember the photo of Mayor Daley, beaming and pointing at the 15,000 guns? Why *is* he beaming?

M. says: "Do you know what that means? What does it mean that we're collecting all these guns? I'll tell you. It means we're a depot. Chicago. They're coming in here from all over the country."

New York has three times as many cops. What does it mean that in Chicago, without trying, we're collecting three times as many guns?

"It means guns are coming here from Ohio, from all over. This is where people from all over are coming now to get the guns."

M. shook his head. "When I was a cop in the Gangs Unit, that was my goal, to collect guns. Every night I'd try to get, oh, at least three. I'd go into empty buildings. A lot of guys didn't want to work with me."

He paused. "I used to grab kids who had cocaine or other drugs. I'd look to see how much it was. Depending on how much the kid had, I'd say, 'This will cost you seven guns.'

"'*What?*' the kid would look at me. '*Seven guns?* How am I going to find seven guns?' I'd say, 'That's not my problem. But you've got thirty minutes—make a call.'"

So he got many guns until word came down: "Stop doing that."

As M. said, our guns in the city come from the suburbs, like those in Kane and DuPage counties, where the big gun fairs are held. I've never gone out. It's hard to imagine, though in one of our groups, a man had gone out to look. He said he went around and argued with the dealers. I imagine it as a big Wal-Mart.

Yes, the murder rate's fallen. But they're all out there stockpiling, in DuPage and Kane, and driving back to the city. The kids are doing it. Everyone's doing it.

We're all waiting for the next recession.

Or until all the community groups and guys like M., exhausted, say "OK, let it go."

Meanwhile, our group goes down to Springfield to lobby.

Gun control? No, forget it. We lobby to *stop* bills, like the bill that would permit people to carry around concealed weapons. There's a U. of C. professor who says that in states with these laws the murder rate goes down.

Concealed guns. In restaurants. That's public policy from the U. of C.

What's it like, I asked M., to be sitting with these guys from the university?

"I'm uncomfortable after a while."

It'd bother me, but I ask him, "Why?"

Pause. "It's hard to sit that long. I feel the bullet in the back of my spine."

UNLIKE ME, M. GOES DOWN to Springfield. And the new groups keep forming. There are two I found out about the other day: Prayer Coalition for Reconciliation and Families and Friends of Murder Victims. These two are out in Aurora, on the border of DuPage County. M. sighs; there are many gun control groups he still has not met.

Well, as Tocqueville said, Americans love to form associations.

I had read a story about the Aurora group. There was a big picture.

Women in black held fifty crosses, each cross with the name of a child. Someone released a hundred balloons.

I SAY NO ONE like me is ever shot. And that's true, but I was at a meeting and saw two middle-aged white men like me. Why are they here?

Their kids were murdered.

Now it's interesting to look at the men, because fathers in such meetings have a different look of pain than mothers.

Not more pain, just a different kind. Someone in a gun group told me, "You're talking to them, but you have to be very careful. Watch out especially with anyone who says 'I'm fine now.'"

No, people like me or the German artist will not be shot, I think. He and I were single. But it's possible to be a parent and have a child offered up as a human sacrifice. That's one thing that would scare me about even adopting.

One Sunday at St. Clement's, a Lincoln Park parish, one of the kids most loved, we were told, had been murdered a few blocks away. People prayed. "It's incredible," I thought, "to be young and in Lincoln Park and to be killed within yards of a Blockbuster."

His mother, one of the finest people in the city, was the inspector general at the Department of Children and Family Services. And this is the agency that deals with kids who are most at risk of being murdered.

And here I have to say, if I had a kid, I'd immediately leave the city. It's not even an issue.

Should I wait for the revival of the central government? The mayor likes to say that people like me are leaving because of the collapse of the public schools. Does he believe that? Look at the Catholics. They had their kids in Catholic schools, but they left the city in droves.

I'd go to Oak Park. It's Hemingway's birthplace, of which he said: broad lawns and narrow minds. Yes, but now it's full of liberals who did their doctorates on Hemingway.

Are they there because of the collapse of the public schools? I know people say this, but I don't believe it. They'd be there anyway.

I would be there, I know, and I'd be more likely to skip my kid back into the city to be taught by Jesuits. No, the reason to go out there is biological: it's the Darwinian instinct, to protect the young.

I want them to run free, and not be killed.

I have talked to a lot of friends who have moved. "Our first day out there," a friend of mine said, "my oldest son—he just got on his bike and took off."

Up and down the broad streets.

"Back in the city, we had to drive them everywhere."

But out here? Run. Fly! Let them loose like birds.

Up and down. Fly!

It's a Darwinian thing, don't you think?

ELEVEN

I'd Be Lonely
in This City

I TOO MIGHT RUN AWAY, BUT THE IMMIGRANTS NOW KEEP ME here. Thank God for the new ones, from Asia, from Europe. I'd be lonely in this city if Congress ever cut them off.

What would I do when there's no catfish in the clay pots of the Lao restaurants? No Lucky Strike stand at Broadway Kabob. No Korean girls, ravishing, to whom to hand my shirts.

It's true suburbia has immigrants, almost half a million. About the same as the city, oddly enough. But they're too spread out, galactically.

I like the immigrants in blocks and grids. It's the way Jefferson wanted it. I have the feeling I can get abroad. It's hard to live here, in the Midwest, and feel cut off. It's not so much the Midwest as it is being on this island, the North American continent, which is cut off from the real world, over on the Eurasian mass.

And there's no one to talk to about the outside world. In America, the only people interested in foreign policy are the isolationists.

It's maddening to come back from Europe. There's no news. I talked to my friend Father C., back from a year in Europe. What's it like to be back?

"Depressing. There's no news."

Even New York, or even Washington, it's like the Midwest: I pity them, they don't know it.

I was out here, cut off, during the collapse of Communism. Now I admit that was in the news. Next to bigger stories like CONGRESS CONSID-

ERS CHANGES IN MEDICAID. I had a strange feeling that year. On the one hand, I felt I should be living here, being a lawyer, etc., in Chicago. But I also felt I was meant somehow to be living in another city.

Where did I want to go? Warsaw, Budapest, but mostly it was Prague.

I was telling my brother one night in Greektown, "That's where I should be." I'd seen pictures of the crowds in St. Wenceslaus Square. Soon I'd see those pictures in the Art Institute of Chicago.

So I wanted to go there, live in history.

"Ah!" my brother scoffed. "There's nothing happening in Prague."

"What?"

"No, you want to see the future? I'd go to Mexico City, with your friend Grogan. He speaks Spanish, right? That's the Third World! That's what you want to see!"

Well, I sulked, and I never did go to Prague. He ruined it for me. Whenever I thought about it—well, maybe he was right, and I should see the Third World. And the funny thing is, I think about this even now.

Where is the second, unlived life I should be living? Is it Mexico City? Or is it Prague?

"MEXICO CITY," SORT OF

Of course I have a sense of Mexico here.

About a quarter of Chicago is Latino. I tell people, "It's the second-largest Spanish-speaking city in the U.S." (I don't count New York as a city.)

"You're comparing it with L.A.?"

"This is where they come after L.A."

But why compare it with L.A.? It's more interesting to compare it to Mexico City. Now don't laugh, just consider:

Both have large numbers of Spanish-speaking peoples. Both are in the middle, not on the coast, but in the middle of North America. When I read of Cortés and his men coming up the causeway that runs along the Lake Texoccoco, I often think, "It must have been like Lake Shore Drive."

But of course Chicago is just a toytown, compared to Mexico City. Or compared to many of the great cities rising in the Third World.

Sometimes I wish we were a mega-city, which is a city of ten million or more. Of the forty mega-cities that are now on the planet, only four, a pitiful four, are still in the developed world.

All the great cities in the world are now in the Third World. But Chicago has the tall buildings.

We're the trompe l'oeil of a world city. Though slowly, on the street, we're speaking more Spanish.

I LIKE THE IDEA, as in a novel:

"I, a lawyer, headed north, as far north as the Port of Archangel, until I found myself one day in one of the great Latino cities."

Except it's not great. Nor Latino, yet.

It's partly because many of the Mexicans have been here since World War I, not II (or really, since the Revolution of 1910).

Also: they're "immigrants," often, not from Mexico, but from California. It's natural to come here. They're just Californians, looking for a better life.

At any rate, Latino but not immigrant. Indeed, is Mexico a foreign country? Big issue. It's hard to be foreign, or an immigrant, when you can tool off in your minivan to the Mother Country for the weekend.

But the main thing is, they're too spread out. There's no apartheid-like isolation. The boys date Polish girls, etc.

It's hard to see them in one place. And some Latinos, the old ones, have gone native. During Harold's election, a few white leftist types went into Latino wards. To their shock, the Machine guys . . . Latino, of course . . . couldn't speak Spanish any more.

On the other hand, the whites could. They'd picked up Spanish in courses at Michigan or Yale.

BUT SOMETIMES I DO SEE the city as Latino. One August night I got in my car. Past the Loop . . . I just drove south, twenty-six blocks.

Dark, dark.

Empty trailers. Rail cars.

It was a boiling night, when old people would die, as their windows were shut tight, in terror of breakins. But it seemed dark, cold.

The Loop far off, spiraling like Andromeda.

And suddenly:

KABOOM!

Light! Mariachis! Dirt Amocos! Men in ten-gallon hats. Bakeries. People jamming the sidewalks. And the Buicks are bumper-to-bumper, I can't move: thick smoke blacking out the moon.

Didn't L. say a few years ago, "Let's come back some night when it's really hot?"

Constanza said: "This is just what it feels like in Bogotá or Panama City." Yes, but it's like two, three blocks of it. Then . . . poof.

Back to the empty trailers.

BUT FOR THIS, it's hard to believe Chicago is slowly turning Latino. But one day, a professor had to show me.

"Let's think of city officials," he said.

> Police chief? Latino.
> Fire chief? Latino.
> School board president? Latino.
> Daley's chief rival? Latino.

Now that was 1996, and I admit this lineup has changed. But still . . .

I was so out of it. Where'd I been hiding, Prague?

But most other whites have no sense of this. None.

Still I can see, to quote a friend, "the mayor really sucks up to them." Daley's appointed most of the Latino aldermen.

And he lauds Latinos at every chance. I heard him the other day at a lunch: "Oh, the Latinos, the immigrants, they have family values. They're a model," etc.

There's a nasty little subtext. They aren't like *those* people, "you know who."

It's annoying, to hear Daley go on and on: How wonderful, they're poor, but two parents. Isn't that wonderful? Two-parent poverty.

Indeed, says V. at the Latino Institute: Latino poverty is increasing, while black is actually in decline. Many experts would say it's a different kind of poverty:

Black poverty, until now, has been chiefly welfare poverty. Latino poverty is mostly "working poor." That's a bit simple, but it helps to keep it simple.

V. has found, in the Chicago area (not just the city), that one in four Latino working families are "working poor." That means they make up to 125 percent of the official poverty line. But most of these, 70 to 80 percent, are actually *under* the poverty line, $12,000 for a family of four.

But as the mayor says, isn't it wonderful the families stay together? After all, he's one of the employers paying them the low wages.

YES, MR. MAYOR, but how much longer will "family values" continue at these wages? As an academic told me, "The longer they stay like this, poor, in the city, the more they'll pick up . . . bad city habits."

Guns, dope, gangs. Two parents, but the kids are dying on the street. It's tough to raise a family with under $12,000 a year.

"Many of them work full-time, too," V. says. "They're in America, they're playing by the rules. And they're poor."

And not a little poor. Really poor. And what about the other families that are well off, middle class? On $18,000 or $19,000 a year?

Yet curiously, immigrants are the majority of our factory workers. I don't mean just Latino, but "foreign born." They have over half of the city's factory jobs.

Recently I had a meeting with workers at a little tile factory on the West Side. I had two men at either side:

One, for English to Spanish.

The other, for English to Polish.

Did anyone speak English? I read constantly about America's "High Performance Work Place." "Employers put a premium on skills."

One of the skills they value most, at least from what I have seen in my (rare) visits to Chicago plants . . . is the *inability* to speak English.

Anyone who speaks English and wants a factory job in Chicago seems, to me, to be at a competitive disadvantage. I'm sure this is wrong, but I'd be wary of speaking English in a job interview.

Now it's true this is lower-skilled factory work, but we're at least exporting some of this stuff. Unlike me and my friends, many of these factory workers are out there competing, truly competing, in the global economy.

V. points out this, too: The less educated Mexicans earn more than the more educated Puerto Ricans.

"I thought," I said, "the more educated, the more income."

She shrugged, as in: I know, but that's what the numbers show.

But it's a mistake for me to paint the Latinos as the poorest of the immigrants. I asked my brother the other night, "Which do you think is the poorest immigrant group?" (I knew he'd never guess.)

"Vietnamese," he said, calmly.

OK, I guess people know this.

Anyway it's complex, since not all the Latinos are immigrants. The question, though, that interests me, and many others, is, "How does this affect the blacks?" How does the immigration affect the chances of the black poor? After all, the percent of foreign born in Chicago is nearly 20 percent. One in five. So? What effect?

I've read a few articles that go back and forth, but what convinced me is a talk I had with Douglas Massey, author of *American Apartheid,* a superb book about ghetto life.

"Look," he asked, "where are the black poor worse off? In Chicago, an immigrant city? Or in Philadelphia? Which isn't?" (Or in New York, the World City? Or in Baltimore, which isn't?)

He sighed. "Believe me , I moved from Chicago to Philadelphia. It's even bleaker for the poor in Philadelphia."

Of course I'm pro immigrant, and easy to persuade. I hope to God he's right.

It would be fascinating to live in a Latino city, and I had a sense of this, though only once. A crowd had come, in the late 1990s, of all times, to City Hall. They were the Latinos from Pilsen on the South Side, and they wanted Daley to stop the use of tax increment financing (the "TIF") to soup up the commercial strip.

Pilsen has long been a "port of entry" for Mexican families. With family values. Only now the mayor's TIF would replace them with childless yuppies.

That's mean, and unfair, but basically right.

So the Pilsen people came down to stand outside his office, and make him withdraw the TIF. I went over, as I was supposed to be one of their lawyers.

It turns out, on the fifth floor of City Hall, about two hundred and fifty of us were roped together. Literally. The police ran a rope around us, and we had to stay inside it.

The crowd began to chant:

Daley come out.

Daley come out.

You pushed us out of Taylor Street.

You pushed us out of Wicker Park.

Now you push us out of Pilsen?

No respect.

No respect.

Daley! No respect.

Daley, oh Daley!

This went on like a litany, but here's what was amazing, to me. Everywhere around us there was press, asking questions. Holding cameras.

Now as T. points out (she was there), any other group would have dropped everything and begun talking to the press. But the leaders of Pilsen?

They talked to us! Not the press. Not the anchors. They kept talking to us, the two hundred and fifty or more who'd taken off work to come down to City Hall.

This *was* a Latino city! I stood near a woman with a floppy hat, looking as if she had just come in from Buenos Aires, 1940.

Daley come out!

Of course everyone knew Daley was not there. I liked the Mayor's staff guy, who'd come out half-smiling. S. said, "The mayor's guy who speaks Spanish." He gave us their press release, one white sheet: the note of surrender. The TIF would *not* be introduced in the City Council tomorrow.

No, no! The crowd now demanded, "We want the mayor to sign it!" "No," the lawyers said, "it's on his letterhead, that's good enough!"

BUT I'M SURE in a few months there is going to be a TIF. Maybe in ten years, the old Pilsen will be gone. (There is some protection for existing homeowners making $40,000 or more, but none for anyone else.)

By the way, the Latino aldermen, many of whom Daley appointed, say nothing when he moves Latinos. In a way they're like the black aldermen under the Old Daley many years ago.

But no one can say Latino wards are dull: they have organizers. Sometimes an organizer will be killed. Assassinated, in fact. I think of Rudy Lozano, or Arnold Mireles. Nothing like this ever happens in a black or white ward.

I left City Hall, desperate to learn Spanish. I've always laughed at the debate here . . . Should we make English "the official language of America"?

Come off it: English is the official language of the *world*!

Yeah? People say. But what about America?

You'd think I'd have been required to take Spanish.

Once I made a stupid remark to a French-speaking person from Belgium, which has two languages. "It's lucky," I said, "you grew up speaking French and not that other thing . . . Walloon?"

"Oh no, I was unlucky," he said. "Because all those children, the Walloons, know, from the very start, they have to speak another language."

But it's too late for me, I think. My friend L., when she took Spanish, used to gloat about this.

"Oh," she said, "and I'm so tired of these 'oppressor languages.' It's so good to speak a 'language of the oppressed.'"

This really irked me: "The only reason Spanish is now a 'language of the oppressed' is because once it was a language of some oppressor."

Maybe we *should* refuse to learn Spanish! Do it to protest Cortés.

IN AMERICA both parents now work, so I read of the pressure to bring in more immigrants, mainly to raise the kids.

A few months ago at a dinner party I was listening to a woman talk about her maid, who's Latino, from the maquiladoras, just over the border:

"You know, she's just twenty-one years old . . . I'm much older, but I feel like, she's teaching me. *I'm* the one learning from her!"

I stared at her. Her voice sounded odd as she told this story:

"She's from a very poor family. They had to kick her out when she was thirteen. And up here? I'm sure she sends home ninety percent of what she makes. So she has no money."

"But the other day," the woman went on, "she saw something on TV, oh, it was 'Adopt a Child' in Africa or something, for thirty dollars a month. So she came to me. Did I think she could send them . . . oh, twenty dollars a month instead? It's OK, they didn't have to send her the child's picture or anything. Could she give *me* the money? Could I do it? Could I send the twenty dollars for her?"

It seemed this story had popped out of her by accident.

"That's . . . some story," I said.

She turned away, as if embarrassed.

Ever since that night I've thought, "Why not let them raise our kids?"

PRETTY CLOSE TO "PRAGUE"

It's hard to prove this, but there's a theory why Chicago is turning Latino, with no one noticing. No one saying, "Who let these Latinos in?"

It was Massey, again, who pointed it out to me. "Why in Chicago," he asked, "is there no anti-immigrant movement, as there is in California?"

Because the white ethnics here have their own, uh, "Mexicans," to protect. White European immigrants. The Romanians, Russians . . . but above all, Poles. From Poland. Many Poles. Tens of thousands. So how can the whites here complain about Latinos? We've got our own illegals to hide.

I say "we" and that's ridiculous. "We" whites in Lincoln Park are innocent. We don't even know the Poles are here.

Yet they are, officially, coming in, some years in bigger numbers than

Mexicans. Here's a question I toss out at parties: "In 1993, who emigrated to Chicago in bigger numbers, Mexicans or Poles?"

Poles, of course.

Poles	10,651
Mexican	8,911

For years I'd cite this number. People would say: "Can't be true!"

But they've never been to a Polish restaurant. Or nightclub. They see words like "European" on posters and don't know what it really means.

No one I know but me has ever seen the Polish phone book.

Of course today many Polish immigrants go directly to suburbia. Mike Royko had a theory as to how the different ethnic groups carved up suburbia. They move where they have their cemeteries. The Polish family, for example, drives out to bury Grandma and then looks around and thinks, "Say, it's pretty nice out here . . . why don't we stay?"

In time Poles, Indians, etc. move out there directly. Never even see Chicago. But others are stuck in the cities, and are in factories, and they're poor.

I know their secret places, and it's odd to get in my car and feel, well, I can *drive* to Europe. Even the people in Manhattan who go to Brighton Beach never know the pleasure of getting there *by car.*

Let's say it's too late for a movie, and it's Friday night. Well, let's go to Europe! Get in my car. Just find the big MAGIKIST neon sign, and it's straight on till morning.

I PULL UP to the Red Apple, which is a restaurant and meat market. And the meat market—it's like a singles bar.

Girls in white aprons dangle sausages. Boys in motor caps hold up their hands. There's no singing, but otherwise it could be the film *The Umbrellas of Cherbourg.*

A young girl, holding up a blob.

Wobble.

Pop.

Right in the guy's hand. Over a stack of Polish *Playboys*.

Some of the girls smile: as they do in Europe, that sly little smile. But the guys? Never. I often think it's the language, with all the *y*'s and *z*'s and *sh*'s. How depressing to spend your life down there, at the dark end of the alphabet.

I suppose another, better reason is, people are unhappy when they have to leave their homes.

You could say, "Who needs Prague?" But of course you still do.

I'm sure some Poles are willing to work around the clock. But others must be miserable. They grew up expecting to live like Europeans.

Or sit in cafés and talk about magazines like, *To Exist*. If they had to be wrenched away to somewhere, why not Paris?

They ended up in Chicago. Like kids who couldn't get in the good schools, Princeton or Yale. Indeed, the ones we get out here are those who couldn't make it in New York.

Though that could be said of all of us.

I once met a Polish journalist based in New York. "Oh yes, the ones in Chicago—we regard them the way you would your, oh, your 'hillbillies.'"

And many in Lincoln Park speak of them in ways they'd blush to do with Latinos.

"Oh, they're all anti-Semites, you know." How often do I hear that.

"All of them?"

Well, no. There may be some exceptions.

But this irks me because in the unions out here it's the Poles or descendants of Poles who taught me the words "freedom," "liberation," "justice."

On the other hand, I remember a shocking moment. It was in a bookstore, the Polonia, which serves cappuccino. There was a signing for a book, *Europe,* by Norman Davies. Big crowd. I'd come feverish with flu, but I needed a Europe fix, very badly.

Davies was eloquent. He noted that Poland was not "Eastern Europe" but the very heart of Europe. It *was* Europe. Maybe not to Lincoln Park. But it was. And the Poles, applauding, loved him. Yes. Not Eastern, but Central Europe. Yes. That's us!

But when Davies spoke about Russians, the tone became ugly. Were the Russians "Europeans"? Ugh.

Not even human.

I feel like raising my hand to ask . . . if the Russians aren't really Europeans, how can the Poles be in Central Europe?

I wish they'd think about that before they start tearing into Russians.

I go sometimes to openings at a Polish art gallery, just to meet the Poles.

"Oh," I say, "I hear Poland's booming."

"Oh? Where do you hear this?"

"In the *Financial Times*."

They look at me strangely, and I note around the city that Polish boom time or not, Poles keep coming in.

The phone book must be getting bigger, and I remember the moment I opened it and was thrilled.

Ah, Polish! Which meets *my* test for a "language of the oppressed," i.e., nobody I know is bothering to learn it.

It's the new high-tech Poles I feel sorry for. They come in 747s and some do get rich, because they've learned our new computer language, which is digital, and it's the new language of the oppressor.

But it's sad how they have to give up, here in America, the dreams of living like Europeans. The promise of European life.

In the 1980s I once dated a Polish woman who had a job as an au pair. It was tough to make a date. She'd phone at night and talk in a whisper how her two employers, the husband and wife, never told her in advance which night she'd have off. Be firm, I said. She asked for Saturday night off, but they didn't give an answer.

I told her, bravely, I was just driving out and we were going.

I was brave on the phone. "Get ready, I'll be there."

Then panicked, I called up T. "My God, what am I going to do?"

"Simple," he said. "Go up to these two yups and say, 'I'm here for the maid!'"

"Very funny. Seriously, what am I going to do if they say no?"

As I drove way, way out to the suburban home she was locked up in, I tried out various ways of saying: "I'm here for the maid." "I'm *here* for the *maid*." "I'm here *for the maid*."

When I knocked on the door, a man answered. He and his wife, I knew, were both lawyers, and she'd been hired for the two kids.

"I'm here . . ."

I don't know what I said, but he answered:

"She's not here."

"Not here?"

"She left."

Then I remembered at that moment—he was a lawyer. Indeed, *I* was a lawyer. And in that moment all the fear I had driving out was gone, because he was a lawyer.

I knew he was lying.

"Oh well," I said. "Why don't you go look?"

He stared at me, so I said again: "I think you should take a look. I think she is here."

It wasn't with any drama. It was just a day at the office. I ask for documents. "We don't have those." "Well, why don't you look?" Otherwise, I have to take it up with the judge. That kind of tone.

He paused for a second, the way they always do. Then he said, "I'll go check."

I'll always remember the way she looked when she came up the stairs and the way the two kids, clinging, were besotted with her.

I took her to the Everly Brothers, in concert. They do oldies, like "Wake Up Little Susie." It was so far out in the burbs, I didn't have a choice. I kept looking at my watch, at her. What would happen to her when we got back?

I bet she'd rather have been living in Paris.

TWELVE

City of Fabulous Kids

Tᴴᴇʀᴇ's ᴀ ʀᴇᴘᴜʙʟɪᴄᴀɴ, ᴄᴏɴsᴇʀᴠᴀᴛɪᴠᴇ sɪᴅᴇ ᴛᴏ ᴍᴇ. ᴇᴠᴇʀʏ time I read an article on inequality, a little voice inside me says, "Oh well, that's not so bad." But the other day I met a man looking at the old census records of the city. "You know," he said, "it's amazing, how big the gap in the city is now between rich and poor. I was looking at census numbers in the 1950s, 1960s. Even in the poorest wards, in the all-black ghettoes . . . they're still at sixty percent of the city's median income."

Now?

"Oh, it's twenty to thirty percent."

And I thought, "Well, that's not so bad." But I know it is bad. How can we be in the same city together?

ɪ sᴀɪᴅ ᴛʜɪs ᴛᴏ ɢ., the demographer: "What do we have in common living in cities now?" "You mean," G. said, "what do we and the poor have in common, other than a sense of urban space?"

"Yes."

He paused. "Look," he said, with no warning, "do you want to make an 'irreversible commitment' to the city? Then why don't you do what my wife and I did. Adopt a black child."

"I'm not even married, I . . ."

"Ah," he laughed. "See, it's very interesting how your friends react."

WHERE THE ORPHANS BELONG

Could you adopt a Chicago child the way people adopt them from rural China? I was haunted by this idea. This is how I could make an irreversible commitment to the city. If I did this, no one would say, "Well, he didn't go to high school here."

I asked a lawyer I knew at the Department of Children and Family Services: "Is it true? Can I adopt a kid? I always figured, there were no orphans anymore."

"It used to be hard," she said. "But this has just changed, even like in the last year. You *can* adopt these kids now." She gave me the name of a professor who worked with the courts. So I called, to ask the same silly question.

The professor said, with warmth and annoyance all at once: "These are great kids."

"You can adopt them, I mean, like you can adopt from China?"

She said that with so many kids in state care (over 50,000 in Illinois) there had to be rethinking. An expert may scoff at reopening Boy's Town, the remedy of Newt Gingrich, but why not terminate parental rights? "So," she said, "that's what we heard when the court had a meeting of experts, social workers, and they said to us, 'Give these kids a chance to be adopted.'"

Otherwise, they'd just go on as, well, foster kids. The idea is that when Mom goes nuts, and locks the baby in a cage, or just wanders off . . . Well, her kid goes with a foster parent, temporarily. Mom's coming back. When she's better.

But now a growing view is: why not let the kid have a home, permanently?

So as I write this, across the street from me, there are four courtrooms, full calendars, just terminating parental rights. Just to give a sense of the change in terminations of parental rights in Cook County:

| 1993 | 958 |
| 1997 | 3,743 |

Each year it seems to climb.

Now, the professor says, fiercely, "These are great kids."

A white person, taking a black kid. Didn't we create all this inequality? It just looks bad, to open the compound gate, reach out, pull in a baby, raise it up inside.

Doesn't it?

I decided to ask, cautiously: "You know, aren't some of these kids, some anyway, aren't they crack babies?"

She scoffed at this in various ways, but the point I remember is: "Look," she said, "you're taking a risk with foreign kids too."

"No, I, I understand," I said, "but how are you going to get parents for . . . ten thousand kids a year?"

"Yes," she said, "we need people like you to put out the word."

Put out the word? Who does she think I know?

I was depressed about this for days. Four courtrooms, going full blast, and all day long they're terminating parental rights.

I made one more call after talking to the court expert. It was to a number cruncher at the Department of Children and Family Services. How many kids are there, just in the city, with no parents?

His estimate: 8 percent.

"Well," I thought, "that isn't so bad."

But it turns out, these are the kids we know have no parents. He said, "If you ask, 'Are there kids roaming around without parents and living with someone else?' Well sure. There are a lot more. How many, we don't know."

Now I know people are thinking these are black kids. But isn't there something orphanlike about any kid living in poverty, real, grinding U.S.-measure poverty? Jared Bernstein at the Economic Policy Institute once told me, "There are twenty-six million children living in poverty," or at 125 percent of the poverty line. Of course I think, "Well, that's not so bad." But then I remembered two things:

First, 26 million is just a snapshot. Next year, some of these kids will be technically "out of poverty," and millions who were out this year will be "back in." It's not upward or downward mobility, it's just the minor swings of fortune in the lives of people stuck at the bottom.

Second, even the kids out of poverty this year are still really in poverty. Does a difference of $2,000 or $3,000 in family income really matter? There's one number, by itself, that can explain why we have so many orphans in the city. The bottom 40 percent of America, closing in on a majority, have 12 to 13 percent of the national income. The top 5 percent, our elite, has almost twice as much, or nearly 22 percent.

Now imagine if this trend goes on. In a short while, the elite 5 percent could make an annual income that is double, twice, two times, what a whole majority of the country makes. Isn't that what's turning the city into the movie set of *Oliver*?

There's been no inequality like this in our recorded history. The quid pro quo? Make the rich people adopt the kids. Why not? They can afford the maids.

Second, why not open up America (like China) to foreign adoptions?

We can leave the kids on the doorsteps of foreign hotels. Some countries in Europe have so much equality, or so little poverty, you could give the kids to people at random. In a way, it's the philosopher John Rawls's test for a Just Society, though he puts it in other terms. Can you leave a baby on any doorstep?

Well, college is free in Europe.

And if no college, life as a high school grad is pretty nice there too. It's true, the U.S. is still the best for being Millken-like rich, or even the top third. But otherwise simply for "moving up," from the bottom to halfway up, Europe is better than America now.

Business Week in 1994 featured a cover story on this. What are the chances for a Dane at the very bottom to move up? Nine out of ten.

What are the chances for an American? One out of two.

In which country would you drop your kid at random?

I STOOD AT MIDNIGHT

Now the Clinton era has an answer: Job training.

Many of my friends, fellow Democrats, would tell me: Let's forget collective bargaining, that's archaic, let's just skill these children up.

And who can be against this? Not even Republicans can rouse themselves to attack so dull a public policy.

OK, I used to think. Let's do it. It used to intrigue me. Did Democrats, CEOs, Republicans, did they really want to skill people up? I mean, did they really want to pay people a higher wage? Why would they want to change the distribution of income in this way?

But I always assumed people were serious. Clinton was. And that's why I thought I could do something about child labor.

I remember the night I saw it the first time. 1991. A recession year. It was midnight. And I admit, I kind of stumbled on this by accident. It happened because one night I ran out of coffee.

As I looked around, I began to notice something odd: The "superstore" was manned, if that's the right word, by children.

What month was this? October. I looked at my watch, it was 1 A.M., wasn't this a Wednesday . . . a school night?

Every kid here seemed to be about sixteen or seventeen years old.

At the cash register, I stared at the clerk and then asked her, "Uh . . . pardon me, but how old are you?"

"Oh!" she gave a little gasp.

"No, no," I said, "I mean . . . what's the average age of people working here?"

She seemed to relax. "Oh, maybe, like, sixteen to . . . like, twenty?"

Like, twenty, was like the manager.

ABOUT TWO NIGHTS LATER, I was having dinner with two schoolteachers, Cappy and his wife.

"A lot of the kids," Cappy said, "work forty hours a week."

"Gee, do you think they should be working past midnight?"

"What's the alternative?"

"Forbid it."

"You want to FORBID IT?"

"Well, working that late. Don't you think they should be home in bed?"

Voices rose.

"Tom, that's sometimes the ONLY income these families have . . ."

"Yes," his wife said, "what would their parents do?"

"Hey, maybe we'd have to hire some adults!"

And I began to see, at midnight, the kids are all over the city:
Color coding at Wal-Mart
Cleaning urinals at McDonald's
Holding butcher knives in the deli at Dominick's.

It began to haunt me that these children were working as I slept. Then I read a report by Joseph Kinney at the National Safe Work Place Institute, which was then in Chicago. Only four states then set any limit on how late the kids could work. And how many kids worked?

Over 2.5 million, and typically they worked twenty-one hours a week. Now it's true, some of the kids are middle class. Adults like to think they all are: "Oh they do it for the clothes."

But the kids I saw that night, I knew something was wrong. What were they doing working past midnight?

Now just as in the case of TB, I knew there must be some old law about child labor. Sure enough, there was, or still is one: It dates back to the New Deal. Our child labor law, passed in 1938, prohibits fourteen- and fifteen-year-olds from working late, but sixteen and over can go straight on to morning.

Except . . .

Yes, there's a clause that says the Secretary of Labor can prohibit an occupation that is detrimental to the "health or well being" of a sixteen- or seventeen-year-old. So? Isn't working past midnight detrimental?

Soon I had met teachers and even some kids, with the help of Joseph Kinney, and we decided to bring a suit in 1993.

It's true I was now suing Clinton, but I thought he would welcome it. I'd be a hero.

"Thanks," the president would say, "for bringing this to our attention. These kids should be studying algebra, science, languages . . . skilling themselves up for the new world economy."

Right from the start, everything went wrong.

First, I went to the most prominent Clintonite I knew and explained what I was doing.

"Oh no!" he groaned.

"What?"

"This is just the kind of old liberalism that gets us into trouble. It goes against the whole thrust of what we're doing. What we're doing now is

'School to Work.' This is the kind of thing we want to encourage. Apprenticing kids, teaching them skills . . ."

"Skills?" I said. "What do you mean? These kids are cleaning urinals at 1 A.M."

"'School to Work,'" he 'said, louder. "That's where we should be putting our emphasis."

And as I now know, Republicans are even more upset. Do you think we could pass the child labor laws today? To the Right, the problem is that the younger kids can't work past midnight too. "Oh you liberals, you're all in favor of midnight basketball, etc. Look at these teenage homicides. This wouldn't be happening in our cities if more kids were working."

OK, that's not an exact quote, but it's the gist of material people sent me from the *Washington Times* and other right-wing organs.

Save the children. Let's put them back in the mines.

And the liberal left?

"Oh," said a child advocate, "I don't think this suit is a good idea."

"You're against it too?" I said.

"I'm not saying that," she said. "But have you talked to the children?"

"No,"

"Oh!" she said. "Why don't you talk to the children, find out what *they* want!"

ACTUALLY I HAD TALKED to the children. The first one was H., who was one of the kids the teachers told me to see. He was in a better job. He did light afternoon work. He was brought out to see me by two women in white. We sat in a clean, well-lighted place as he talked about his former life.

"Kids do it for the clothes," he said.

Shit. Just what I didn't want to hear.

"Uh, what do you mean," I asked, "by clothes?"

He stared at me. "Look," he said, "you're a lawyer right?"

"Yeah."

"If you were my dad, I could say, 'Look, maybe you're not rich, but you can get me cool clothes.'" He paused, gloomily. "The kids with good parents, they don't have to work."

"What do you mean by . . . good?"

"Oh," he said, "uh . . . like fifteen thousand dollars a year."

I soon realized by "cool clothes" H. meant simply clothes. And this kid knew about child labor. He knew child labor the way Huck Finn knew the river.

For example: "Never work at a Pepe's."

"Why?"

He thought. "Just never work there. That's all I can say."

"What about McDonald's?"

"They're OK, but . . . don't work at restaurants that serve real food. They're worse than the ones that serve fast food." He went through each of the big discount stores. "And V.!" he said. "Never, never work there. They love to keep you late." He kept saying how he wanted to get them. "Do you know what they do?"

"No."

"See, they take kids in the city, and ship them out to the suburbs, and . . ."

"Don't the kids know?"

"No, no, man, they don't know. Look, you apply for a job and you say, 'It's got to be from four to ten.' And they say, 'Oh, well, we close at ten.' But that's a lot of, uh, bullcrap. They *close* at ten. Sure. But that's when you *start* working! You got to do like inventory and close up and . . ."

Then he got to the chilling part: The bus would come around and pick kids up. "Only you got to go to the other stores and wait for the kids . . . and you get back to the city like at 2 A.M.!"

"And at Thanksgiving, they close at eleven and at Christmas they close at midnight, and right before Christmas . . ."

"Wait," I said, stopping him. "Wait, how can a Pepe's be worse?"

"Believe me," he said. "Pepe's is worse."

IT'S AMAZING HOW many jobs a kid can fill in America now. I can grasp why full employment doesn't mean inflation. You can always hire more kids.

So for Alan Greenspan, this is good. But is it good for the children?

There's even more evidence now about the harm this does to kids. They fall behind in school, get in trouble, drop out. Still, these are kids. And 26 million are in poverty. And the ones like H., and the others I represent, if not technically poor, are in the same fix.

Now to me, the high school these kids were in seemed wonderful. Once I got to ask the kids in class what country each was born in.

Jordan.

Philippines.

Romania.

Guatemala.

I could almost weep. Is this America, or what?

They came from every country. Yet now they were all the same. Each kid, regardless of race, origin, religion, each one flipped you the finger the same way. Each, that year, was listening to Kurt Cobain.

I went to the principal. I tried to explain what it meant to me, to be here. He nodded, like the abbott of a monastery. He knew I was having a mystical experience.

"I know," he said, "I couldn't do anything else but this." He told me the school had twelve . . . *twelve* . . . bilingual programs.

Now I knew why I hated child labor, and the kids dropping out. They should be here, skilling themselves up.

Until this suit, I was always bored by talk of school reform. But now it seemed to me of the highest importance.

The big issues here are to raise the test scores and keep the kids from dropping out. As to the scores, the Board has a certain power to manipulate them. Hold back kids. Focus on certain schools at the median. As to dropouts, that's *hard*. The dropout rate is over 43 percent, though it's true many get their degrees later. Still I heard stories of how you can walk into some of the city schools on a nice spring day and there aren't any kids there.

At that time, the mayor's program was to decentralize, and give more power to the local councils.

Later the mayor's program was to centralize: take back the power from the local councils. Indeed, right now, there are two sets of reform laws on the books. One set of reforms saying decentralize. Another set of reforms saying centralize.

But which reform works? I asked the principal. What is the one thing that will help kids learn? It's not, I am sure, manipulating the scores.

Here is what he said (I remember writing it down): "The only thing that's ever been proven to work, and I mean work every time, always, is this . . . Raise the wages of the parents."

But he also encouraged me with the suit.

THE THING THAT WORRIED ME was that people would sniff and say, "Oh these kids do it for designer clothes, designer jeans."

I said this to a teacher in a cafeteria. "Look around here," she said. "You see any kids in designer clothes?"

The kids, in black and white, looked like POWs.

"No."

"See the ones with the long, long jackets? You can tell, they're the ones who work late. They wear these coats that scrape the floor." And she told me they flip them over their heads like bedrolls. She sent some of them out of class to the school nurse, who was used to seeing kids. They weren't really sick. They just needed to get some sleep.

I nodded, and thought what a wonderful thing it was, "I'm helping these kids . . ."

And all the time, without my knowing, the kids I was helping were dropping out of school. One day the law student who was helping me said, "I can't find any of our plaintiffs."

"What do you mean?" I said. "How can we lose our plaintiffs?"

She said, while the suit was pending, they'd been dropping out of school, one by one. "And no one knows where they are."

That was the incredible thing to me. But why would anyone know where they were? Technically they had parents, or a parent, but they didn't really live with any adults. Or they lived with an older sibling, etc.

I was in a panic. What if the government lawyers found out? "Well find them!" I snapped at her. "Go over to the school. Someone must know."

What a time to lose the kids! I was now going to meet with an official at Labor. Now the position was: "Oh, the law doesn't give us the power to set those hours." But as my lawyer friends agreed, the words in the old

New Deal law ("detrimental to well being") were big enough to give the power, if they wanted to use it.

I had the pictures of the kids in the file:

M., she was tall, shy. She had found herself working over forty hours a week, didn't know how to ask for overtime. She had become pregnant, or married, or something, and dropped out.

Then there was A., who worked at a hardware chain. The school counselor kept calling her boss to let her off the night before the college boards. Even her older sister called, "Let her off this one night." NO.

I also had a picture of G., who worked at the McDonald's the kids called "McCrack." She got off at 1:30, when the buses had stopped running.

And finally there was C., who worked at the big discount store. I just remember he was tall and so thin, his knees knocked together like a baby doe's.

Gone. How could they be gone?

I kept thinking about the lost kids as I went into the Clinton official's office. It turned out he was pretty nice. When I started to argue the legal issue he stopped me. "Let's assume we have the authority to do this. Why should we?"

"Why? Why should you? Well . . ." I wasn't ready for this so fast.

"We don't have the staff to do this." He went on to say how they didn't have the staff or personnel any more to stop the sweatshops.

"Besides," he added, "here's what bothers me. I'm thinking of the parents of these kids. Raising them in the city. Isn't this a way for the parents to keep these kids under control?"

What?

"What?" I said. "The parents . . . These kids aren't 'under control,' these kids are *out* of control!"

I was so angry and hurt, because he was right in a way, the Labor Department was overwhelmed enforcing the laws we did have. So as I often do in such cases, I became self-righteous, and went on, "Oh these kids don't even have parents," which is true enough, but beside the point.

Anyway the Labor Department didn't settle out of court. And in the end we lost the case.

Oh kids! Where are you now? I'm sorry I couldn't do anything for you. And I guess maybe the Clinton Democrats are right: If I had really wanted to make an irreversible commitment, I should have picked out one of you and paid for your college.

GIVE THEM A BLACK BOX

You can't save everyone, right? At least with America's weird growth of inequality, you can't. The other day I came across this graph in the London *Financial Times*:

Where Pay Inequality Rose

Ratio of 90th to 10th percentile of the gross earning distribution of men

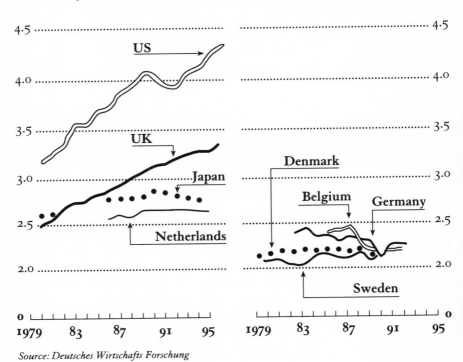

Source: *Deutsches Wirtschafts Forschung*

Scary? That's why at a dinner party a teacher like C., eyes shining, will talk about saving *one* kid. "Roberto," he says, and he looks at his wife, "we drove him up to Ann Arbor, that's what we have our eye on."

Strange, it's like Sophie's choice, which one will we try to save. For a week or so I had a fantasy of *being* a teacher, though I wasn't serious. It started when my friend Father G. said that my old teachers, the Jesuits, had opened a school.

But this school was not for the elite, like St. Ignatius, but for the poor.

"It's a trade school," he said.

"The Jesuits, a trade school, like a plumber?"

"No, no, this will be more like hotel management."

Ah. How Leninist of the order to think of taking over the Hyatts. The name of the school is Christo Rey. Well . . . couldn't I go down there and teach hotel management?

That's the future, for kids in the bottom half, i.e., jobs where they wait on people in the 5 percent.

I often think of myself going down there to Pilsen, after I've learned Spanish, and picking out the brightest kid, in the Jesuit manner:

"Now this boy or girl could be a concierge at the Drake."

NOW OF COURSE one could say: But isn't this America? Why not save all the kids? This is what Clinton likes to say in the State of the Union. When I go to D.C., and talk to the policy wonks, it's the opposite of talking to a teacher. Down there, the Democrats talk about sending all the kids to college. Save one or two? No, no, employers are *demanding* more skills, they aren't interested in low-skill workers. We'll just send everyone to college to meet the growing demand. Every week there's a story about how Silicon Valley needs another six battalions of computer engineers. Or a story in the *Wall Street Journal,* how all the new jobs are management jobs. And on and on.

For years I've seen such stories, and it amazes me, because for years I have been following the dull, grim, Victorian-type reports of the Bureau of Labor Statistics. This started when I first wrote away for the BLS study, *The American Work Force, 1992–2000.* No one ever talks to the BLS staff. They always interview professors, CEOs, White House policy wonks. All the BLS does is count the beans, and what they report isn't very pretty. I remember the shock of flipping open to Table 3 of that report, "Occupations That Will Grow the Fastest by 2000": the thirty jobs on the list include manicurist, security guard, janitor, home health aide.

Are the schools failing us, when this is our list?

The horrible thing is, all the kids I lost in my lawsuit—I'm sure they all got jobs. Indeed, child labor, cleaning urinals at McDonald's, isn't so far off from the jobs they get as adults. It confuses me to read, as I sometimes do in a journal or paper, "The demand for low-skill workers is in decline." It seems to me that the demand is bigger than ever. That's why inflation is low. The job mix is in a downward spiral, i.e., more and more low-skill jobs. If the mix is going up to higher skill management jobs, that would be reflected in the median wage. It's not.

Yes, there's a shortage of computer engineers, but when you look at the hard numbers, it's tiny. That's why the Urban Institute has been arguing for years against raising the quotas for foreigners. We can produce the high-skilled workers here. It's still the case, in 1998, that the sum total of *all* our computer engineers, in *all* of America . . . is one third the number of people just working away at Wal-Mart, which now employs 700,000!

Yes, at one company: the scanners, the colorizers, etc.

Even the people who work in manufacturing are low-skill. Impossible, right, since America is so productive? In 1997, in Britain, there was a report by the National Institute for Economic and Social Research. What industry in America has, the report says, is a huge elite of engineers. Nothing like it in the world. That's why everyone else in the plant can be low skill: in manufacturing, over two thirds of our work force is low skill (Germany's is 29 percent).

Our factories look like our country, i.e., an elite telling the low skills where to move things.

IT'S DISTURBING to walk around the city. What do I see people doing? Or to walk in a factory, as I sometimes do. Poor people, no English, do they have skills, or do they need them?

But suppose we had the high-skill workers we always say we want. Suppose we set up our workplace more like Europe. What would happen to the profit margins?

Do the elite really want people to have more skills? If they have more skills, who's going to park the cars? Or bus the tables? Or do all the things that I see people doing in my city?

I want to believe in public schools. It's not controversial, like unions, collective bargaining. We can change the income structure, and no one will raise a fuss.

What's wrong with this way of achieving the Promise of American Life? It's what Clinton wants to do. In every State of the Union, until now, there's a line or two somewhere, which implies grandly we'll send everyone to college.

How can there be a gap between high school and college graduates' incomes if . . . well, if everyone goes to college?

Now I know Clinton doesn't mean this literally. But what would happen if we double the amount of college graduates?

First, it's impossible to imagine. Even now, if the percent going to college remains constant, it's estimated that by 2015 the cost of college tuition will have doubled.

But isn't that like a tax on kids to let them get the same sub-Dilbert–type jobs?

Second, there's a glut of B.A.s now, with one in five in noncollege jobs. That by itself is OK, as long as the supply of B.A.s stays fairly steady. What's more depressing is the kind of work we now call "college jobs."

To the BLS, a "college job" is any job the boss wants a B.A. for and actually fills with a B.A. By that technical standard, here is what we now call "college jobs" in the BLS studies: legal secretary, insurance claims adjuster, manager of Blockbuster, assistant manager of Blockbuster.

Will doubling the number of people bidding on these jobs change the way we live?

BUT OF COURSE we aren't going to double the number of B.A.s. We need too many people in low-skill jobs.

That's what depresses me most of all. I think of all the orphans, or kids without parents, and all the jobs—busboy, valet, assistant manager at Blockbuster, circling around them.

Of course I should be more upbeat. That's what my friends say. One of them invited me to be on a panel on education. Of course she just asked me to talk about child labor.

Still, I was amazed to listen to the others, how bright the future was, etc.

First there was a businesswoman, who said, "I'm in my seventh career!" She went on, "The old way of educating, that's obsolete.... For example, I was in marketing management. But I was trained originally to be a doctor, and ..."

I've forgotten some of her careers.

Then came a professor of education, and he held up a black box:

"See this box? In the future, there will be a black box on every desk ... just think, a child sitting here, in five minutes ... five minutes ... will be able to download the *entire* Library of Congress."

Then came a cultural critic, who asked, "Who is going to *control* the black box? We have issues of democracy. We have issues of control. Who's going to control the black box?"

The public school teachers, out in the seats, said nothing. But the two panelists became more agitated. Who's going to control the black box? Is Bill Gates going to control the black box?

Are we going to let Bill Gates determine how fast children can download the *entire* Library of Congress?

My God, this can't be what people are discussing. But now it was my turn. This made no sense. My lawsuit on child labor, it has nothing to do with this.

Think of something.

So I asked the thirty or so people: "Are you all teachers in the public schools of Chicago?"

Yes.

"Well ... from what I read, and the way the job structure is set up, the kids in this city ... you think they'll be in the top third? No. Middle third? No. Bottom third? I don't know why these kids would even try."

A teacher shouted: "That's what they do ask: 'Why should I even *try?*'"

Yes, more angry voices. I thought about these kids I had lost . . . I actually hadn't thought about them for a while, but now, I was on a roll. Little black box. Come on, where are they going?

Now the professor blew up: "There's so much, so much that I disagree with . . . I don't know where to start! What are you saying, 'Give up'? Give up? You? Who are you? I know what life is like for these kids. I taught in the public schools. I know. I *know*. But I'm not telling them to give up . . ."

How dare he lecture me? "I'd forget about this black box," I grumbled.

I turned to all the teachers: "Look, I'm not a teacher, but you ask about the new global economy, and skilling them up . . . Well, I'd just teach the kids two things. Two. First, 'How can I get this kid, in my class, later on as an adult . . . to vote?' Second, 'How can I get them, later on, as an adult, to pick up a newspaper?'"

Pick up a newspaper. Take an interest in civic affairs.

"Oh!" the professor snapped. "You know what that means for these kids? That's fifty cents a day! Three dollars a week! But a computer . . . they can read it on-line, for free."

OK, let them read it on-line.

Anyway, the panel was mollified I'd made that concession.

But the teachers began scoffing: "Read a paper? What are they supposed to read about, some *murder*?"

Another said, "The papers?? They have these stereotypes about African American males. These kids don't want to read about stereotypes."

Now a third teacher spoke up, intoning: "I find what works with these kids . . . be sincere. Be sincere. Who you are. My kids, they know I'm sincere. They look at me and know, 'He's who he is!'"

Someone told him to stuff it.

Most of us were shouting now, about newspapers, and black boxes, and why should we even *try*. And when it was over, a teacher who I really did think was sincere came up and said: "I'll tell you what I didn't like. You don't give people any hope. You don't."

"Don't? What? Because I said, people should go out and vote?"

Oh, lady, I . . . ah! I thought that was the purpose of education, once.

Maybe I was thinking, in some way, of all the John Dewey I had read in college.

It vaguely stirred in my head: Isn't that what Dewey said? The purpose of education wasn't to skill kids up for the New World Economy, or to have seven careers, like the businesswoman who was the doctor. No, wasn't it to get people to vote? That's what Dewey wanted the schools to teach. Not to get ahead of the other kid, but for all the kids to act together. Dewey's still our master on how to teach kids to live in a democracy.

Indeed, it's the rest of the developed world that vindicates Dewey. He argued against "private collectivism," i.e., big private business. And "public collectivism," i.e., the government.

He and his disciples thought that we should teach our kids to act collectively, *outside* of the state: i.e., to form unions, to "vote" on our wages. It's a mistake that Dewey cared more about "how to think" than "what to think." It's true he didn't want kids to memorize the Great Books. But at least by the New Deal, he and his disciples argued that we should teach our kids, in the schools, how to act collectively.

Some of his protégés even started a magazine, *The Social Frontier,* at Columbia Teachers' College, and that's the message.

Don't trust business. Don't trust government. But act collectively as a group to keep an eye on both.

Dewey's disciples then would say that is the most crucial of all skills that schools need to teach kids.

The 26 million kids, sloshing around down there below the poverty line.

Dewey would say, I believe, that the schools should teach these kids how to act as a Madison majority-type faction. How to vote, the way Europeans do, and fend off those who drag their wages down.

IN *Working Under Different Rules* (1994), Professors Freeman and Katz in a way back up this idea. They say you can determine the distribution of income in a country—Germany, Sweden, America, Italy—by the degree to which citizens in voluntary associations, as Dewey imagined, fix their wages *outside* of the government.

Indeed, this one thing, citizenship, so affects everything else . . . well, some say you can be put down in a country, unknown, Ruritania, and walk around for five hours, and know by the end of it how Ruritania sets its wages.

But here's the exciting thing about Dewey and his disciples: They thought democracy could be a science. Not just one faction bashing the other, like in *Federalist* No. 10.

It was the touching belief that people in a democracy could learn to act scientifically. And think what life could be like! People in other countries, not just economists, but the common person, the citizen, think and talk and write about this: How can we in our country act together and be happy and prosper without the shocking inequality of America?

What works. What doesn't work. What should we keep. What should we try. This is what Dewey imagined the majority of us doing, what he imagined the schools teaching us how to do.

For example, does raising wages improve the mix of jobs available? Some economists believe this. David Soskice at Oxford University. To some extent, Robert Gordon at Northwestern. It's the idea that just by raising wages slowly, we push the economy into higher skill, higher value kinds of work.

Isn't this the kind of thing Dewey and his disciples meant when they told us democracy should be a science?

This is what children in a democracy should be learning, instead of cleaning urinals after midnight at McDonald's.

GET A JOB

But what if democracy in Dewey's sense is only possible somewhere else? Then the kids should learn to work long hours, and show up on time.

A friend of mine points out this is really all that many a business person asks. "Just get them to *show up.*"

Forget the black box. Or downloading the Library of Congress. Just at least teach them the skills of getting on the El, showing up, holding the broom.

That's what much of the welfare reform really consists of. Maybe if there is one thing we should do as citizens in the Clinton era, it's to teach people to show up.

Fill out applications.

Hold the broom.

I was involved briefly with a volunteer group that simply worked with kids, eighteen or nineteen years old, to get them jobs as movie ushers. And it's not so easy to be an usher, or take the tickets. You have to teach the kid to show up. Fill out the application. And above all, get through the interview.

I was supposed to help the kid get through the interview. That meant, I too needed a mentor to tell me what to tell the kid.

"All these kids," my mentor said, "have gaps in their lives that have to be explained. I mean, these are great kids. They're hardworking. They're in this program, right? But they have to learn how to do an interview. So the interviewer says, 'I see you dropped out of school. Why?' Now what's the wrong answer? The wrong answer is, 'I was pregnant.' The right answer is, 'I did a foolish thing, but this has helped make me a more serious person. I went back to school and now I have my G.E.D.'"

"OK," I said. "Right answer, wrong answer."

"Or they say to the kid, 'Why did you leave your last job?' The wrong answer is, 'My boss was hitting on me.' The right answer is, 'I felt I needed a new challenge, I wanted to grow as a person.'"

"OK," I said. "I have this."

I looked around the room, and I was impressed how many of the business people helping these kids were black.

I did this for a while. And all the time I hoped Dewey, wherever he was, wouldn't be ashamed of me. If he ever did come back, I would tell him: "We're never going to do in this country what you thought we'd do, raise the wages of the kids generally. So at least let's teach them to park the cars."

So I sat there silent when I was told:

"Tell the kids not to ask about how much they'll make, or about benefits. At least not the first interview."

I know that's wise. It bothers me, though.

And what's so wonderful is that there are volunteers. And the kids come in, one by one, out of the 26 million who (this week at least) are in poverty. They just want an adult to help.

They come here on their own, no one pushing them, with wild ideas of what a job will be like: dangerous fantastical ideas of what a paycheck can do. They'd do anything for a job. One of my mentors told me, "These kids are really, really serious."

THIRTEEN

In the "White City"

WHAT HAPPENS IF A YOUNG MAN FINDS NO WORK, OR scorns the low wages? I guess I already knew the answer to this. But sometimes, it takes a European to show me my own city.

Anyway, this story begins on the balcony of a German official. Sometimes I'd go to meet groups of visiting Germans, e.g., lawyers, or students. We'd look out at the city at night and ooh and ah at its beauty: the harmony, the sense of symmetry and number, like a Pythagorean speculation.

"Oh, it's wonderful." "Perfect."

To impress them, I'd tick off the other things they had to see. Wright Museum? "Oh yes, we have seen this already" Newberry Library? "We have seen this already."

Wait, you've only been here a day!

OK, they're efficient. Irked, I'd list other things. "Yes, we have seen this already!"

Then, one night, to show off, I urged a young German lawyer to see a place that, to my shame, I myself had never seen. "Oh, you must see our Night Narcotics Court!"

"Yes, I have seen this already."

Come on, I blew up. How could you? He was going to be a lawyer in the consulate, so in New York he'd gone to see it. "It is fascinating, yes?"

I was annoyed, since I'd never seen it.

Now it makes sense a lawyer in a consulate would see it. There is a chilling story that I heard about a German boy:

Once it seems a young boy, seventeen, came to O'Hare to see a family member. He was carrying a little dope. He didn't know what a crime it was. He was arrested, and taken to jail. Before anyone could find out where he was . . . he'd been assaulted.

So that's why it's good for them to be aware of our Night Narcotics Court.

Still, I was irked that this young lawyer, smug, was saying, "I have seen this already."

Yeah? I was going next week, damn it.

THE LAW OF HALLUCINATION

I needed a guide, a criminal lawyer. I called J., who once had been a "public defender" or P.D. "Yeah, it's fascinating," he said. "I'll take you."

We would go to the criminal courthouse on the South Side. The poor sit next door, in the county jail, which gets now over 90,000 admissions a year.

Then they sit there for months, he told me, as they're unable to make bail. Late at night many are called over for "trial."

Tonight I would really see my city. I could already hallucinate this: the clock striking twelve, the poor spilling into the halls, vendors selling Hogarth prints. But when we got there it was empty. Night Narcotics? Everyone had gone home.

"Usually they're spilling out into the halls, but tonight . . . ," J. said as we looked in each court.

At last we found a room with a judge, so we took seats in the back. J. happened to know the judge.

We sat with the women, who were all black. Almost all the people here, except the officials, were black, with very few Latinos. The women were waiting for a glimpse of a son or a brother.

There was a strange feeling to all of this, as if the court was holding, as a school would, an open house for parents.

In the back, J. was telling me about a particular judge. "His trials would go really late. He used to be called 'The Prince of Darkness.'"

But now the Prince has cut back a bit, since one night out in the parking lot, one of the jurors was raped.

I saw a woman who looked like the judge's clerk. "Who's that?"

"State's Attorney."

She was in a tent of a dress, and she sat up there as if she were the judge. As each man came up, she would mumble very fast, as if whispering Hail Marys over him. (It turned out, she was reading the charge.)

I looked at the women in back of me. How could they hear this? Then it shocked me again how everyone was black. "It's like a plantation," I said to J.

"That's exactly why I got out of it," he said. "At first I'd kid myself, 'Oh, I'm defending people.' But then one day I realized, 'No, I'm really just one of the overseers.'"

The judge took a break, and we went back to see him in chambers. He was a guy like us, and very natural. I wanted to ask him about the jail being overcrowded. Did he worry about this?

But the judge wanted to talk about the decline of the family. That's what he saw up on the bench. I'd like to have told him, why won't you sit with me? Sit with the women, just there for a glimpse of a brother, a son.

I thought this spoke well for the American family.

Anyway, did he think about the overcrowding?

"No," he said, "I can't let myself think about that."

But he said he disposed of cases at a very fast rate. He checked something. "This past year I've done over 2,000 felony dispositions. Second best, here in the building."

He may have done two or three while I was watching, but the S.A. mumbled so, how could I know?

"So you do eight or nine felony cases a night?"

Yeah.

Now most people here go on probation. After all, they've already been in jail for months.

In fact, that's why the P.D.s are so restless. There's nothing up here to try. Why do it, if you can't get any trial experience?

We talked to a P.D. He had only one trial coming up, and it was stupid. "You want to hear his defense why he wasn't dealing? He says, 'I've got two pairs of sneakers, I got a white pair and a black pair. Now . . . the night I was arrested, I was wearing the *white pair*. OK? And *never, never* have I dealt any drugs wearing the *white pair*.'"

"Good argument," J. said.

"And you know," he sighed, "I have no choice but to go to trial."

Where had I heard this alibi? I'd read something like it in a Nelson Algren short story.

Was a black kid by accident using the same alibi a Polish kid had used years ago?

It made me feel, for the first time, that maybe very little of this had to do with race. All that night, I would think of Algren. He's the city's literary icon, who wrote in the 1930s and 1940s about blue-collar life. He is famous now mainly because his lover, for a while, was Simone de Beauvoir, the French writer who was the lover of Sartre and author of *The Second Sex* and many other books. It's incredible to me that once *she* lived here, with Algren, in Chicago! I read somewhere that one night Algren brought her down to the jail, next door: he wanted to show her the electric chair. It's sad to think of him, desperate, doing this for a date . . . show her anything to get her to stay.

And the sad thing is the jail's so much more impressive now. In de Beauvoir's time it had only two divisions. Now it's shot up to . . . eleven! Once you could walk around the jail. Now you get in your car and drive.

That's what J. and I did.

First we said goodbye to the public defender, and I felt sorry for him. It's a tough life, no money. The other day I ran into a woman I know to be a P.D., and she was waiting on joggers in a shoe store. She has to work there on weekends. The idea that a lawyer like this would have to put shoes on me, like a pasha . . . it was unbearable.

J. and I left and as we drove around, J. pointed to the divisions, and what each division was for.

"That's for the women . . . that's for people with AIDS . . . "

Each division is huge, all eleven. There's one white blazing block after another.

It reminded me, a little, of D.C., all the monuments, white as human bone, but the jail is bigger and scarier than any memorial. It is a whole White City, and that was the name, by the way, of the city's first world's fair. It's the White City where people came to see the country's future.

"This is the city's future," I thought.

I told J. how on a boiling, airless, summer night, I had come down here. It was the humid night on which hundreds of old people, their windows locked tight, would die of the heat. I had stopped right in front of the jail, and I thought I heard screaming. I turned off the AC and rolled down the window.

"*Aayyyieee . . . !*"

"*Ahhhh!*"

At barred windows, men were screaming.

"I can't believe it," J. said. "They're all air-conditioned."

"Well, maybe I was wrong." But I dreamed about this for days.

Then we were quiet, just looking at this . . . thing.

"You know," I said, "it's actually kind of nice."

J. nodded.

It was—nice clean lines—though I didn't care for the razor wire around the top. I remember a friend who said of Ceaușescu's palace in Bucharest: "Can I be the only one who think it's, well, nice?"

It also appealed to me as a civil servant. It shows the government can still build something. And at least it's new. On the South Side, in the 1980s, except for a new ballpark, who was building anything?

"Think of all the money going into this," I said.

"Yeah," J. said, "and over at Robert Taylor you don't think they see that? The money going into the jail?"

And it sucks in civil servants, not just criminals. The kitchen is huge. As I later found out, it's the biggest kitchen in the whole Chicago area, except the one at O'Hare.

The jail has to feed at any given time only about 10,000 prisoners. But there are the guards, other staff, and if you think of all the people passing through—90,000 in the course of a year—it's much bigger than any ward in the city.

Just as a civil servant, I could feel the pull of the thing. There are many "policy types" who find themselves, often against their will, working on "the jail." My friend M., for example, wanted to be an urban planner like Jane Jacobs but soon found herself working on the jail—in particular, services for pregnant women.

"How," I said, "do they get pregnant when they're in jail?"

Well, maybe before jail.

And her boss ended up on jail issues, when she was in turf wars with jail and prison officials over how to use county land. She wanted to do industrial parks, but, well, she was recruited over to the other side.

But the county is careful how they build it. One division at a time. One bond issue at a time. Never too much debt, ever. That's the old Dem Machine way. "The Machine," says a friend of mine from the Harris School, "they always wore green eyeshades."

Look what the county pols get: new bonds; tons of money: a budget of $150 million; jobs, jobs, jobs. (Not just in the kitchen either.)

And the voters don't even see it. Who knows, or cares, what's going on, or not going on, the way we do with Streets and Sanitation or the parks.

Anyway, this is what I now took out-of-town friends to see instead of steel mills. Once or twice someone would call later: "Why'd you take me to see that? I've been dreaming about it every night."

But dreaming about it wasn't enough. After Night Narcotics, I was determined to go in.

LIVING LIKE IT'S PARIS

I had a chance months later to go inside the jail's hospital. The doctors there asked me to their weekly luncheon. I was to talk about a challenge to a law that required a doctor to be present when a prisoner was executed. It's fascinating how many doctors, even the Republican ones, hate this. It violates their canons—the first step down the road to being "Nazi doctors."

So I gave my talk in a jail that could have been built by Albert Speer. After lunch, a Dr. Mike, whom I liked, took me on a tour.

Well, it is a hospital, but it seems at first like a refugee camp. The men are in brown jumpsuits, with big white letters, "D.O.C."

But it was shocking how thin they were. Really, really thin. As I came down the hall, I had to step over them.

I was expecting, oh, big, violent men. But these frail men, they'd need a nurse to help them to hold a gun.

Then I saw that this was an asylum too. One man, with dreadlocks, was rolling his head, sitting in a kind of trance on a mattress.

Another man was rolling under a bed.

Though insane, they were in a jail. Dr. Mike said, "The P.D.s figure, better to get them in here than in some asylum like Manteno where they'd never get out."

But how in the name of God did they get this thin?

We went to X-Ray, and a technician told how he screened every prisoner. "I can tell from the shape of the lungs, I believe, whether a person is 'HIV,' so do I tell him, or no? As a lawyer, what is your opinion?"

Once I attempted Foucault's *Madness and Civilization*, and before I gave up, I read this fact: In Paris in 1700 over 1 percent of the population was "confined." Now this haunts Foucault, but why? The number in Chicago has to be higher. There's this jail, then the downstate prisons, then the asylums, then the out-of-state prisons, where some of our Chicago locals end up.

It would seem that over the course of an entire year, well over 3 percent of Chicago may be locked up. And that's now, with a falling crime rate.

What happens when there's a recession? Or when the crack babies get older?

That is, if they're ever able to hold a gun.

Now it may not be that bad. But I was lost in all this, and said to Dr. Mike: "Did you ever read Foucault's *Madness and Civilization?*"

He stopped, and gave me a big grin.

"Great book, huh?"

I really liked this guy.

Now I met Dr. Ann, who said, "Well, of course you must go on and see the jail."

Now? I begged off. "I'm not strong enough," I thought.

But the next week I *did* want to see it. So I phoned her, and she set it up with a captain in the jail.

I was ready for something awful. I called up my friend Father C. to keep me company.

We met Captain T. in one of the "new" divisions. He is rotated out every three months to another division, so that neither he nor any other captain can get too "close" with the guards they supervise.

First we went to Maximum Security. Now here for once I saw some whites. It turns out, if you're a serial killer, you can't get out on bail like other whites. Remember, no one in jail has been convicted, but for a few special cases. Most simply lack the money for bail.

But Maximum Security is a different world. These guys are in here, period. Even if they're white. Two guards showed us around, as if it were Madame Tussaud's Wax Museum.

"Now here's Clepper."

"Kepler?" This seemed familiar. The astronomer?

I looked at the door, and there was a tiny hole and an eye looking out.

"Yeah," said the guard, "this is the guy who killed the fifteen prostitutes. Put them in the trash bin."

Oh.

The eye bobbed, violently.

"What's this guy doing over here?"

There was an inmate here watching TV, but in a creepy way, with a wild look in his eyes.

"He's watching a video."

"What?"

"*Seven.*"

"*Seven,*" I gulped. "The serial . . . the slasher movie—*Seven*?"

"Yeah," said the guard. So? What difference did it make.

He then explained this was a twenty-two-hour lockup, then one hour the man is "exercised" and the other he's allowed to watch TV.

Every door we passed, the guard would tell us about the man, and an eye would bob up and down as we talked.

In a while I was caught up on the *10 O'Clock News.* And the guard talked about John Wayne Gacy, who killed all the boys. Did you know Gacy?

"Oh, yes I had to 'recreate' him." That means, give him recreation.

Now we went upstairs to see where the men were recreated. We went by a TV room, with several TVs blaring. Off the TV room was, well, it was kind of a basketball court, but a crazy third of a court, where men ran up and down.

"What do you think?" I said to Father C.

"I don't like the way they're playing, it's too loose."

It was obvious, he said, the way the court was misshapen and crazy, someone had decided, "This should not be a normal game."

I looked back at the TV room, and the captain said, "See the pay phones, the way men are lined up? Each gang has its own phone."

Men in rows waited their turns.

The captain went on, "We had a woman guard come in at dinner and say, 'OK, line up. The G.D.s are over there. Latin Kings are over here. Neutrinos, over here.'"

"'Neutrinos'?"

"People who aren't in a gang," the captain replied. "I said, 'Look, you can't say that.'" How can the State of Illinois line them up in gangs?

"Do the guards," Father C. said, "do they go sour?"

"Oh, I'm sure they go over to the gangs."

(I don't think this is what Father C. meant.)

Go over to the gangs? I was shocked.

"Why did they become guards?" the captain went on. "Why do people go into gangs? They want structure. For one, it's a positive thing, for another, it's a negative."

I said, "But the charges could flip?"

"We had a guard, he came at midnight and took off his shirt, the prisoners took off their shirts, they took a photo of their gang tattoos. . . . One of the girlfriends of the gang members sent it here. Like she thought: 'Hey, this is weird.'"

I looked back at the court. Young men running up and down, it's like a pajama party. I can see how you're a guard, and lonely, you might want to jump into the game.

Now there are over 3,000 jail employees, and for most of them a job like this is like a life raft. It's a fabulous job, by South Side lights. It has security, benefits, and it starts at $32,000 a year.

But the trick is not to stare and stare at the men on the court, and one night . . . take your shirt off, and go over to the other side.

I looked around at the guards. Not to worry.

One was fat, Buddha-like.

And the woman guard next to him? A county official's girlfriend.

They won't go over.

It was hard to look away from the game. "They're in great shape," I said.

It was evil they were in here. It was jail, after all, and they were just too poor to post bail. On the other hand . . . I thought of the men, crumpled, lying on the floor.

Do you throw them back on the street? The one service in here that's really decent is the health service. When they come in, what do they weigh?—160 pounds, average.

When they leave?—180, average. Or so I was told by one of the docs.

And what's the difference?

"They're off drugs."

And "on food"? And if I looked at the court, and the men running up and down, and turned away from the TV room, where men were piled up at phones, and where even when it's not "overcrowded" legally, it's still much too crowded, and if I just stared at the young men in brown "D.O.C." pajamas up and down the court—well, the place was electric with health.

But my God, they've not been convicted of anything.

Anyway, the captain took us back to his office, and then he tossed on his desk Bic pen–like things, with razor nails.

"'Shranks.' See how they twist them into knives? We find 'em all the time."

The captain told about his life. "I'm a flower child from the sixties." But he took a job here, as a temporary thing, and it's turned out to be life.

I kept staring at the Bic pens. Hard to believe they cut throats.

(I'm writing with one now.)

So why, I asked, do the numbers at the jail get bigger and bigger?

"This place," he said, "everything you saw . . . it shouldn't exist . . ." He meant there were too many people here. Then he said the usual Chicago thing: "I'm sure this doesn't exist in any other city . . ." when it always does.

When Father C. and I left the jail that night, I needed a big jolt of Italian, with a lot of red wine. So we went to Taylor Street, where the S.A.s and P.D.s sometimes go.

"Well," he said, "you go. What's your impression?"

"What's yours?"

"You go first."

"Well," I said, "it shows government can build housing." And I pointed out there was the kitchen (look how many jobs), and the clerks (look how many jobs), and the guards (look how many jobs).

In its dark way, the White City was "the City of Fabulous Jobs," wasn't it?

No. Yet it seemed to me the Old Mayor, the first Daley, might have been proud of it. But even that was too mean a thing to think.

White blazing block after block—and now up to eleven! "Why didn't they just build one big one all at once?" he asked.

"More frightening."

"For whom?"

We were quiet.

Stop the damn thing at eleven divisions! My God, I didn't want it to be the twelve-gated city, the one St. John sees coming at the end of time.

"OK," I said, "your turn."

It was now he talked about the basketball, and yet he must have thought of it as a city too, because he paused and then seemed to start all over: "In Europe you know the city was a neutral place." A low voice, intense. "Paris. Paris was a good place. Or at least neutral. But here. In this country, the city got stamped as something evil."

"Well?" I said. "After tonight, don't you think, it might *be*?"

OK, he said, but who made it evil?

A pause. I ordered.

But then I thought, as I drank more wine, it wasn't so "evil," was it? First, think of the game, I mean even the way they played.

Second, the captain. Decent guy, I thought at first. The whole way he changed, as he talked of the lockdown that he'd ordered that week.

When we finished dinner, I told Father C., "It's ten o'clock, the prisoners are in bed."

We're still up. But they're asleep.

One thing that hit me, as we left, and the men went off to their cells, the captain said to one or two: "You have a nice night." It would take sixty pages to describe the tone of his voice. And in the end, I couldn't. It was hard, but with feelings, but hard, etc. They responded like a crew on a ship. "You have a good night, too!" Just two or three exchanges like this.

I thought maybe all over the city we should have been calling out: "You have a nice night."

And they'd call back, "You have a nice night, too!"

FOR THE NEXT WEEK I was troubled by the idea that men were waiting six, nine months for trial. Shouldn't we be trying the cases faster, moving people out of here?

The council of lawyers urged me to talk to more P.D.s, and when I did, I was dismayed.

"Try the cases *faster*?" They were already overwhelmed. No, no, said the ex-P.D. I was told to call.

"Look," I said, uneasy, since I knew how little I knew, "I'm just trying to figure out . . . I'm trying to help." Then I had the nerve to preach about what I saw.

She blew up: "Look, you want to 'do something'? Do something about the bail laws. Or about the drug laws . . . But don't go around saying we ought to try cases faster . . ."

Yes, what was I saying? I thought of Night Narcotics Court, and the S.A. in her tent, and how she and her judge, all mumbling, did eight felony cases!

But do something about the bail? That meant going down to Springfield! That means passing new laws. So what should we do? Maybe we should do nothing. There are some liberals, even P.D.s who say this. "Some of them are better off in there." They aren't strung out, they get their health back.

When I told this view to a prison reformer, much later, he sighed: "I'm still shocked about the jail. But it's getting 'politically incorrect.' 'Well, what's really so bad about the jail?' I have to keep saying, 'But they haven't been convicted of anything!'"

Over the years, people like Clarence Darrow have come down to see the jail. Darrow went in 1902, and one of the docs gave me a copy of Darrow's speech, "Address to the Prisoners in the Cook County Jail" (1902). Why are you here, Darrow asked? Because you men don't have enough money.

He seemed to fix on the idea of Thomas Buckle the historian, that the price of bread would determine scientifically the number of people in a jail. And the P.D. I had lunch with said there is a yuppie businessman he knows who has worked with these guys and says: "If they can get up to eight dollars an hour, that'll do it. Then they don't end up back in jail."

As I read this speech, I felt a shiver, because, well, that night in the jail, hadn't I felt this way, too? I could imagine Darrow saying, "You men are here because no one's pushed your wages *up!*"

I kept thinking, this speech makes even more sense today. We let wages drop, and the jail kept growing, exploding like Lincoln Park. Two cities, each white hot, each growing in the shell of the old silver city.

And which one is growing faster? Last year the number of people in all the jails, all over America went up 9 percent.

Can Lincoln Park (greater) really grow faster? With violent crime down, it's hard to believe the jail can still keep growing faster. But maybe it's just that the bottom fifth has gotten poorer. And what happens, God help us, if the boom stops?

IT'S A FAULT of mine that I once read Augustine, the church doctor, and I've wondered what he would say about our two cities. His definition of a city is rather odd. What makes for a city, he says, is to have a people united by their love for a single thing. In the City of Man, it's the love of self. In the City of God, it's the love of God.

Now an earthly city is a mix of the two: it has a bit of the City of God and a bit of the City of Man. And it's just as true, it seems to me, of Lincoln Park and the jail.

It may seem the jail as a city is Hell by definition, i.e., a place to punish, each "self" locked up in his or her little cell.

Ah, but remember, there's overcrowding, and didn't I see community? People eat together, play games, run up and down a court.

Of the two, the jail may be the city with the lesser "love of self." It has the captain after all. And the P.D. who works in the shoe store. The guards who cross over to the other side.

Or the doctor who came to the jail and said, "This man needs air!"

and "This one needs light!" and complained and complained until someone said, "Doctor . . . this is a prison!"

These good people live in Lincoln Park, but they're only alive when
they're down here.

And what about Lincoln Park, i.e., its love of self? Of course there are
the people up there who volunteer. But it's very hard for any of us to think
of the two cities the way Europeans do, when they first show up, i.e., it's
all one city!

Maybe it is, in Augustine's sense. It's not that in Lincoln Park we have
people using shranks, but we have our ruthless types who downsize for no
reason or wordlessly, bloodlessly cut someone's throat.

When the Just Judge comes at the End of Time, which of the two
cities is going to have a lockdown first?

WHAT'S GOOD ABOUT CHICAGO is it's big enough, barely, to have a
large evil like the jail. But it's small enough, barely, so many of us can hear
the shouting.

I think.

But then I'm so insular about my town. I have no idea anymore
whether I became obsessed with "the city" and quoting Augustine *before* I
came to Chicago . . . or instead, it was the coming and living here that
made me so obsessed. At any rate, I now have a public policy to recom-
mend: To walk around the city. I really think it could change our lives.

It may seem unconnected, but I always think of this story, which my
father told me: When he was a boy, in the 1930s, the Depression, his father
would take him around. They'd pass the boardinghouses, flop houses,
and my grandfather would say to my father: Look how they're all full of
men. You wonder what became of the women?

I tell this story because until I went to the jail I was wondering: What
became of the *men*?

Oh, I saw men selling flowers on the ramps off the interstates. My
brother and I were just talking about this. Where *do* these men come
from?

But I'd forgotten the men, really. It's easy in the current debates . . . all
I hear or read about is, "How do we get jobs for these welfare mothers?"

President Clinton. Mayor Daley. The Fortune 500. Working round the clock to find them jobs.

But what of the men?

Then I went to the jail. Later by accident I was at a Mass at Notre Dame de Chicago, which is on the South Side, and out came a sister from St. Leonard's House. Now St. Leonard's is a halfway house for ex-offenders. The nun was saying, "We need volunteers. Look, I realize this is not for everybody . . . but they're just scared young men, they're not hardened criminals . . . They just need someone to talk to. Maybe you can help them find a job!"

Who? Us? Help find a job?

I looked around and the people here were blue collar or even immigrant, with a small knot of Catholics from the U. of I.

We're supposed to do it?

I wonder where Clinton is, Mayor Daley, the Fortune 500. Why aren't they doing this?

Oh, they're busy. They've got to help the women.

This must be the only country where the first priority is to get jobs for mothers of nursing infants.

And the men?

Well, we have a nun working on that.

IT WOULD BE DIFFERENT if we walked around the City. Alan Greenspan couldn't talk the way he does. Why is there no inflation? He thinks, childlike, there is some magic productivity beyond what we can measure.

Why doesn't he walk around? See all the jobs, jobs, mostly silly jobs, we have been creating . . . and the people willing to work two of them. And all the people sitting in the jail.

We can tell ourselves at the moment the city is at peace.

Peace. The shooting is down, a bit.

Peace. The poor have work.

Peace. More people in the jail.

But it's a false peace, or dangerous peace, which brings, each week, a few more people in the jail, a little more inequality, a little more instability.

But there's no need to worry, because the boom will go on and on.

But if you're not sure it will, you can always read Darrow's speech. And I found out my own partner . . . but that's not right: hero, mentor . . . Leon Despres . . . is writing a piece to introduce a new edition. In fact he met Darrow once. He told me the story about the speech, how a prisoner was asked what he thought of Darrow's speech and shook his head, "Too radical."

Maybe the truly radical thing is he went down to see the jail at all. And throughout the history of Chicago, there have been people like Darrow who go down to see the jail.

Well, Darrow. Algren, who brought de Beauvoir. Harold Washington, who went down there at the start of his campaign. Len himself, writing the introduction now. My friend Bob Lehrer.

In each period or time, the idea pops up, "I have to go down there." And someone really does go down.

A doctor, or a P.D., or someone with a copy of Darrow's speech.

It's terrible, and it's like an aural hallucination, to think of that speech, to have the idea of "City" echoing in one's head.

Think of doctors in the jail.

Or even a doctor like Augustine.

And it's why people keep coming down, over and over, even against their will, helpless, because they have to look at it, they have to see it, the jail, the White City.

Epilogue:
The Promise

I PUNCH 10

Novembrer 5, 1996. A WHIFF OF MAJORITY RULE, IN MY OWN city!

Today, this election, the Democrats take back the Illinois House. It's because, many say, people "punched 10," or voted slate.

In Illinois, I can do a slate vote, and give my vote to every Democrat.

One needle. One hole.

But it's a dark thing.

This day, I held the needle up mid-air, and thought, "This is like voodoo."

Now, I scoffed at people who punched 10, instead of voting line by line in each candidate race. Once I thought, only a stewbum, a sewer inspector, would punch 10.

But then I thought about Gingrich, and the Republicans in Springfield. What a way to show my contempt.

But I can't, I went to college.

"Oh go ahead," a voice said, "no one'll know."

So, I . . . did it.

I stumbled out, and ahead of me on the sidewalk was a woman, well dressed . . . rushing away . . . click, click, click.

She'd *really* punched 10. She'd been behind me in line.

I could walk fast, catch up with her. "I know what you did."

All that day people would come up dreamily: "I did something very strange today."

"Yeah, you punched 10."

"How did you *know*?"

Later the General Assembly, in lame duck session, made it illegal to do "slate voting" at all.

WELL, WHAT OF YOUR HERO, MADISON?"

I'm sure that's what my enemies would say. "What would Madison, who hated faction, say about punching 10?"

Yes, well. All Madison did was punch 10.

After 1787, he was a hack for Jefferson, who was away in Paris at the time. He was Jefferson's capo. Madison was the guy who raised the money to put out pamphlets on the sex lives of the Federalists.

The point is, he expected us to punch 10. Yes, there are checks and balances, but they assume, in the first instance, that people will come out to vote.

If people don't punch 10, the Constitution doesn't go.

Sure they expected people to punch 10. It was remarkable back then if We the People could put the needle back in *any* hole: the per capita consumption of alcohol was astounding. In *The Vineyard of Liberty* (1982), James MacGregor Burns indicates each American may have consumed up to several gallons of rum or other hard stuff each year.

Man, woman, child. Rum. Wood alcohol. From stills.

Yet drunk, they elected Washington. Drunk, they elected Jefferson.

Somehow, as a people, they blew on the flywheel. They made the Constitution go.

JEFFERSON IN PARIS

Of course, was Jefferson so great a choice? He gets knocked a lot by scholars now.

A friend, a lawyer in D.C., just read *American Sphinx,* and he talked about it at lunch:

"You know, it turns out, Jefferson really wasn't too bright."

"Yeah," I said, "I used to hear that from a professor I had."

"No," he said, "really not smart . . . He was over in Paris, you know, when they wrote the constitution. And he never really did seem to grasp it."

It's true, Jefferson missed Philadelphia. On the other hand, ever see the movie *Jefferson in Paris*? Nick Nolte as Jefferson.

How stupid was it to miss Philadelphia wood alcohol for Paris and the state dinners?

Bragging about the "American model." Dining with George Soros. Sitting next to actresses like Greta Scacchi, who whisper: "Tell us about the American model."

Back then, to brag about the American model was to brag about democracy.

Alas, if Jefferson were now in Paris, he'd be expected to brag about our:

Low wages.

Flexible labor.

And the key is that our democracy lets it happen, i.e., people *don't* vote, they think government can do nothing about this. But a necessary condition of this American model that we boast about in Europe is that less than half the country votes. No majority rule: that's how we can downsize, etc.

That's the new American model.

EXCEPT FOR BEING UNMOORED from majority rule, isn't it nice to live in America, and be in the top third? Sure, America's great, up here. But looked at from the top down, a lot of countries are pretty great.

The special thing about America used to be: the promise in it, looked at from the bottom up.

Now it seems the promise is locked up in Wall Street, like a gated complex. But even though the middle class is "in it," it's still true:

(1) The vast majority, 60 percent of households, are locked out.

(2) Even for those of us inside, the gap between rich and poor has grown.

(3) Many of the middle class are worse off during the bull market than they were out of it.

Indeed, half the work force still have no private pensions. And the other half? For many, their 401(k) balances would barely see them through a year.

Though you can also use your VISA to buy into mutual funds. (It's funny, even in the Roaring Twenties, people couldn't do that.)

But the worst part of a bull market is this: it turns the "promise" into a speculation. It's no longer a payment in return for work. It makes, from time to time, for "consumer confidence." But it doesn't make for civic trust.

It turns us all into Board of Traders, cruising the singles bars at night.

Though I must say, my broker's a good guy.

CROLY IN THE KITCHEN

Christmas 1997. A friend takes his wife to the office party. On the way home she cries. She found out what the workers in the factory make.

"Hey," he says, "I don't set the salaries."

In fact they probably went up. It was a good year.

After twenty bad ones.

But isn't it better that a child is fed? Yes, be grateful for a boom. But there's also a boomlet in soup kitchens and pantries. All through the 1990s and through the boom, the number of food pantries has been climbing.

In Chicago alone, there are four hundred "providers" or pantries. The number served by the Second Harvest, a national network of food banks, rose to 21 million in 1997.

It's hard to measure how much poverty is up until the next census, but we can count the people lining up at pantries.

Yet it's odd, I never see the pantries anymore. "That's because," John Donahue told me, "they site them out of Lincoln Park now."

Donahue runs the Chicago Coalition for the Homeless. All the shelters are now sited out of Lincoln Park.

"That's sad," I thought, "they put them out of the reach of the volunteers."

The only way I can see the hungry now, as the city blooms, is to pick up a government report and imagine them. The U.S. Conference of Mayors put out one report.

Homelessness . . . up 3 percent.

The back of the report is the best. Terse, one-line bulletins, city by city:

"Can't cope . . ."

"Many new soup kitchens, but . . ."

Really one city is like any other.

Now it's surprising in a way: food's cheap, housing is dear. So how can hunger be going up? I suppose, to hang on to a place to live, you might even take food away from a child.

The mayors take up the point that D. made at the Illinois Hunger Coalition. "We've had an 800 number for six years, but this is the first year we've gotten calls from so many people with jobs."

That's what we're bragging about in Europe. The American model. People with jobs lined up for food.

And not just food. The National Coalition for the Homeless did a study of selected cities, like Atlanta. In 1986, less than 2 percent of the homeless in Atlanta had jobs. In 1997, nearly 40 percent of the homeless in these cities had jobs.

But just think: half the homeless still don't have jobs. So Clinton in Christmas of 1997 announced a new program, $1.2 billion in job training for the homeless.

For what?

It reminded me of an eerie moment when I talked to a woman at the Illinois Hunger Coalition.

"We are doing job training," she said. "In food preparation."

"To work in soup kitchens?" I asked.

"No, no, in restaurants. That is something we know how to do. How to serve food."

The training center is called Oliver's Kitchen.

The pantries themselves are like little Olivers.

WELL, IT'S A BAD time for Progressives. Or liberals. Maybe we need a new name.

I had lunch the other day with a law professor, in his eighties, an old New Dealer, and he laughed at how the names had changed. "After

World War II," he said, "we stopped saying we were 'Progressives' and began to call ourselves 'Liberals.'"

"Why?"

"Because we didn't want to be tied, in 1948, with Henry Wallace and the Progressive Party."

This started us on the old Progressives and who they were.

"What did they have in common?"

"What did Theodore Roosevelt and Bob LaFollette have in common?" he laughed. "I'd say nothing."

This sent me back to read an extraordinary essay by one of our real heroes, Sam Beer. It's a piece partly about Croly and other Progressives, entitled "Liberalism and the National Idea" (1965). Beer argues that the Progressives, the real Progressives (like Croly, LaFollette) had two great concerns:

Inequality.

The growing power of big business.

Yes, just like now. Richard Hofstadter makes the point in *The Age of Reform* (1955) that they also worried about the stagnation of wages.

My first shock was to realize "America then and now had the same evils: the *same ones* exist today." Except ours may be worse.

The distribution of income? In 1997, a boom year, the poor actually had a drop in income a U.S. census study claims.

Stagnation of wages? Ours has gone on much longer than in Croly's time: a record fifteen years, 1979 to 1994.

BEER'S ESSAY TAKES the liberal movement from Croly in 1909 through the 1960s. And for me, there was a second shock:

What's different about liberalism now, in 1965, the essay argues, is the emphasis of Democrats on education and job training. Nearly a third of John Kennedy's new programs dealt with education. And Lyndon Johnson's were doing this even more . . . education, job training.

My God, I thought. The people who now say they're "New Democrats" like to claim, "We have to move beyond the liberalism of the 1960s, to things like education and job training." But what they mean is, "We have to move back to the liberalism of the 1960s . . . to things like education and job training."

Because this was the moment when liberals broke with the old New Dealers and Progressives. In the 1930s, liberals said, "We'll raise your wages," but now:

"We'll invest in you, and then you go and raise your own wages."

Yes, and a decade later the decline of wages would begin.

FOR YEARS I THOUGHT, "Why not pick up Croly's book and read it?" For years I'd wanted to, but just lacked the nerve.

Once I ordered *The Promise of American Life,* and went to the bookstore and Greg, the clerk, gave it to me.

"Oh God," I said, "this is impossible to read."

"Don't buy it then," said Greg. "There are other books."

Yes. Graham Greene novels. But what if this one's the American cabala?

So I read it, sort of, and it's a jungle in there, but every so often I'd come into a clearing. For example, his wonderful sense of democracy. It's that form of government that results in continuous social improvement, that is, pushing up wages: not every year, of course, but over time.

I'd just put it this way. Democracy is that form of government in which the majority faction at least keeps its steady share of the national income . . . but what would Croly make of our modern history? How can it be a democracy? Either it's not a real democracy or the majority has an entrenched disdain for its own well-being.

As Croly wrote, our democracy is not about a "safety net." Or "equal rights." Or "equal opportunity." That's not the Promise of American Life. And even Teddy Roosevelt knew it, once Croly said it. No, the promise is the standard of living goes up, continuously.

Then came OPEC.

Iran.

Flat wages from 1979 on.

Now no one wants to promise. "We overpromised, etc." But Croly is clear that not to promise is worse.

If we don't promise, people will disengage. Indeed, it's clear in the book: Croly warned us, people will stop voting.

This isn't England, or France, where we're all related, part of a tribe. If people are to extend themselves as citizens, there has to be a quid pro quo. Otherwise who cares? Why come to the U.S.?

It is often said that the Democrats in the 1960s promised too much. But in what way? If we wanted to eliminate poverty we could have. We still could. If we wanted the median wage to rise in a broad and long-term way, we could do it. Most developed countries have essentially wiped out poverty. Over the decades, many of these other countries had a true "continuous social improvement." Also, Croly seems right: in a democracy it is even more destabilizing to *under* promise. A friend told of a professor who went to the Third World, and saw a sign in a crowd: NO MORE AUSTERITY! GIVE US PROMISES!

AN ECONOMIST FRIEND once had this idea. I'll try to quote it right: "A country can survive a declining median wage, like us. *Or* it can survive rising inequality, like us. But no country, not us, no country . . . can survive for long both a declining median wage and rising inequality."

Well . . . for much of the 1980s and 90s we did have both. Thank God . . . and I mean this . . . the median wage did stop its decline in 1996 or so. So for the moment that doomsday switch has been flipped off.

But the other switch? Inequality is still rising.

Worse.

The reason people in the middle got paid last year is that economic growth is so white hot.

There was enough money to go around was after the top 5 percent have been paid off. But how often will that happen?

Consider the changing share of the return to labor and capital in just the past few years. Since 1991, there's been a change of 3 percent more to capital. That's huge.

Why did that happen? The better schooling, education of . . . stockholders?

An economist at the Economic Policy Institute says, "It's as if since 1992, for each one percent rise in income, working people lost three-eighths of one percent to Wall Street!"

Even Rhodes scholars, if they ever really do go to work, make that much less as a result.

NOW THIS IS ALL WELL SET OUT by my betters, economists like Richard Freeman or Lawrence Katz at Harvard, or Lawrence Mishel and Jared Bernstein at the Economic Policy Institute.

What else explains it? Even Alan Greenspan said in his testimony before Congress in 1997 that he was puzzled why little people can't take their share.

It violates the rules of the market. Except the real problem is, people are powerless to take their little share, or even hold the share constant, as a majority in any other democracy seems able to do.

NOW SOME SCOFF OVER THE YEARS: "Oh it's only the kids who lose out." The under thirties are starting out as citizens. Why teach them to give up on the promise of American life?.

But meanwhile, it's the kids who have kids. That's why so many children grow up in poverty.

Second, we pound the very ones who give up early on the Promise of American Life. And we still ask: Why did young people stop voting?

HUMPHREY-HAWKINS DAY

"I suppose," one might say, "there's some little law you'd like to suggest?"

Yes.

Now I know it will trivialize everything to come up with an answer. A law. "You think it can all be fixed by a little law?" It makes my whole argument ridiculous.

On the other hand, I'm trying to be a citizen.

The first problem is, of course, the structure of the Senate. I admit, it is a difficulty. But things did happen in the New Deal. And it's conceivable, barely, we could arrange to readmit some of the larger states as "two states with one capital" or "three states with one capital" (California, New York). This would push us a bit closer to one person, one vote.

Well, I'd try it.

But let's suppose we do get closer. What then? Let's suppose the voting rate slowly goes up, and one day, by accident or otherwise, there's a Democratic majority. It would be good to take the big New Deal laws, reread the preambles and purposes, and then update them.

I have a favorite I'd like to update from the 1970s, the Humphrey-Hawkins Full Employment Act. There's a law with plans! it was the last hurrah of the New Dealers.

I've always had a crush on Humphrey-Hawkins, if only because it forces Alan Greenspan to get up and testify. But here's how I'd change it:

Humphrey-Hawkins says the goal of the U.S. is full employment, and this used to be, when Hubert Humphrey was alive, the very definition of "continuous . . . improvement." Full employment meant: higher wages—a better life for the high-school grad, for everybody

Now alas, it means homelessness and soup kitchens.

So let's redefine it. Or have a new Humphrey-Hawkins goal: Each year the president would have to report to the country "the living wage unemployment rate," the percent of job holders and jobless from households that are under a new, revised poverty line. Get rid of the old poverty standard, which is out-of-date. Then the president must say:

How many in the workforce are from households that can't meet the new standard?

How do we reduce it, by what measures, over two years?

We'd have a much more useful debate about *that*. And it may just be that everything we did to lower "living wage unemployment" would also help the middle class.

THE STATES WILL BE OUR HOMES

Perhaps this era of "Big State Government" will last a thousand years. Many hope so.

There's even a book, *The New Promise of American Life,* by Lamar Alexander, the Tennessee ex-governor who ran for president. He argues, contrary to Croly, that the "New Promise" lies in giving more power to the states. Of course since he's been a small-state governor, he should think this. Well that's reasonable, given he was out there, lonely, like Clinton once was.

How can other people believe this?

Well, it is said the states are closer to the people. They know where to site the soup kitchens.

I've always been intrigued by the Tiebout thesis, which was developed by the economist Tiebout in the 1950s. If we give more power to the states, Tiebout argues, people will be happier and better citizens, since "like-minded" people over time will regroup themselves into states that most fit their views, e.g., on the liquor tax.

The states will be like little communes. The people who want higher liquor taxes will move to state "X." Those who want low liquor taxes will move to state "XXX."

Most American conservatives seem to think people are billiard balls that can be rolled from state to state, e.g., by liquor taxes. ("I'm sorry darling, we're taking the kids out of school, and leaving our families, because state XXX has the cheapest gin.")

Only a conservative could be so tone-deaf to family, friends, school ties.

It's clearer now than in Croly's time that the states are powerless to budget the big stuff, like wage levels or standard of living. Indeed, the more we "devolve" power to the States, the more it seems each state is alike. Vermont has the same inequalities as South Carolina.

Even mobility from state to state is dropping. Why move?

HE TRIED TO BE FAIR

It's in the graveyards, the city graveyards, that I can imagine what we used to have.

About a year ago, Ed. S took me to one I wanted to see, way on the South Side: where Harold Washington is buried. It was dark, the last day of November. We went with his son Ed, and he pointed out the graves of politicians, and city workers.

Sewer cap inspectors. They lay in rows.

Young Ed was saying, "You know in Madison" (he lives in Madison, Wisconsin) "up there people serve on the park boards, police boards . . . without pay. They serve for free."

I could hear the dead groan.

Old Ed shook his head. "I bet it's like the school board in Chicago used to be . . . they'd serve free, but, they have the contracts, the concessions, to put erasers in the classes." Stock the candy machines, etc. Yeah they serve for "free." Those concessions are worth millions.

Well, in the old days there was money to go around. Back then, people here believed in *The Promise of American Life.*

Even in death.

Even then people went on voting. The dead would dutifully awaken.

We passed the grave of men larger than life, like Jim Colusemo.

"Old Jim, he was in the tenderloin district."

"Tenderloin? Meat packing?"

A pause.

"Prostitution."

"Oh."

More history. The day went on. We came to the grave of Cecil Partee who, it seemed only a year ago, was state's attorney. He was dead already?

"Poor Cec," Ed said. "He used to run with Paul Powell."

"Pol Paul?"

"Paul *Powell.* You know. Who used to stuff the cash in shoe boxes."

And I could imagine what the city was like. Just then Ed told me to come over, he pointed to Harold's grave.

I came over, sadly, and read the marker.

Harold Washington

1922–1987

"He Tried to Be Fair"

"Fair? Fair? I thought the whole point of Harold was that he *didn't* try to be fair."

Ed muttered about a strike Harold didn't support.

Well, he did try, but thank God he never tried too hard.

THEN I SAW SOMETHING, it still haunts me, like a curse put on the city, on everything, on the promise of American life. It's biblical. We'll never get rid of it. It's down here among the soup kitchens, it's been sitting here for years.

Ed knew all about it. He brought me over to see it.

"Camp Douglas Memorial."

"Let me look."

I went up. I knew a little about it, it's a mass grave for Confederate soldiers. Rather, it's a mass grave for the prisoners of war. Young kids, often eighteen, nineteen brought up from the South.

"They only had their summer clothes, then typhus swept them off. They died here in the thousands."

This was the North's Andersonville. But as Ed said, "They took the guy who ran Andersonville, and hanged him . . . They took the guy who ran this place and made him a general." I went up and looked at the names:

Gibbs, Gibbs, Gibbs, Gibson, Gibson . . . It's as if in the whole South they only had ten last names.

Unlike the Vietnam Memorial Wall, the bodies of the kids were under my feet. Kids named Gibbs, Gibson, all rolled underneath. It's strange to look down.

I thought of the massacre of Polish officers at Katyn.

And a few yards away there's a statue of Lincoln, trying to look noble. Where was *he*?

A friend of mine said, "The Civil War was not worth it. At some point the slaves would have been let go."

And I thought how if the North had let the South go, and just had its own country, we'd be today a social democracy. We'd be like a country in northern Europe. We'd have a New Deal, more equality, and there wouldn't be this thing I'm staring at:

There wouldn't be this curse.

"You're awfully quiet," Ed said.

Acknowledgments

First, and most of all, to Linda Healey. The best editor I could hope to have, and better than I deserved. There'd be no book without her.

Second, to professor Samuel Beer, who, it often seems, gave me every good idea I had.

Also, to Jim McNeill and Josh Mason especially, and to Stephen Holmes, Tony Judge, Joel Brenner, David Shipley, Kathleen Hobbins, Theresa Amato, Andrea Laiacona, Terry Donovan, and Ed James who either: 1) checked the book, 2) urged me on, or 3) heard me moan about it all at dinner.

To Amy Gray and Denise Hoffman, for all their help in the final assembly.

To Len Despres, who really did show me my city. What a gift to see the city in the company of Len and his wife, Marian.

Finally, to my colleagues Sarah Vanderwick and Jeff Boulden.

Oh, one more: To all my friends and family who've been telling me, "Just write a second book so we can have another party."

About the Author

THOMAS GEOGHEGAN'S essays and commentary have appeared in the *New Republic*, the *New York Times*, the *Washington Post*, the *Chicago Tribune*, and *Slate*, among other publications. His previous book, *Which Side Are You On?: Trying to Be for Labor When It's Flat on Its Back*, was a finalist for the National Book Critics Circle Award and received a special citation from the PEN/Martha Albrand Award judges. Geoghegan lives in Chicago, where he is a practicing attorney.